Foucault,
Subjectivity,
and
Identity

Foucault, Subjectivity, and Identity

Historical Constructions of Subject and Self

Robert M. Strozier

WAYNE STATE UNIVERSITY PRESS   DETROIT

Library of Congress Cataloging-in-Publication Data

Strozier, Robert M.
Foucault, subjectivity, and identity : historical
constructions of subject and self / Robert M. Strozier.
p.   cm.
Includes bibliographical references (p.   ) and index.
ISBN 0-8143-2993-4
1. Foucault, Michel.   2. Self (Philosophy)—History.
3. Subject (Philosophy)—History.   I. Title.
B2430.F724 S875 2002
126—dc21
2001005612

For Carolyn Merlo

CONTENTS

7

Contents

PREFACE

This book is concerned with the notions of subject and of self that have developed during the history of western thought. When I began to think about writing this book, I realized how difficult it was to do that—that is, to *begin* to write about subjectivity. It is not merely that the term "subject" has a rich and varied history in the west, for that indeed would be a motive for writing the book. There is rather the difficulty of a beginning, the stance one must take and the assumptions one must make in order to initiate a discourse on the notion of the subject. It has often been said that the inquirer can only discover what his or her initial perspective allows, but an inquiry into "the subject" can be even more difficult because the inquirer is already a subject; this, along with the evanescent character of the referent, makes matters unobligingly oblique.

This difficulty may be overcome somewhat by a beginning based on some of the more ordinary meanings of "the subject." Generally the term is applied to human beings, whether in philosophy or in general discourse. There are numerous exceptions to this: test subjects may be human, but more often than not they are from the "lower" orders of animal being. However, exceptions aside, there is a close historical relation between the terms "human nature" and "the subject."

Moreover—and in contrast to the above relation—the terms "individual" and "subject" are so closely related that the phrase "the individual subject" has become a common one. This human being is unique, different from other humans—with the difference emphasized. But "individual" is another slippery term. In contrast to the above, Foucault uses the term "individual," that is, *individuum,* to signify the human material entity (including mind); for him this is the stage prior to becoming a subject, that is, a *cultural* subject.

"The subject" as a referent seems similar to the representations called "optical illusions" that appeared on matchbook covers and other cultural ephemera in the past: a set of stacked boxes or an outline of a solid geometrical figure that, when focussed on long enough, turned into a stack of a larger number of boxes or turned inside out. I spare the reader the almost inevitable reference to Escher. Thus we have a subject matter that dances its independence of the inquirer, and one that will not even appear in any guise until a number of assumptions have been made. "The subject" is an elusive subject.

In order to begin the book, I found myself forced to make several of the assumptions already mentioned. First, that subjects are generally human beings, with the exception to be noted later in Lucretius: the *clinamen* or swerve of the atom that initiates creation in the field of downward-passing but untouching atoms identifies the swerving atom as a nonhuman, nonintentional subject. Except for the case of Lucretius (who writes of human subjects as well), the general assumption that subjects are human raises the question of what human nature is and therefore what the possibilities of subjectivity are. (Incidentally, one of the arguments of the book is that there is no human nature; but this point will appear in its own time.)

Considering human nature and its broad as well as individual differences allows consideration of subjectivity to open out along two broad and complex avenues. First is the notion of the subject as a foundation or as an origin of thought, action, and change. This subject is the a priori, the preexistent platform or basis from which thought, action, and reaction emerge; these functions are then said to make the subject manifest in somewhat the same sense as Aristotle thinks of substance as the first category, one that is modified by attributes of quality, quantity, and so forth (compare Balibar 1991, 33ff.; Critchley 1996, 13–14; and Guzzoni 1996, 202ff.). Second is the notion that the subject is the result of some enculturating process. In the first case the subject is the given; this subject produces culture and knowledge; the other subject is produced by culture.

Kant offers a clear instance of the first kind of subject. When he begins the *Critique of Pure Reason* he assumes a normal human nature with aesthetic (that is, having to do with sensible perception), cognitive, and rational faculties. Kant thus assumes that these human capacities provide the foundation for the production of knowledge—although he is careful to argue that limits do apply to human knowledge. More emphatic versions of the subject as foundation exist throughout western history; for the followers of Pythagoras the warrant for belief and action is the simple fact that "ipse dixit," that is, the master himself said it.

The Greek Sophists argue that to learn to speak well one must imitate the master orator, whose capacities for excellence are in evidence from the outset, without benefit of imitation or training. Such early instances of what I call in the book the "capital-S subject," or simply the "Subject" (after Althusser), devolve into more popular versions of the same: the great "man" theories that refer history, change, and (usually) progress to the causative intervention of an intermittent series of great minds. Medicine, science, technology, politics, and other disciplines have often taken up this sort of explanation to account for their own evolution. The humanists of the Renaissance maintain that the given of human nature was *oratio* (and often *ratio* as well), the capacity to speak and act or to give communicable form to thought and things. The Subject is one in whom these capacities are given as complete or perfect; other subjects with similar potentials must needs imitate the words of the Subject in order to actualize those potentials and become effective speakers. This is a continuation of the Sophist tradition mentioned above.

Another variation of the subject as foundation or origin is the late modern version of "the individual subject" mentioned earlier—that is, of the subject as unique—and this is probably for the general reader the way in which subjectivity is normally perceived. According to this version of the subject we are self-founded as individual subjects or selves as a given. We actualize this potential by self-reflective insight: we have the capacity to stand outside ourselves, examine the cultural forces acting upon us, and to find our true selves in contrast to this alien other. This historical version of the subject as self has its proximate roots in Descartes's formal construction of self-reflexive examination, but it reaches fruition in the nineteenth and twentieth centuries. Afterwards structuralism and poststructuralism begin to challenge the claims of a self-founding subjectivity.

In the book I begin with this notion of the subject as foundation in what I call the Sophist notion of the originating Subject. It is, in the history of the west, arguably the most powerful version of the subject, and demands pride of place.

The second avenue along which subjectivty can be pursued is intimately related to the notion of subject as foundation, but in a peculiar way. Both notions derive etymologically in the romance tradition of languages from the same Latin verb, *subicio* (or *subjicio*, to place near or under). Two opposed substantives derive from this verb: *subjectum* (in Lewis and Short, "that which is spoken of, the foundation or subject of a proposition"—that is, that which has *already* been placed under, so that it may serve as the foundation) and *subjectus* (from the past participle, "an inferior, subject"—that is, subject-ed or subjected to something prior). *Subjectum* would eventually be applied to humans considered either generically or individually foundational, as in Protagoras's claim that "Man [*anthropos*, i.e., human nature] is the measure [*metron*] of all things." The *subjectus* is produced by being "brought under" a disciplinary or cultural apparatus or "subjected to" that regime. Etienne Balibar speaks of this as the "citizen subject" (1991, 40ff.), and as noted just below, the political subject. The two lines along which subjectivity is conceived appear in the Sophist-Renaissance notion that there are two kinds of subjects, one the foundation and the other to be formed by submitting to the discourse of the Subject.

The subject in this sense of being subjected has also been a continuous feature of western thought, although not one as likely to be appreciated by actual humans, especially in modern times. From ancient times down well into the eighteenth century, this version was used most frequently to refer to the political subject, or those subject-ed to power and authority of both legitimate and illegitimate kinds—that is, almost everyone. But with the "death of the king," real or supposed, a somewhat different version of this subject has emerged. Foucault argues that monarchy has given way in the modern age to a power-knowledge network of discourses (for example, medicine) and disciplines (for example, pedagogy) to which the modern individual is necessarily submitted in order to be produced as a cultural subject. The individual is nothing more than material prior to being produced as a "discursive subject" (the current term).

My claim that there are two primary and competing versions of the subject in western thought is something of an assumption, but a working one. They are inevitably joined versions as well as separate ones. The two versions, insofar as they indicate distinctly different kinds of subjects, derive from the same verb. In many theories focused on the originating Subject there is a necessarily conjoined subject-ed. From Descartes on, self-reflection entails a split subjectivity: one subject possesses the gaze, or the position of knowledge, and the other is subjected to that gaze. Contemporary arguments in feminist theory and cultural studies often foreground the notion that discursive subjects must recognize their subjection and work to change it. What is assumed is that discursive subjects have agential capacity, at least after they undergo the self-reflection described above, by means of which they create themselves as authentic beings. Then they become originating subjects.

On the other hand, understanding the itinerary of the subject in western thought requires the heuristic opposition. At least some such similar opposition would be necessary, one that would, as in this case, allow opposed versions to define themselves against the other. And, in fact, it is rather easy to find forceful versions of each pole of subjectivity in western thought that are very close to being discrete. It is usually the case, however, that one discourse on subjectivity will contain both versions of the subject, as noted above.

These are the parameters within which the book on "the subject" takes form. However, I make no attempt to present a continuous history of the subject—something that is perhaps no longer possible—but an analysis of particular historical moments and eras during which subjectivity becomes a crucial issue, or when the groundwork of a particular notion of the subject is laid, one to be articulated and exploited in later eras. These are, I hope, moments that can be shown to be important to western thought about the subject and important to what we are (as subjects) at the present time.

This book is organized along several lines. First, beginning with chapter 1, the book is a study of a number of representations of subjectivity during the history of western thought, and it includes several dominant themes of that history: the prior Subject, the self-reflexive subject, the subject as mind or act, the self-founded individual subject, and so on. Second, beginning in chapter 2, it is an analysis of Foucault and his notions of self and subject as they develop within his work. My interest in Foucault ranges from his influence on gender theorists, in chapter 3, to the historical precedents of genealogy, in chapter 4, and to his notion of self-relation and how that is represented in the classical era, the Renaissance, and the modern world.

Following Foucault's insights, questioning and complicating them—this has allowed me to inquire further into the issues concerning subjectivity and the self that have been sustained within western thought. This is the third line of development of the book: examining how self-relation is complicated by the notion of interiority in antiquity in chapter 5; extending the twinned notions of self-relation and interiority to the Renaissance in chapter 6; and confirming Foucault's argument that the modern version of identity is the result of these same twinned notions. Human identity in the modern age—who we are, historically—and its emergence is the subject of the final three chapters of the book.

Chapter 1 focuses on the notion of the prior Subject. It introduces narratives of origin, which are fundamental to western thought and histo-riography and which usually entail the notion of the subject as origin. In particular, what I will call the Sophist narrative of origins, which took shape in the ancient world, provides one of the fundamental positions against which subsequent notions of subjectivity may be gauged because it institutes and consolidates the notion of the prior Subject or the subject-as-origin. I have constructed this notion of a Sophist narrative and theory of origins from suggestions by various ancient Sophists and others, none of whom, incidentally, has ever been thought of very seriously as a theorist. But this Sophist theory, so called, represents a fundamental notion of subjectivity present throughout western thought.

Chapter 1 also has its own itinerary. Narratives of subjective origin tend to be narratives of reproduction. I have taken up two narratives of origin, that of the Sophists and of Freud. By reading them together I have attempted to understand how each constitutes and supports the other, especially in terms of how the nature of authority is determined and how, in terms of sexual difference and gender, reproduction occurs. Freud's narrative is more productive when considered as prior to the Sophist narrative, and an analysis of the former explains how authority comes to be recognized as benign and how women are excluded from (cultural) reproduction.

Chapter 2 raises a number of issues central to subjectivity in the contemporary critical world. The fundamental issue here is whether there is or can be a "subjectless poststructuralism." This question has been bandied back and forth for a long time now; my extended encounter with the middle Foucault suggests new issues and permutations within this recent debate. Other critics and reinventors of the subject are also under scrutiny in this chapter.

Foucault's first genealogical attack on the notion of originating subjectivity is direct and as such invites recuperation. The structure of his genealogy of punishment and the disciplines, with its origin in the Subject, guarantees this. The issue is played out here against the background of the Sophist notion of origin, which I have reinvented for this chapter in order to emphasize the occulted return of the Subject in the discursive subject— that is, the subject constituted by discourse or culture but which, according to the current narrative, retains the potential for origination, agency, and change. This is one of the central issues of the post-theory world.

There are substantial moments when Foucault is able to produce openings toward a subjectless history. In the period after *The History of Sexuality*, volume 1, Foucault realized that there was a subject after all, and that the modern subject was historically formed as self-reflexive and therefore self-constituting. He was then able to utilize this self-reflexivity to begin to construct a genealogy of this historical ontology of self-constitution. This later phase of his thinking is the subject of chapter 5 and the following chapters.

Chapter 2 ends with an analysis of Michel Serres's contribution to a subjectless history, here on a cosmic as well as a local scale. Foucault in the best moments of his genealogical phase points toward Serres; but Serres, like Foucault in his lesser moments, fails to cross over into a subjectless scientific reading.

Chapter 3 continues with Foucault's genealogy in order to examine how it operates within the contemporary scene of activist theory. Prominent in cultural studies and other strategies of the postpoststructural era are concerns with the notions of agency and resistance. These are theoretical issues: the agenda becomes one of discovering ways to put poststructural thought to work in determining how gender or race or sexual preference have been produced, and how they may be disrupted.

In analyzing Judith Butler's *Gender Trouble* in relation to Foucault and genealogy, this chapter suggests a return to the theme of gender exploited in chapter 1. But the perspective is different here. Butler, the best representative of poststructural gender theory, utilizes Foucault to construct an argument for naturalized gender formation. She also argues that Foucault reverts to sexual nature as a given, and then moves beyond him to produce an agency with the potential to disrupt gender determination. This disagreement is central to our understanding of both theorists. We are able to see what the implications of Foucault's genealogy are, and what specter of subjectivity lurks beneath the surface of Butler's notion of agency. The main points are that Butler can be seen to return to a traditional notion of subjective agency and that her utilization of genealogy paradoxically excludes history. At the same time, understanding what Foucault's genealogy is and what it is not emerges from the confrontation with Butler.

The first part of the chapter situates Butler's argument, particularly her derivation of agency and resistance from discursive gender formation, and points to the problems mentioned above in her narrative of the production of agency. The second section is based on the distinction between genealogy and discourse, the former conceived as the representation of the contingent process within which discourses emerge, join, conflict, and so forth, over a period of time. Butler calls her perspective genealogical, but it is actually discursive; in other words she conceives of one dominant discourse—the masculinist—and a future liberation from it, or history as the future.

In addition, certain aspects of Foucault as genealogist before the final shift in his thinking can prove counterproductive for an activist theory in need of agency. Here there is no distinction between the natural and the naturalized (both are the same historical phenomenon), and therefore there is no basis for characterizing the naturalized negatively. History is the result of a contingent process, so it is arbitrary and does not provide a basis for determining the value of a discourse nor a reason for dismantling it.

The final section of the chapter takes up the universalizing and essentializing tendencies of theory that undermine an activist theory such as Butler's, especially in the absence of a genealogical perspective, or one which foregrounds history as contingent process. But the question here is how Butler can be reassessed, not merely as an activist whose recourse to theory produces an entrapment, but as a practitioner with a new sense of the paralogical possibilities of theory.

Chapters 3 and 4 together form an extended consideration of Foucault's genealogy. Chapter 3 looks at Foucault's influence on gender theory. This allows for the development of arguments that define and sustain genealogy as a theory or method of explanation. Chapter 4 takes another look at genealogy, this time from a more abstract perspective that attempts to identify what *kind* of explanation genealogy offers. Here, against the background of ancient materialism, I attempt to define exactly what history is and how it occurs according to genealogy.

This entails analyses of Foucault's conception of a material minimum (the issue raised by Butler against Foucault), and his conception of process—the level-to-level relation within process as well as the diachronic succession of stages of process. Foucault's genealogical analysis, seen against this background, becomes a marvelously complex rendering of materialist thought; but the *aporias* in material method tend also to reappear in Foucault as limitations on the explanatory potential genealogy offers. This part of the extended meditation on Foucault also sets the stage for Foucault's next move in his long journey through the problematics of subjectivity.

Chapter 5 moves to this most dramatic and well-known shift in Foucault's thinking about the subject. This is the shift that leads to *The Use of Pleasure* and *The Care of the Self*, texts that exhibit a perspective substantially different from that of the first volume on sexuality. The shift provides a new basis for genealogy, now founded in the present in the historically constituted self-reflexive and self-constituting subject. This is a return to the subject, but as a historical and not a transcendental phenomenon.

Chapter 5 begins with an analysis of this shift and its implications, and then moves to an analysis of Foucault's treatment of self-relation in fourth-century B.C.E. Greece and the later Hellenistic and Roman periods. I reread *The Use of Pleasure* and *The Care of the Self* in order to produce an analysis both founded on Foucault's and critical of it. The period of Foucault's concern includes two epistemic shifts toward interiority as the focus of philosophical activity, but both are beneath the level of his analysis. These are important shifts in that the form of self-relation is inseparable from the notion of interiority, but this relation doesn't surface in Foucault in any significant way. In the third volume on sexuality he offers a general characterization of the five-hundred-year period beginning with Hellenistic thought that is inaccurate and alters the contours of the actual thinking in the ancient world about self-relation. Two final sections of the chapter treat Epicurus and Seneca as a means of directing attention to this problem in Foucault's argument. The analysis here of the divergent forms of interiorized and exteriorized self-relation prepare for the later versions of self-relation treated in the following chapters.

Chapter 6 marks a departure from my direct concern with Foucault and the various stages of his insight. This is necessary in one sense because Foucault did not have time to complete his genealogy of self-relation, that is, connect the end of *The Care of the Self* to what he had written earlier about the seventeenth century and afterwards; nor had he time to rethink his earlier writings on the modern era in terms of his new perspective—or not enough time to write about it.

In fact we are left by Foucault with about twelve hundred years after the Romans and before the modern era without knowledge about the direction his genealogy of self-relation might have taken, or with only a few hints. It is thus easy to assume a Christian era in which self-relation consisted in the hermeneutic of the self followed by the self's submission to a licit/illicit code of behavior. While I obviously cannot complete the genealogy of self-relation during this period, I do attempt to break away a part of its assumed solidarity. I do this by focusing on the thought of a number of humanists during the fourteenth and sixteenth centuries in order to develop the character of self-relation during these periods.

As a means of separating these two centuries I return in this chapter to the notion of interiority as a focus of theoretical and philosophical activity and its connection with self-relation. Specifically, Petrarch represents the fourteenth-century focus on interiority; self-relation during this period takes the form of self-focus or the return to the inner and undisturbed self, along with the production or augmentation of the interior self. These facts emerge from an analysis of some of Petrarch's religious and moral treatises and the letters on imitation in the *Familiari*.

In contrast, interiority as the central theoretical concern has all but disappeared by the sixteenth century, being replaced by the assumption that the text or performance is central. This is a "communicative" era somewhat similar to the second half of the twentieth century, in which, first, interiority only becomes viable through its representation and then, later, with poststructural thought, doesn't exist at all or is constituted by the text. In the sixteenth century, mind also ceases to exist except as the motive for representation, and as a consequence self-relation is transformed. In the humanist tradition of imitation of the century—this tradition is central because it is one of the most elaborate forms for producing subjects during this time—self-relation literally disappears, being replaced by a self-other relation—that is, to the model—by which the learner becomes a competent speaker and actor (of courtly skills, of virtue, and so on). This sixteenth century appears in a number of humanists from Peter Bembo, Castiglione, and Melanchthon through Erasmus, Ascham, and Montaigne.

Chapter 7 chronicles the return in the seventeenth century to a focus on interiority and the necessarily a priori return of the self to the self as an initial theoretical gesture—a renewed and intensified form of self-relation. Descartes, the primary example here, marks the shift from a moral ascesis to an epistemological one and opens the way toward the constitution of that most typically modern creature, the subject of knowledge.

Foucault's insight concerning self-relation as a primary part of the modern version of human nature, and his subsequent utilization of that historical nature as a means of constructing a genealogy of self-relation, came at the end of his life. As mentioned earlier, Foucault never had a chance to write about the middle ages, the Renaissance, and the modern period in terms of self-relation, except in some few essays.

The issue of the modern period in Foucault is a complex one. In Foucault's pre-self-relation texts it is an era of the increasing penetration of scientific discourses and disciplines into the body, and the constitution of the individual as a subject through the creation of new, interiorized identities. Self-relation is absent from this earlier description except in the impulse to find out who we are and how, historically, we came to be what we are. Chapter 7 is an attempt to do what I imagine Foucault might have done: to reread the modern in terms of self-relation, beginning with Descartes and, within limited scope, to trace the development of issues arising from that new identity formed by cognitive self-relation down into the twentieth century.

The issue can be put simply: the shift of confession, for example, from the religious to the secular arena leads to individual self-constitution by means of the recognition of identity through the production of interiority in self-decipherment. Two facts intervene here in a causative manner: in Descartes the self-inquiry is now epistemological, an attempt to determine a subject capable of knowing itself and thus capable of producing true knowledge of the *res extensa*; then, too, as Foucault notes, what is produced from a structured self-inquiry no longer dissipates with absolution but becomes the primary material from which the modern attempt to invent "man" can be accomplished—by the various emerging sciences and disciplines such as medicine.

In Descartes and for some time after him, at least until the end of the nineteenth century, there was compatibility between the interiority of the individual as self-reflexively produced and the emerging scientific disciplines and discourses. These discourses are constituted by the information drawn from individual self-inquiry in a variety of venues and in turn constitute or subjectivate individuals—that is, as subjects—in terms of the now-systematized particularities of their thoughts, feelings, and intentions. But once interiority is produced and systematized into a series of identities that are used to constitute subjects, that same source of interiority becomes historically oblique, denying the reciprocity and continuity between interiority and objective knowledge. The individual can now argue a unique interiority by claiming that this interiority is no longer accessible to knowledge. The result is an intensification of identity as interiority that characterizes the first part of the twentieth century.

The chapter begins with an analysis of Descartes as a means of establishing the new subject of knowledge, which itself becomes in time the object of discursive knowledge. I continue the genealogy of self-relation as constitutive of identity as interiority by reference to literature and the novel from the eighteenth century to the twentieth. The novel provides through its narrative structure a unique insight into the changing relation between scientific knowledge and self-knowledge, as well as clear evidence of interiority as identity.

Chapter 8 returns through some philosophical texts to the genealogy of modern self-relation and the continuities between self-knowledge and objective knowledge that are sketched out in chapter 7. The texts at issue here are the first two Critiques of Kant, of pure reason and (pure) practical reason. In the *Critique of Pure Reason* Kant may be said to deny the possibility of self-knowledge, but on the other hand the structure of the text assumes the existence of a prior subject of knowledge that produces objective knowledge through its (the text's) analysis of the interior faculties of a normalized and abstract human nature. Kant would thus seem to promote objective knowledge almost exclusively and give foundation to the scientific enterprise of modernity.

The *Critique of Practical Reason*, however, assumes that self-knowledge—of the self as a noumenon or origin—precedes objective knowledge of moral behavior, and so promotes the continuity of the relation between self-knowledge and objectivity more directly. But the first Critique reverses Descartes's order: objective knowledge in the form of the aesthetic and the analytic necessarily precedes the (failed) attempt to produce self-knowledge; the attempt is itself necessary yet secondary. Then, too, in the *Critique of Practical Reason,* self-knowledge is the result of a speculative assumption (one which is illegitimate from a theoretical perspective), not an ascesis or the production of the subject of knowledge. The issues in Kant that both promote and depart from the historical ontology of modern "man" add texture and complexity to the genealogy of modern self-relation proposed in chapter 7.

Chapter 9, which also develops analyses of Descartes and Kant in terms of the constitution of the modern episteme, derives from a late Foucault essay entitled "What Is Enlightenment?," which is an attempt to specify a self-reflexive turn in Kant in the philosopher's sense of his relation to "the present moment." The chapter contests this insight and then attempts to assimilate it by a return to the first two Critiques. At issue are Descartes's and Kant's—each in his own way—constitution of the subject of knowledge and the necessity of that subject's transcendentality or removal from the empirical/historical realm to its role in producing objective knowledge.

This chapter thus reiterates the previously discussed relation of the two kinds of knowledge during the first phases of the modern era and clarifies and strengthens that link. The Kantian ahistorical subject defines an essential part of the discourse of modernity; it is this transparent subject and object of knowledge from which scientific knowledge is produced. On the other hand, it is this same subject that, by a later turn of the discursive element, becomes obscure, demanding autonomy, ahistoricality and escape from determination by scientific discourses.

1

How Men Invented Themselves

Theories of Origin, Subjectivity, and the Monogendering of Reproduction

This book develops in relation to Michel Foucault's changing notions of subjectivity, beginning with his arguments for a discursive subject and ending with his ultimate notion of the self-reflexive subject and its "historical ontology." But the book must begin "before" Foucault, primarily with subjective theories of origin that emerge in the ancient Mediterranean world. It's not that Foucault failed to recognize such a subject—the one generally referred to as the humanist subject. In fact his original attempt was to confront this version of subjectivity with his own version of the subject as constituted by cultural discourses. He also, not incidentally, came back to this humanist subject, although now as historical rather than ontological. But more about that later.

Despite this general familiarity with this so-called humanist subject by Foucault and everyone else, I have felt the necessity of grounding it in the ancient world and of giving its rationale in full. This is justified I think by the power of this notion of the founding subject and its pervasiveness throughout written history; we need, in short, to think this version of the subject *through*. This necessity leads me to narratives of origin, which make up much of the core of western thought. And though it is unlikely that today we would be able to return to them unproblematically as constituting knowledge and insight, their significance within the tradition of the west was for a long time unchallenged. What I have chosen to look at here are two narratives of subjective origin, by the Sophists and by Freud, in *Totem and Taboo*. The points at issue are two: that culture is produced by the Capital-S Subject; and that within these narratives gender is occulted.

Ironically, what I am calling the Sophist theory of the originating subject doesn't have a precise historical origin, nor is it a fully developed narrative. Nonetheless, following the lead of Richard McKeon in his various works on the history of philosophical systems, I have constructed this theory of the Subject as the origin as "Sophist." Although Isocrates, Protagoras, and other Greek Sophists such as Gorgias were not philosophers in the traditional sense, various statements they made have philosophical resonance, and Protagoras was certainly taken seriously—philosophically— by both Plato and Aristotle. McKeon, for example, argues that Protagoras's best-known maxim, which claims *anthropos* as the "measure" of all things, represents a choice of philosophic principle significantly different from those of Plato, Aristotle, and Democritus (1954, 108–18). Such a "philosophic" choice is important to McKeon's system of philosophic history, and I have chosen to use this construction of the Sophists as important to the tradition of subjectivity. It may be countered that the Sophists were merely teachers with philosophic pretensions.

The Sophists are certainly often dismissed as nonphilosophers; but since there are no universally agreed upon notions about what constitutes and limits philosophy, and since certain Greek Sophists claimed to be philosophers, many commentators have accommodated them to some degree. W. K. C. Guthrie typically treats them as concerned with the ethical and political, that is, with practical philosophy (in Aristotle's scheme), and attributes to them an (philosophical) attitude of skepticism and doubt about the possibility of absolute knowledge.

Richard McKeon makes the same point, that Isocrates, a Sophist,

> included philosophers in his conception of Sophists and gave systematic exposition to the doctrine that opinion alone is possible, not truth, and that its criteria are practical and aesthetic. Men who are well endowed by nature and prepared by practical experience can be made more skilful by formal training. Such training and knowledge are concerned with words and discourse, and it is the master who is the object of imitation. In this tradition art is conceived . . . as a skill in using language acquired by imitation of great models. (1954, 111–12)

McKeon is here positioning the Sophists on the one hand in relation to Plato and on the other in relation to Aristotle and Democritus; simply put, McKeon uses the Sophists to represent one of four modes of philosophizing—the Sophist mode as a kind of anti-philosophy, for example, in its denial, against Plato, that there exists more than human knowledge.

Isocrates' "systematic exposition" in *Against the Sophists* amounts to a rehearsal of the rhetorical triad, *ingenium,* art, and practical experience, along with a catalog of what the art should include: invention, arrangement, style (1945a, 14–19). And clearly Isocrates considers himself, along with other deliberative orators who are concerned to offer persuasive guidance to the state, one of the "devotees of philosophy" (1945b, 48 and passim). And Isocrates admits Sophists in general into the philosophical camp, including teachers of ethics. A recent book on Isocrates shows how he avoids the position of teacher in his written works; the book also argues that the distinction between rhetoric and philosophy was introduced by Plato and Aristotle to "legitimize their own technical emphasis" (Too 1995, 151–232).

The issues here are double. Can the Greek Sophists be seen as important to philosophy? The answer is yes, since they stand at the origin of a tradition within which systematic assumptions are made, ones which rival or replace the assumptions and arguments made by those whom no one would hesitate to call philosophers. The assumptions of the Sophists may indeed be less subtle and the systematics less articulated (McKeon 1952, 168ff.), but the question is actually whether we will allow the Sophists to operate within the same arena as the philosophers.

Second, what are those assumptions? While it is not my task to renew philosophical interest in the Sophists, we might consider the claim often made from within the rhetorical tradition from Cicero to Ramus that philosophy, politics, literature are merely different forms of speaking. Isocrates in the *Antidosis* makes a similar kind of argument when he says: "With this faculty [of speech] we both contend against others on matters which are open to dispute and seek light for ourselves on matters which are unknown; for the same arguments which we use in persuading others when we speak in public, we employ also when we deliberate in our own thoughts" (252).

The central Sophist issue for the matter at hand can be situated in McKeon's claim that the Sophists "deny . . . the upper half of the Socratic distinction between being and becoming, knowledge and opinion" (1954, 111). Isocrates does indeed argue that truth resides in the orator's skill and honesty of character (1945a, 15ff.; 1945b, 274ff.). But it is also clear that for the Sophists opinion is truth—in the sense that there is no prior recognizable cosmic truth but that "truth" in specific circumstances must be determined for an audience or a community by persuasive arguments produced by effective speakers. This brings truth down to the opinion or position of the most powerfully persuasive individual orator, one who is able to assemble the most effective arguments. It was Protagoras who was said to have first maintained that "there are two sides to every question" (Diogenes Laertius 1925, ix, 51)—thus necessitating a more effective speaker to settle the question.

Protagoras's most famous philosophical statement to the effect that "Man is the measure of all things, of things that are that they are, and of things that are not that they are not" (ibid.) can be read in several ways. Aristotle takes it up seriously as a universal at least three times in the *Metaphysics*. But the Sophists in general might be said to interpret it as a particular: the singular individual speaker establishes or founds truth. Such a notion is clearly implied in Isocrates' argument that the master "must in himself set such an example of oratory that the students who have taken form under him will, from the outset, show in their speaking a degree of grace and charm not found in others" (1945a, 17–18). Absolute knowledge has been put aside for the truth of the unique individual as the originator of a human tradition. The Subject is the Sophist principle, comparable to Plato's Forms and Aristotle's prime, unmoved mover.

But why Freud? And why *Totem and Taboo*? Why not Kant on the "Conjectural Beginnings of Human History"? The former text is of course central to Freud's notion of the origin of culture as well as his construction of the Father as original Subject. In a number of ways the text is a narrative of subjective origin which complements the Sophist theory, one which pretends to historicize the time prior to culture (and the Sophists), as Kant's does also, but which is written later and certainly influenced by Sophist theory in one form or another. Freud's story on the one hand is about sex, turmoil, killing, and repression (as progress), while Kant conjectures that humans develop through a series of changes based on their use of reason—which indeed does "violence to the voice of nature" (1963, 56). Kant's history begins not with Freud's clamorous horde of men fighting over sexual rights to the women but with the heterosexual couple, who become gradually, through reason, part of a social and civil order. Reason, for example, turns the natural sexual instinct into love. Incidentally, only if humans were to live lifetimes of eight hundred years or more would there develop strife between father and son or brother and brother.

But one thing that should concern us in an age of cultural criticism is gender. And if Freud's story is more tumultuous than Kant's, they both do the same work on gender: they create a singularly masculinist narrative. So either narrative at this point would do. The question that needs to be asked along the same lines is: why does the Sophist notion of Subject through most of its history apply only to males? This is another reason why the chapter is pre-Foucault: his work on the subject is pre-gender in that his view of the formation of subjects doesn't always descend to the level of gendered subjects. In his works on self-relation women are excluded by the texts he analyzes, and in his genealogical work gender plays a small although significant part. Masculinist discourse is simply a fact in Foucault.

In chapter 3 I discuss some feminist criticisms of Foucault's genealogical theories of the subject, but aside from that gender is not an issue in my book. Critiques of Foucault by feminist theorists do clarify the former's thinking, and these critiques have to do with gender. Here, "at the beginning" of the Subject in chapter 1, I think gender is also a necessary issue. We need, as I have just said, to know why the originating subject is always masculine—at least in theory. I have used Freud's narrative as the prior one in order to explain why the Sophist theory is always and exclusively about males, or why, in the words of Irigaray's phrase, "the woman? She 'doesn't exist.'" In addition, Freud's narrative is fundamental to the critique of our own thinking about gender. Whatever imbalance this creates with respect to Foucault's lack of focus on gender and my own in chapters 2 and 4–10 will, I hope, be outweighed by the attempt to explain why women were always excluded from cultural reproduction.

One of the grand narratives cited by Lyotard, the narrative of origins emerging from Kant's Critiques, is an instance of a later notion of the originating subject: the rational Enlightenment subject. The late Foucault pointed out that however disinclined poststructuralism was toward Kant's foundation of knowledge, moral behavior, and aesthetic judgment in the essential faculties of the human subject, it was nonetheless bound by this historical narrative of auto-representational, originating subjectivity produced by philosophical self-reflection. In point of fact, our "historical" essence (Foucault 1984) or construction allows for the self-reflexivity to question whether we as subjects are essentially originating and self-reflexive. And either way we are stuck with a narrative of origins.

By the end of the eighteenth century Kant's narrative is a familiar one, and even long before that. His account of knowledge leads back to earlier narratives of origin, particularly as relates to human subjectivity. According to this Sophist theory there exists a Subject that is the origin of discourse and culture; in general it may be argued that this theory contains the possibilities of most theories of subjectivity which follow historically in western thought.

Aristotle provides a revealing addition to this Sophist notion of origin, pointing out its humanist and nonscientific context. He argues, against Protagoras's maxim, that substance and real objects determine perception

25

and thought and not the reverse, and further that the senses are accurate. So man is a *subjectus:* "man is measured" rather than the other way around (1941, Bks. 10 [1053a 31–b 3], 11 [1062b 12–1063a 9]). But Aristotle illustrates, along with the Sophists, the ancient commitment to the explanatory potential of the notion of origin—Aristotle by the way of the four causes. In the productive as well as in the natural sciences, "anything which is produced is produced by something" (ibid., Bk. 7 [1033a 24] and passim). Aristotle's philosophy of causes leads ultimately back to the prime mover, eternal and unmovable itself but the cause of subsequent motion—the ultimate origin. The human subject can serve as an origin in Aristotle's scheme only as the efficient cause or with reference to only one cause among the four causes that are used by Aristotle to construct the abstract, multiply determined and comprehensive classificatory system that underlies his philosophy. It should be added, however, that Aristotle in the *De anima* does treat the mind as the unmoved cause of local motion (B434b 30–435a 1); at such times he "sounds like" a Sophist. But Protagoras's claim would ultimately fall under the practical sciences such as ethics or politics, in which the end is action, not knowledge or production.

Aristotle's notions don't replace the Sophist Subject, nor do they deflect its historical influence. For example, the Sophist prior Subject "is" the Kantian human subject, that is, the *subjectum* or *hypokeimenon,* what, transcendently, precedes, underlies, and "supports" representation. (Kant is in many senses actually an Aristotelian, although his "I" is not a substance.) Although not a subject of discourse or constituted (historically) by discourses, the Kantian subject is also *subjectus* or "receptive." On the other hand the Sophist Subject is nonreceptive, since its originating act is *pure* precedent; the subject which imitates is both *subjectum* and *subjectus*— within an already constituted discourse, but able to stand *outside* discourse (that is, self-reflexive, able to see itself within discourse, representing itself to itself) enough to be able to innovate and divert the discursive processes. Kantian subjectivity is thus either Subjectivity per se or a subjectivity that repeats the Subject: posterior to the instituting act but also repeating and re-"claiming" it.

This reproduction of the Sophist Subject is often a matter of tradition and influence, for example, the relation between the European Renaissance and ancient Rome, but even the attempts in structural and poststructural thought to dissolve the Subject-as-origin have led to only problematic and recuperable success. One of the signs of the decline of theory—that is, of poststructuralism—has been the claim of the late eighties that it is politically necessary to theorize an agent of resistance.

Subjectivity and origin are closely related notions in the western tradition, and Sophist theory stands at the "origin" of this identification, at least given the manner in which "western" is traditionally figured. There is a related necessity in western thinking for a "nature" which precedes and determines culture. The Sophist notion of origin may seem to support an essentialism; for example, Kant's notion of an essential human nature as the foundation of knowledge is easily analogized to the Subject/subject conception of *arché*. On the other hand, the Sophist Subject stands as the critique of essentialism, since the act of the Subject is "natural" *and* "arbitrary"—specifically, without precedent—simultaneously; or, the act of the Subject institutes such oppositions as nature/culture.

Essentialism as recently discussed assumes a stable and determinable opposition between essence (or nature) and accident, even if the history of metaphysics belies such a claim for stability of essence (Fuss 1989, 20–21). On the other hand, the Sophist theory parallels essentialism since, like the act of the Subject, essence (as origin) is opaque, a mystery. Against this idea of essence or the "given," poststructuralists have argued that culture precedes nature in the sense that culture always promotes the construction, retrogressively, of the nature in the form of an origin so as to describe, regulate, or justify itself in terms of its own "discovered" original principles.

What follows is a summary version of some of the implications of the Sophist theory of origins.

I. The Sophist Subject institutes culture and discourse. In a system in which the novice imitates the master in order to become like him in grace of speaking, effectiveness, and achievement, the obvious question is: who has trained the master? This leads, theoretically, to a narrative of a tradition which descends from an origin (here, of training) constituted by the act of an originating Subject. Prior to this originating act there is no discourse, no culture, no rules, and, if the context is expanded beyond simply the acquisition of effective techniques—that is, if the context is anthropological, social, or historical, as is the case in Cicero's *De inventione*—no society and no law. The act defies categories: it or the acting Subject constitutes the nature upon which culture is founded (for example, the rules of discourse are renderings of the texts of the Subject); at the same time, since there exists no nature which precedes it, the act is completely arbitrary; and it produces both nature and culture as well as the categories and oppositions—such as nature/culture—at the same moment.

II. Reasoning about the Subject and its act is always retrogressive: in Cicero and Lucretius (the latter's subject is not a human agent), culture or the material world which we experience results from the precedent act by some unknown man or the arbitrary *clinamen* at some unknown time and place: "incerto tempore ferme / incertisque locis" (Lucretius 1963, 2.218–19, 259–60, 293). Thus the Subject has already disappeared, as well as its instituting act, into culture or materiality. In Lucretius, *tuché* or chance is introduced into the system of material determination by the *clinamen*. Freedom of action results, according to Lucretius, from the repetition (literal or figurative) of the *clinamen* within each successive stage of material interplay (ibid., 2.251–93). Later we will see that Freud's narrative entails retrogressive or "deferred [*nachträglich*] obedience" of the sons for the father they have killed (13, 145).

III. At the same time the "causality" of the Sophist narrative of origins establishes difference: the primary act of the Subject is an opening up of different-iation and the beginning of history or process. Equally important is the always maintained difference of Subject/subject, the master versus the novice. The Subject, although already absent, is the standard or origin; a naturally well endowed pupil may only become *like* the master by assiduous imitation of the original act or text. Differences arise in systems based on imitation about whether to follow the rules abstracted from the master's works or whether to imitate such texts directly; but no system questions the a priority of the Subject and its difference from the subject.

IV. The subject becomes *like* the Subject if successful, yet is never identical to it. In Roger Ascham's system of imitation for training young sixteenth-century "scholars," the pupil engages in an elaborate process of double translation in which he repeats a Ciceronian text. A later chapter will offer detail on this method, but its end is to produce a student able to deal successfully with the speaking situation Cicero faced, using exactly the same words.

Adaptation, which is a regular feature of systems of imitation, points to the difference of Subject and subject. The subject never becomes identical to the Subject, or is able to surpass the original and instituting act. But the subject must enter an ongoing process of culture and adapt his acquired skills to new speaking situations: the subject is the Subject in originating or creative potential to the degree that a situation within the process is like the situation prior to the institution of the process itself. The subject is within process—that is, part of the process and formed by it—and at the same moment "outside" and with the (Subjective) potential to divert the process. Incidentally, this notion of the subject "in/out" of discourse (philosophically, *subjectus/subjectum*) is a fair general description of postmarxism's and others' attempts to deal with their own theoretical need for agency at the same time they yield to the pressure from poststructuralists to erase the originating Subject.

V. The difference between Subject and subject can never be closed, since it is the motive or productive force which drives the system; yet the subject is always the Subject: his act represents the (absent) Subject and is a weak repetition, in process, of the act which institutes process. Since the Subject is always absent, the subject is its guarantee: the Subject needs the subject as much as the other way around.

This notion of original subjectivity persists in western thought up to and even within the poststructural era as primary metaphysicality. Deconstruction recognizes, for example, that the erasure of the subject means its reappearance in another place—somewhat like the successive takes of Gödel's theorem. Multiculturalism and the arguments about marginality which are popular nowadays have as much to learn about the persistence of the Subject. In the postpoststructural era, one of the first traditional notions to make its reappearance is original subjectivity (Dews 1987, xii–xvi, 6ff.). The condemnation of the Subject—that is, as centered and hegemonic—continues, but that the notion of the "marginal" subject is a repetition of the Subject in terms of its agency (the subject *is* the Subject) is clearly repressed. There is also a tendency to attempt to reclaim this notion of a central subject as a strategy on behalf of the marginalized subject, as in Spivak. Yet the notion of strategy here entails a Subject prior to both central and marginal subjectivity.

There are two interesting aspects to the Sophist theory of the a priori Subject. First is the fact that it is "naturally" gendered, yet there is no mechanism apparent in this theory of the origin and originality by which it is restricted to males. By the time this theory of origin arrives on the scene, gendering, or rather monogendering, has already occurred. This is an important issue because the Sophist theory is a theory of reproduction.

The theory of the originating Subject is also both authoritative and benign, and this seems uncharacteristic: it might be expected that the power allotted to the Subject would give rise to resentment in the suppressed subject. Yet aside from occasional claims that the Renaissance poet, for example, can contend with and even surpass his ancient model (Spenser, and Ovid—and even here the sense is that the poet can surpass other poets in attaining to the original or ideal expression), hostility even in this mitigated form seems never to surface. The competition of Subject and subject is structural, founded on the difference of levels on which the system itself is based.

The Subject/subject relation must be kept open, but it remains a benign relation, uninflected by negative affect. It is difficult to conceive how this benign theory, with its obvious and utilized political implications, persisted in western Europe until the early modern age. By that time, according to Foucault, sovereignty had its negation (e.g., Foucault 1979a); but on a parallel track benign theories of literary, historical, and other cultural forms of authoritative subjectivity persisted. Even in politics. Borch-Jakobsen shows how the "benign" myth of the Subject/Father operates in twentieth-century fascism, along with Freud's version of the organic unity of *Führer* and *Volk* in *Group Psychology* (Borch-Jakobsen 1991, 68–72). For Borch-Jakobsen this political myth is a repression of the failure of identification of the masses with the leader.

The Subject/subject difference, which parallels the father/son difference within the family structure, the absent negativity, and the general androcentricity of the Sophist theory suggest another narrative of origins: Freud's, in *Totem and Taboo*, concerning the establishing of the primary social and legal institutions (which he considers universal) from the killing of the Father of the "primal horde" by the group of "brothers" (or "sons,") held in check and cast out by the Father. Here the structural hostility is the motive force, although it is in later stages subject to repression. Otherwise, or even because of the difference of hostility/benignity, the two narratives of origin referenced here bear strikingly similar features and seem inevitably related. Freud is historically posterior to Sophist notions of origin, yet his text stages an origin prior to that of the Sophists.

The somewhat tortuous process by which these narratives intersect raises another question: which narrative of origin is the original one? In a literal historical sense, Freud's narrative is yet another example of the attempt, almost coextensive with the tradition of western thought itself, to explain culture and language by inventing or constituting its origin. Freud's original notion in *Totem and Taboo* was to draw a parallel between primitive behavior and contemporary neurosis. Further, Freud's narrative exemplifies Sophist Subjectivity, although invertedly, in that culture results from the murder of the Father; on the other hand, the Subject has always already disappeared from the scene in Sophist theory. And if the Subject is acted upon by the group of subjects in concert, the prior coercive acts of the former stand as the original cause which leads to the demise.

The negativity of the father/son relation is of central importance to Freud's narrative. It was written well after the counter narrative to benign authority was instituted historically, and clearly makes use of the ambivalence in attitude toward authority. Yet since the narrative claims to represent the history of a period—in fact, the beginning of history—well prior to the Sophists, then it might be useful to consider the increasing repression of hostility toward the Father over time in Freud as historically connected to and the precedent for the benign Subject/subject relation in the Sophist theory. Is the Sophist narrative then subsequent to the Freudian narrative—the former of which it is only possible to construe after the stage when antiauthoritarian hostility has been successfully repressed?

Freud's "prior" narrative is androcentric, but unlike the similar Sophist narrative, the mechanism of exclusion is more apparent in Freud, amounting to a redoubled exclusion not often noticed. Is Freud's then the prior narrative with respect to gender as well, explaining why the Sophist narrative is naturally and without question exclusively male? The importance of this question lies in the claim that the Sophist theory of subjectivity is the ground of most of the consequent notions of the subject in western thought. Is it possible to construct a narrative of the origins of narratives of origin of the subject and gender exclusion? Is this simply a return to the structuralist critique of the origin, an origin that turns out to be the site of an already gendered culture?

Freud's narrative of the origin of culture may thus precede and explain both the benignity of authority and androcentricity in the western tradition—as long as it is remembered that history/narrative is culture's own story, its normal mode for the invention of itself. One further question: what, at the origin, is the relation between these two characteristics of culture, benign authority and the exclusion of women? how does the latter lead to the occulting of hostilities?

Specifically, these two narratives of origin reflect on each other in terms of their multiple historical relations; this allows for some insight into how theory (en)genders itself and how it explains itself in a way that makes monogendering culturally necessary. The relation of the two narratives suggests how the explicit mechanism of monogendering operates within theories, especially theories of origin, and how this leads, in the Sophist narrative, to an explanation of reproduction which requires the participation of only one gender, excluding, repressing, or denying the existence of the other. The monogendering and the notion of benign authority appear coextensive. The two together are keys to a narrative of the origin of the understanding of western culture's theorizing of itself.

《◎》

Any inquiry into narratives of origin would eventually come across Freud's famous story of the emergence of civilization in *Totem and Taboo,* first published in 1913. The story is also recounted briefly in *Group Psychology and the Analysis of the Ego* in 1921 (Freud 1955, 135), where there is little mention of the rivalry among the males *for the women.* Freud's ventures into social anthropology have always been taken *cum grano salis,* but the narrative does have value in terms of the "desire" of western culture; in other words the narrative can be read as the social anthropology of anthropology. The story in *Totem and Taboo* is an interesting example of the western tradition's male- and subject-centered narratives, all founded on the Sophist narrative of the originating Subject; but if we wish to take Freud's version—because it claims to explain the emergence of authority—as the origin of the Sophist narrative, the *Totem and Taboo* narrative is even more interesting: it explains, as noted earlier, why the latter narrative assumes a benign authoritative relation between the Subject and the subject, and why in it reproduction seems only and naturally to require one gender, the masculine.

Freud's narrative is prior in the sense that he constructs the process from prehistoric times through successive and closely related stages of social organization: from the "primal horde" to the return of patriarchy in familial and political organization. There are four stages in the process, none, however, explicitly delineated. Freud claims through his anthropological sources that the existence of totemic clans or "bands of males" (141) is an empirical fact; thus he must needs explain that stage of human history by construing a prior stage, as well as subsequent ones, in order to put together a coherent narrative, a causality and the essential "truth" of the present time.

There are several peculiarities of Freud's version of the origin. First, if Plato claims that writing is forgetting, Freud argues that narrative and history are processes of repression. In an explicit methodological note in *Totem and Taboo* he distinguishes between narrative as allegory and as "historical stratification" (Freud 1953b, 149). The odd opposition allows Freud to maintain that each phase of the narrative occults the prior stage and is occulted in turn by the subsequent stage, so that the final stage, "the victory of the son's affectionate emotions over his hostile ones," guarantees the repressed presence of the hostility: emotional ambivalence is preserved by narrative layering. This is a necessary method, given Freud's analogy between the contemporary individual experiencing mental disturbance and the mental lives of primitive peoples: the title of the first published part of *Totem and Taboo* was "Some Points of Agreement between the Mental Lives of Savages and Neurotics" (1912). Yet this is typical of all narratives of origin; the prior stages are necessarily incorporated in the subsequent ones: the origin is always "there" (see also Freud 1961, 68–73).

In the Sophist narrative, to which we will be returning repeatedly in terms of Freud's narrative, the originating act of the Subject is absent because prior, but it is also present in the act of the subject or the one who follows the master; in the *De rerum natura* the *clinamen* is incorporated into every further stage of the material process either as chance or (human) choice; Cicero's and the Greek Sophists' explanation of social organization, as initiated by "some man" who recognized the potential of reason and eloquence, assumes the preservation of his initiatory act in the continuing rational and communicative structure that holds society together; and so on. The retrogression of all narratives of origin—that is, the necessity to constitute an origin in order to explain the present and justify it—guarantees that the absent origin is always present in the current process. Ambivalence and the negative attitudes that are repressed mark Freud's narrative as different, but how these subsequent narratives of origin emerge from Freud's narrative of ambivalence and repression is one of the questions being asked here.

Second, all but the last stage of the Freudian narrative is prefamilial. This makes for a different reading and sometimes a difficult one, since terms like "father" and "brothers," which would seem to indicate positions within a family structure, are absolutely central as narrative agents in Freud's prefamilial story. This paradox often entails Freud's own forgetting or repression, the reverse incorporation of the subsequent stage(s) in the prior. For example, at the fourth stage of social organization, the restoration of patriarchy, "the change in attitude to the father . . . extended to social organization. With the introduction of father-deities a fatherless society gradually changed into one organized on a patriarchal basis. The family was a restoration of the former primal horde" (ibid.).

But the primal horde is not a family. Freud's narrative excludes what is normally assumed as the foundation of the family unit, the biology of reproduction. In the primal horde there is no distinction of levels, of mother/daughters or of father/sons. The women are an undistinguished group of sex objects in Freud's narrative, at least in this first stage; the "father" is at the same time a "brother"—the latter term being one that Freud prefers to "son"—since they are distinguishable only in terms of positionality in a power relationship; and the father does not occupy a position according to the triangulation of the "family." In *Group Psychology* Freud characterizes both the "crowd"—that is, what is of interest in "group psychology"—and the primal horde as "an individual of superior strength among a troop of equal companions." In the same text Freud argues that the family is constituted in part by inverting the hostility of the "father" toward all the other males (Freud 1955, 122, 124–25).

It is the power relationship which defines the position of Father, that is, in control of the group of females and able forcibly to ward off the other males. Even the blood ties, which according to Freud are established at the stage of clan organization, are not familial: consanguinity is merely the promotion of solidarity among the brothers after the father has been killed and the women excluded, a symbol of nondifference or identity among them.

《∞》

The primal horde is prehistorical, preceding as it does, and setting the stage for, the first social act: killing the Father. This constructed notion of a "primal horde" (Freud 1953b, 103n., 125) derives from Darwin who, departing from observed primate behavior, hypothesized primitive human society as centering on the stronger, proprietary male, who excluded the other males from access to "his" females. In Freud this constructed origin becomes presocial and consequently prehistorical—the conditions or situation from which the narrative originates: "we find there [in the primal horde] . . . a violent and jealous father who keeps all the females for himself and drives away his sons as they grow up" (ibid., 141). Freud calls this the "earliest state of society" but at the same time he speaks of the "memorable and criminal deed" of killing the Father as the beginning "of social organization" (ibid., 142). In the same sense the primal horde is a family—a social organization—and it is not.

As noted above, Freud does not connect knowledge of the biology of reproduction with any level of social organization; and anthropologists have often noted the lack of connection between sexual behavior and biological reproduction among "primitive" groups. At any rate, nature and instinct seem to consist for Freud in sexual desire and the narcissistic desire for control. Both are "givens" in the Father of the primal horde. Sexual desire is based on sexual difference: the desire of one body to *incorporate* sexually with the different or other. The "given" here is the "natural" (heterosexual) desire of male(s) for females, and a hierarchical desire, since it is not necessary that the females have reciprocal desires. Much of the later Freud, Lacan, and subsequent theoretical analyses have been inclined to deny that "nature." But Freud here makes the unquestioned assumption that there exists a heterosexual nature (distinct binary gender, opposite-sex desire) which is in place prior to culture—in the same way that the incest taboo assumes heterosexuality.

It is interesting that Freud constitutes and represses this, hetero-sexual desire and consequent intercourse, as a form of (unstable) social organization—whether connected or not with biological reproduction. This sexual/social relation of all the females to the dominant male constitutes a social organization (although not a very politically correct one, from which Irigaray develops an economics of scarcity [1985, 170, 174]) that Freud does not recognize, partly because, as we shall see, he prefers a narrative of monogendering; that the primal horde constitutes a social organization is repressed. Culture must *overcome* nature, it seems; this seems clear in Irigaray's claim that feminine sexuality/desire is the foundation of male discourse, but is also excluded.

Nature is a peculiar thing in Freud and in psychoanalysis in general. It has been argued that feminists gravitate toward psychoanalysis as an effective anti-essentialist discourse, one in which sexual difference and heterosexual desire are not givens but are matters of cultural subjectification which can be transferred from a universalist to a historical reading (Fuss 1989, 6). However, it is generally understood that Freud's career is split with respect to the question of sexual differentiation.

Until after 1920 or so Freud treats sexual difference and hetero-sexual desire as natural, and that period contains *Totem and Taboo; Group Psychology* is at the margin. For example, the Oedipus complex meant in this early period that desire operated along heterosexual lines. According to Juliet Mitchell, Freud was so focused on gaining acceptance of the notion of infantile sexuality that he was unable to broach the question of the de-termination of sexual difference as anything other than natural (Foucault's notion of the nineteenth-century deployment of sexuality, focused in part on "children's sex," makes this statement a complex one).

After 1920 Freud gives the castration complex much more impor-tance, and makes sexual differentiation a consequence of the response to that threat. It is also generally argued that Freud's ideas about what was given or natural began to change long before 1920—that is, during the period when he came up with the primal horde narrative and even before (Mitchell and Rose 1982, 9ff.; see also 106–11 and Freud, *Three Essays on the Theory of Sexuality* [1905], 8, 145–47fn., esp. 146, on the interim concept of bisexuality).

Freud's problem in the anthropological narrative lies in his need to "go back to the origin" in order to explain culture: the origin requires an initial situation "in nature"—what else does "primitive" mean?—including subjects with natural drives. This locks Freud into natural sexual difference and heterosexual desire; the threat of castration operates by implication in the narrative, but it is the result of the competition which arises from natural heterosexual desire; hence a narrative of origins must support and repeat the notion that culture is an emanation of (sexual) nature. Origin *is* nature. The opposite problem has similarly severe repercussions. If, for example, the penis (that is, the supposed natural) only takes on significance in terms of the external "law" of castration, what accounts for the constitution of this law and culture as so founded? Hence the narrative of origins *in nature*.

This problem is complicated further by the refusal within gender studies of the eighties to accept either sex or gender as natural. Judith Butler's *Gender Trouble* is a sustained argument that heterosexuality and binary gender form an arbitrary, historical discourse which alibis for itself by constructing, a posteriori, its own origin "in nature." However, the application of discursive theory raises questions of the grounds for distinguishing the naturalized from the natural and, as Foucault discovered, questions of the origin of discourse itself (see chapter 3). Freud's narrative of origins is in the above sense clearly an alibi similar to Lévi-Strauss's: culture is the institutionalization of an already given male hegemony or binary sex/gender hierarchy. But the identification of nature as alibi escapes Freud: for his narrative nature is present and determinative in/of the origin.

In *Totem and Taboo,* then, there is a "nature" at the origin. Yet what is interesting in this text is the *denaturalizing* of sexual difference as the foundation of culture. It could be argued that in the early Freud this should be the key to any culture which develops, but in both *Totem and Taboo* and *Group Psychology* he seems to frustrate that naturalist tendency: first, heterosexual union is without stability (assuming, as Freud suggests, that "brother" succeeds "brother" in the power position as Father over a long period), and social *order* comes about only with the laws and stability of the clan; or the primal Father is free and antisocial, unencumbered by his sexual activities—in fact, made independent by these activities. In the latter case, "the father of the primal horde owing to his sexual intolerance compelled all of his sons to be abstinent, and thus forced them into ties that were inhibited in their aims, while he reserved for himself freedom of sexual enjoyment and in this way remained without ties. All the ties upon which a group depends are of the character of instincts which are inhibited in their aims" (Freud 1955, 139–40).

The agents in this passage from *Group Psychology* are full subjects, and heterosexual desire is natural. The forceful inhibition of the latter instinct leads to the formation of the homosexual clan and the total exclusion of women. In this way, paradoxically, heterosexual desire leads to its own repression; it is both the foundation of culture and the absence on which the first society, the clan, is structured. And shortly before this passage Freud has been discussing the infant's undifferentiated sexual inclinations (137).

According to the narrative of the primal horde, in his "nature" the father is not different from the brothers: they possess the same "craving for power and sexual desires" (Freud 1953b, 143) as he; the only difference is in his dominant position in the power relation. This identity of desire among the males is based on sexual difference, or the difference of gender, which is clearly prior to and the basis of the social organization that Freud represses. Freud's version of the origin of the social is rather in the act of killing the father, itself a social act because the brothers must act in concert in order to eliminate the primal Father (141). In this sense they cancel difference—of power—by killing and consuming the body of the father, by incorporating it, producing identity and equality among themselves; at the same time, however, the act introduces difference: the powerful brother, once killed, is produced as the Father, as (non)existent on a different and higher level.

The production of the Father is problematic in Freud's naturalistic narrative, since outside the family the father has no identity (that is, bio-social). The production of the Father, however, prior to biological and social reckonings, or simultaneously with the social, appears to reproduce the original "relation of force"; but it transcends that: the Father is a construction of the brothers' image of themselves, coextensive with their desire or their consciousness of the difference between themselves and the now-Father. In this sense, the killing is indeed a necessity: to constitute the other and simultaneously to subjectivize themselves. In Lacanian terms, nothing of the human order exists prior to the prohibiting/constituting law of the Father, within the symbolic order—in the same sense that the Sophist Subject constitutes the space of the subject.

The difference of power is thus internalized or introjected: the animal becomes human in its first social act, of killing, in reproducing the difference in terms of loss or lack, that is, in terms of the psychic capacity for remorse and the fissure of being which Freud labels ambivalence—that is for Freud the split in a full subject—and which results in further and further repression into an unconscious. Lacan would situate the killing as the moment of subjective constitution and entrance into the symbolic, dependent on their loss/lack represented in and by the production of the Father.

In effect, the brothers misidentify the dead man as the Father and must, as consequently identified "brothers," suffer the difference; it is the condition of their social subjecthood to be "subject to" unsatisfiable desire—for the Father. Constitution of the Father as the position from which the now-subject is "seen" constitutes the "law" of the Father, the "external" (which is now also produced as different from the internal) threat of castration, the "cutting off" of the brothers from their desires—they have, until this point, been "natural" desires for the women—and replacing those with the desire for the Father. Thus what happens in *Totem and Taboo* is the cutting away of the females, or, in a structural sense, the *failure* of the law to produce sexual difference, and success in producing a monogendered social order. However Freud's ideas change about the production of sexual difference under the law of castration, it seems clear that his commitment to monogendering is never superseded. Reproduction is incorporated into identification, and psychoanalysis and its explanation of culture continue to exclude biology: Freud never stops telling stories of the origin.

Borch-Jakobsen, referring to the *Totem and Taboo* narrative in terms of individual narcissistic desire (that is, identification), points out that the Father is "no Father," but "a fellow being" different only in terms of power (1991, 72, 75); the Father is "*no one*" (75), but is created by the brothers in (the failure of) the identification with the now dead Father, in the opening up of difference: the brothers as subjects, able to represent themselves to themselves (auto-representation) only in the difference from the Father. Also in *Group Psychology* the more explicit reference (than in *Totem and Taboo*) to the aftermath of the murder supports the argument that Fatherhood is positionality: "None of the group of victors could take his place, or, if one of them did, the battles began afresh, until they understood that they must all renounce their father's heritage" (Freud 1955, 135). Thus as Freud's narrative begins, gender or sexual difference is repressed and the difference among males opens up; monogendering begins. Narrative is identical to repression: in Freud the repression of the hostility toward the Father, but also of sexual difference.

The parallel between Freud's and the Sophist narrative of origin of culture appears even at this level: the instituting act of the Subject is inversely matched by the killing of the father. Both theories are vague about the time and place of the originating occurrence. Freud's "One day . . ." is matched by Cicero's "at some time, some man . . ." or Lucretius's claim that the *clinamen* moves laterally or creatively "in incerto tempore . . ."—another clear sign, incidentally, of culture's claim to discover/invent its own prior nature. The difference of Subject/subject derives initially from the brothers' invention of the Father, who is at that stage also absent. One narrative instances a positive act, the other a "monstrous" and "criminal" one (another of Freud's anachronisms) (Freud 1953b, 142); this divergence is overcome only at the later stages of Freud's process, in which monogendering and the total exclusion of women has already been fixed.

◖◖◑◗◗

The second stage of Freud's narrative of social development is the totemic clan, which he claims, from the anthropological data he cites, is a social organization still observable in remote locales. This, the first stage of social organization, brought about by the killing and consuming of the father by the brothers, initiates a political equality and brings about "the two fundamental taboos of totemism" or the laws which constitute society-as-ethics and as-morality: the prohibition against harming the totem animal; the prohibition against incest or the rule of exogamy (143).

Narrative is repression: at this stage the brothers reenact the murder of the father by killing and eating the totem animal—which symbolizes the absent father—in the ritual totemic meal; but remorse and appeasement are also evident: "Totemic religion not only comprised expressions of remorse and attempts at atonement, it also served as a remembrance of the triumph over the father" (145). What Freud calls "the tension of ambivalence" is characteristic of the totemic sacrificial meal: killing and atonement. But the killing of the father is also the killing of the strongest brother, and hence the invention of the Father and his "empty" position. In this sense the law of the clan against fratricide redoubles the prohibition against harm to the totemic animal/father: the implication is to refuse the possibility of any brother becoming like the Father, or fulfilling that empty position of power over them and hence invoking the repetition of the killing of the father (146).

The "father" never was a biological parent; his murder merely removes the most powerful rival from the scene. The guilt of the band of murderers is not familial, although Freud projects the family "romance" into the prefamilial stages of social organization and makes it the basis for guilt. But clearly, in Freud's own narrative, the clan is the fundamental social unit, not the family. The guilt is invented or produced along with the murder, by the murder, as a cultural fact. This invention of the Father and of guilt, which makes the totemic and fratricidal prohibitions identical, is ultimately a transformation and removal of the becoming-father: as animal symbolically and as existent at a removed level—that is, just as the Sophist Subject is absented and exalted, removed to an inaccessible because

39

prior plane of existence. Both resemble the notion, generally attributed to Foucault, of a discourse that invents the nature that must necessarily be regulated and distributed by the discourse.

At the same time the totemic meal represents the identity of the father with the brothers—again the reverse repression, a forgetting that the father is originally only the most powerful brother. Consuming the father-brother is not merely to become like the Father, that is, to undergo transformation; it is also a ritual of complete identity. In the totemic meal, similarly, the brothers dress and act like, and generally imitate, the totemic animal "as though they are seeking to stress their identity with it" (140).

Thus, according to Freud, the totemic system is "a covenant with their [the sons'] father" in which the totem promises the benevolence of "protection, care and indulgence" (144) and by which the murderers can say by way of self-justification: had the "real" father been this way, there would have been no need for the killing. Hence the invention of the Father, which then allows for the process of further narrative repression: the removed Father is a Father any son could love. He is first of all dead, and hence no longer physically strong, egocentric, or a sexual rival; (re)invented at a remove, on the other side from life, his cruelty is forgotten and his altruistic feelings toward them are produced and foregrounded. From repression, benignity; from the totemic prohibition an ambivalence that is in the process of becoming a manifest benevolence covering a latent hostility according to the narrative causality mentioned earlier.

The second prohibition, against incest, is also brought about by the killing of the father and the emergence of the clan. In the primal horde, the women exist as the sexual property of the most powerful male. After the killing that invents the Father at a remove, prohibition against incest and the consequent rule of exogamy appear. The prohibition, according to Freud, is both symbolic and practical—an opposition, like many Freud uses to construct his narrative, easily collapsed. Since heterosexual desire is inherent, every brother is a potential Father, and this would lead to "a struggle of all against all" (see also Freud 1955, 135). The resultant choice is symbolic and practical at once: "they all alike renounced the women whom they desired and who had been the chief motive for dispatching their father" (Freud 1953b, 144).

Practically this brings peace, but it also allays guilt. The brothers kill the father-brother because of the rivalry over the women, in order to enjoy them as sex partners. To renounce these objects connotes guilt, "an attempt to allay that feeling and to appease the father by deferred obedience to him" (145). This results, however, in the double exclusion of women. In the primal horde they are "excluded" as sex objects, secondary to the males. Recently, Lévi-Strauss has been held most responsible for this, that is, for a configuration of nature (female) controlled by culture (male) that already subordinates women to a lack which instates male solidarity in clan relations (e.g., Rubin 1975, 171ff., and Butler 1990, 38ff.) In the clan women are excluded totally from social organization. The family does not exist at this historical stage, only the clan and only the single clan; and Freud does/doesn't recognize the horde as a social organization.

Earlier in *Totem and Taboo* Freud discusses the incest prohibition as clan based, not familial, and he treats exogamy in terms of multi-clan groups. But in his narrative of the killing of the father there is only the single clan—a monogendered social group made up of the brothers and excluding women. In the *Group Psychology* version, there is clearly only one horde at the origin (Freud 1955, 135). The strongest argument to the contrary that Freud makes is that exogamy entails a split between affectionate and sensual feelings for women, the latter being allowed exercise only in relation to "strange" women (111ff., 141). As Freud more directly argues, however: "In this way [by excluding women] they rescued the organization which had made them strong—and which may have been based on homosexual feelings and acts, originating perhaps during the period of their expulsion from the horde" (Freud 1953b, 144; see also 1955, 124n., 139–40).

The rule of exogamy can have little meaning in terms of Freud's narrative, since it precedes the opposition between inside and outside; it can only mean the total exclusion of women, since there exists no social organization outside the clan. If difference is necessary to social organization, then in the monogendered clan men are content with the difference of the Father and the more material differences among male bodies. Women are no longer marginalized sex objects; under the double exclusion, they disappear.

Such an argument must be put in the context of Freud's shift toward sexual difference as a result of the castration complex, and not toward the biological or natural predetermination mentioned above. Lacan followed the lengthy psychoanalytic debate about female sexual difference of the twenties and thirties by focusing on the difficulty and precariousness of subjective sexual identity processes. But in 1912 in *Totem and Taboo* Freud was unwilling or unable to deal directly with the issue of sexual differentiation: he assumes prior natural difference as the basis of desire, and then he subjects that dispensation to an *aphanisis,* so that the process of differentiation is projected entirely on males (a condition, incidentally, that appears as "normal" in the Sophist narrative). An example or even a

41

prototype of the process might, according to Eve Sedgwick's work on the homo/heterosexual structuring of culture, be *Frankenstein,* which "loses" the female term, "leaving . . . a residue of two potent male figures locked in an epistemologically indissoluble clench of will and desire" (1990, 187; also 1985, 83ff.).

In the Sophist theory the originating act opens up difference—of Subject/subject, nature/culture, prior/posterior—allowing for process and history to be constructed from those differences. Killing the father inaugurates difference as well—the difference of the father—and leads to cultural process. But Freud's narrative has a prior moment, so that the opening of monogendered difference as social organization also entails, as mentioned earlier, the closing off or repression of gender difference as social foundation; monogendered difference becomes the origin. Most narratives of origin are unable to close off the possibility of a yet more prior origin, but Freud's is particularly vulnerable, since he both suggests and represses that prior origin. Thus the close relation between the two taboos: the totemic prohibition symbolizes the emerging benevolence of, and the necessary repression of hostility toward, the Father; at the same time the object of rivalry—the other of women—is excluded. The killing of the father institutes culture, but of a certain kind, a monogendered one. The relation to the Sophist narrative, which is monogendering—reproduction by means of only one gender—and in which the father-Subject is benign, is beginning to emerge in relation to clan organization; or rather, the reason that the Sophist narrative is "later" than the Freudian is beginning to appear.

Sophist theory excludes women in the same way as Freud's clan. It is not simply that both narratives refuse the notion of biological reproduction; both are protobiological, but they are told from a postbiological perspective. "Before" biology, they discover an origin of reproduction which is monogendered: social and intellectual origins and history are the result of exclusively male reproduction, as in Cicero's explanation of civilization as the replication of a male idea or in the general Sophist notion that novices reproduce the master by imitation (see Jaeger 1944, 3:134).

The postbiological perspective is significant: both Freud and the Sophists—and all consequent theorists of the subject, it seems—seem intent on replacing biological or bi-o-gendered reproduction with monogendering. Freud's narrative actually presents sexual difference as the origin of social organization and then makes it disappear, replacing it with the all-male clan organization. It is as if biological reproduction, once knowledge of it has been established, must have already been made subsequent and peripheral or made to disappear until monogendering is established firmly enough at the center so as to be unmovable—that is, as the way in which culture "really" reproduces itself.

In the nineteenth century when biology became a science and "life" began to be studied, as prior to culture, "great man" theories began to proliferate and intensify; in the twentieth century with the failure of the explanatory power of narratives of origin the notion of an originating Subject has begun to disappear, although it persists in the form of explanations of the shift from centered to marginal subject, in the shift from universal to specific intellectual (Foucault 1977, 205–17), and in every case in which the subject repeats the Subject from "inside" culture or discourse. Monogendering may be experiencing the same sort of disappearing/reapppearing process, since both Freud's and Sophist narratives mark the union of originality and the single gender.

◖(◕◡◕)◗

The benevolence of the Father is already evident at the clan stage, although it is countered by the ambivalence evident in the survivors, in the totemic meal ritual and elsewhere. The next stage in Freud's narrative is the religious, in which the brothers continue to invent the Father as more removed from them and more benevolent, the hostility being repressed by layer on layer of narrative and history: the totem become god, that is, anthropomorphic and more *like*, though further distanced, a god which looks after the interests of the clan without any of its own desires interfering. The continuing total exclusion of women opened up the sphere of men's work—reproduction—in which women were warned, until recently, not to interfere.

This emergent Father-god, anthropomorphic or like the brothers, a sign of the longing to be the Father, is a reduction of the original difference of the Father instituted by the founding murder. This is significant in that Freud's narrative achieves closure when patriarchy is restored, that is, when the father-son difference, having been denatured and subject to a repression, is reintroduced into domestic life. This restoration marks Freud's subsequent and final stage of culture.

The stage of the god as father-surrogate also continues to emphasize difference, carrying further the exclusion, abstraction and distanciation of the Father from the clan. The lessening and increasing of difference is what Freud calls a "more widely separated ambivalence." The process of maintaining difference continues the denaturing of the "dead" Father represented by the totem. Freud generally in his "pre-castration" days conceives of nature and culture in opposition: culture is the narrative of the repression

43

of instinct and the sublimation of its energies, or the disappearance and the forgetting of nature. Even after 1920, the threat of castration is the "law" which brings an end to desire and initiates psychosocial sexual difference. Distancing the Father into a remote and omnipotent god is the sign of this high level of repression, which has begun with the invention of the Father at the clan stage. Although not as unbridgeable as the contemporary sense of the divine-human difference, certainly extreme (149).

Freud evinces little interest in language in his narrative, but the various shifts in conceptions of language implied by his story are significant. At the clan stage—the first stage of social organization and culture—language appears and is based on analogy and identity; in other words it is materially symbolic. The totem is the Father in terms of the human-animal symbiosis as well as the ambivalent relation between animals and humans, above and below each other in the food chain. An overdetermination of identity in nature. The totem animal is a symbol of the Father, existing in its own right as an animal while also signifying the Father. Signification is natural and grounded, without a differential and arbitrary system of signification.

At the religious stage of the process the character of language changes. The Father, formerly represented materially, is abstracted, made "ideal," distanced into an arbitrary signifier, having lost its relation to a signified. The Father becomes, through repression, a pure sign, part of a differential system. Borch-Jakobsen claims that what is significant in the *failure* of the attempt to identify with the Father is reflected here: metaphor, identity, symbol—all turn out to be part of the process of the breakdown of the identificatory relation of representation, so that a nonessential ego attempting to become substance "identifies" with a detached sign, in effect becoming itself a sign within a systematic play which gives it an "identity." It is also significant that in *Group Psychology* the historical movement from group to individual psychology is achieved "in imagination," or in simulacra which have no relation to the objective or "real" (Freud 1955, 136): thought substitutes for action as sign displaces symbol.

Sophist theory is most closely related to this, the religious stage in Freud's narrative. Freud precedes the Sophists, clearing the way for them, narrativizing away the hostility to the Father and eliminating women. The religious stage is a continuation of the clan stage in that the primary social organization—the only one—remains the group of brothers. The invented, longed for, and distanced Father gives rise to a theory of the Subject whose act originates culture and of a benign Subject/subject relation which is unproblematic. The Subject-god-father is, having instituted culture, distanced or absent, yet is present in culture and in the acts of subjects who have the potentiality to divert the process of culture toward better and higher ends. The subject is both the Subject and is not, and this is the largely positive ambivalence which characterizes the Sophist theory of origins. In *Group Psychology,* however, the "father, chief, or leader" is materialized as historically a priori; that is, he stands *before* the group, "free," "independent even in his isolation. . . . He loved no one but himself" (123)—existent, not invented.

On the one hand the separation between the Sophist Subject and the subject is unbridgeable, as in Freud. The Subject is prior, instituting that culture in which the subject is nurtured and able to realize his own portion of originality, so that structurally the subject can never become Subject. Although the subject goes beyond the Subject in adapting to new situations inconceivable to the latter, in Serrean language the Subject is permanently positioned at the head of the stream; everything else is downstream of the inaugurating act. The creative and adaptive act of the subject is necessarily a repetition of this act.

On the other hand the invention of the Subject is the invention of the Father: as always, in theories of origin, subject precedes Subject, since the reasoning is always retrogressive, as in the cases mentioned earlier. The subject *is* the Subject, in that the subject's creative act institutes the conception of the Subject: the subject thus invents the Subject as an identity with itself ("brother") transformed into a difference ("Father"). Or culture inventing its prior nature and thereby justifying itself. Without this prior act of the subject, or as Freud would say, this group of subjects, the Subject is nothing. The benign/repressed ambivalence between Subject/subject then appears as a competition: becoming *like* or surpassing the model by means of which the subject is trained: never succeeding because, structurally, nature precedes culture; and always successful because culture, in theories of origin, always invents its own difference, or nature. This invention at Freud's religious stage and in the Sophist theory is benign, or almost totally repressed.

The Sophist narrative replicates the monogendering of Freud's narrative as well—that is, beyond hostility to the paternal it has already instituted the total exclusion of women, who are the absent ground upon which the amelioration of the father-sons relation can occur. In the Sophist narrative reproduction is totally in the hands of males: the subject is reproduced from the origin in the Subject by imitation; this ignores or diminishes the importance of the biological reproduction of bodies. Closely related to the Sophist narrative is Michel Foucault's account, in *The Use of Pleasure,* of reproduction in fourth-century B.C.E. Greece—incidentally, yet another narrative of origins. In that text it is clear that the reproduction of mature upper-class males is a parallel instance of monogendering. Heterosexual pleasure and biological reproduction come under the economy or the rules of the *oikos,* the household, but the male's prior achievement of self-mastery is entirely and priorly the result of monogendering: as a youth he is selected and trained in self-restraint by an adult male (e.g., Foucault 1985b, 195); and during this time sexual pleasure among males is explicitly included, although the overall relation is problematized and subject to limitation (192ff.).

Foucault's is a more detailed version of Sophist monogendering, yet it also differs from the Sophist narrative in important respects. Freud's and the Sophist narrative exclude women entirely; there is only one gender in the sense that exclusion must precede monogendering. Foucault's history is post-Sophist in the sense that the biological cloning of bodies is regulated as part of household management (although still articulated largely as a regulation of male pleasures). Bi-o-gendering seems to exist here side by side with monogendering, but is in fact peripheral and secondary. Once monogendering has been established as primary reproduction through the explanatory force of theories of origin, women may be introduced and biology allotted its minor role.

Historical research into the origin of patriarchy has not yet revealed an initiating event, but some inquiries uncannily reproduce or parallel implications of Freud's narrative. Women are, first of all, subject to domination in terms of their sexuality and reproductive capacity (in the ancient Near East, c. 3100 B.C.E.), and, as noted above, excluded from the process of representing or the construction of history. The social and economic nonsignificance of Mother-goddesses, state support of patriarchal families, and, with the appearance of the Hebrew religion, the exclusion of women from the God-humanity covenant—these are included in histories of women by women (e.g., Lerner 1986, 8–11 and passim). Such history is postbiological: that is, reproductive capacity is obviously central to the issue of control within *recorded* history (40–49).

It might also be interesting to consider the latest of narratives of reproduction, cloning, in terms of gender and exclusion; it is certainly a test of the "natural."

((◦◦))

Freud's final stage consists in the restoration of patriarchy. It is a continuation of the prior stage of deification of the Father: it entails the readmission of the father, his restoration as head of the simultaneously constituted family, and his emergence as head of state. According to Freud, this is the climax of the "denial of the great crime which was the beginning of society" (Freud 1953b, 150) and the high point of authority. In other words, the repression is so far advanced that the invented Father of the totem-become-god can now be reproduced within the level of social organization, as domestic and political heads. The original invention created a stratification of levels, but that is now reintegrated into the social level. Men can now coexist at different authoritative levels within the social complex as long as they continue to repress their natures/desires, that is, as long as women are literally or virtually excluded. For example: "In the great artificial groups, the Church and the army, there is no room for woman as a sexual object. . . . It seems certain that homosexual love is far more compatible with group ties" (Freud 1955, 141).

Whether women are indeed still literally excluded at this last stage of the *Totem and Taboo* narrative is unclear. Foucault's narrative suggests that the reinclusion of women at this advanced stage may have little effect on the by-now firmly established narrative of monogendering; the institution of the family at this stage may suggest the subsidiary inclusion of biological reproduction, along with sexual object-cathexis of the male towards the mother and other females.

A curious note: Freud in *Group Psychology* argues very strongly for the significance of the leader or chief in understanding what holds groups together. It is not just that members of the group identify with each other, as is well known; identification occurs only because "they all want to be ruled by one person" (121); all this leads Freud to argue that the group is "a revival of the primal horde" (123). Thus group members, who *love* the chief, represent an "idealistic remodelling" of the relations within the horde—or the inversion of those relations. What is curious is that Freud short-circuits the process of repression here and raises more questions than he answers with his explanation.

It is worth mentioning that there are several explicit signs of Freud's exclusion of women in the construction of his narrative. At a few points, drawing on a myriad of anthropologists, as he does throughout *Totem and Taboo*, Freud mentions possible matriarchal stages of the narrative: of such a stage that might have preceded the patriarchal (Freud 1953b, 144); of "mother-goddesses" which may have preceded the father-gods of the religious stage (149); and elsewhere. He is constrained to mention these instances because of the anthropologists' descriptions of ritual surrounding feminine deities, yet Freud's typical gesture is to the effect that "I cannot suggest at what point in this process of development a place is to be found" for *that other gender* (ibid.). The casualness of the exclusion is a sign of its deliberateness. The historical-theoretical construction of origins thus makes clear that the discourse about origins is already male.

This makes a double point: we are, with Freud and the Sophists, always after the origin, or, what is the same thing, prior to it; and there is no origin, neither of culture nor of gender exclusion. There was always culture and it was always gendered. The need to construct an origin of monogendering-as-culture comes from the prior male culture, Freud's and our own. And what is striking in the narrative, as I have said, is not that women were sex objects at the origin but that they were subjected to a double or total exclusion—a monogendering that, once firmly established, can be ameliorated and supported (as well as disguised) by the institution of the family and bi-o-gendering.

It is not ironic that, in the return to Freud, Lacan *loses* the woman: she is not or "not all"—the usual quotation—difference, loss, absence; in his description of the phallic organization of the symbolic order, Lacan finds himself unable to grasp any concept of the feminine (Mitchell and Rose 1982, 49–50, 56–57). But in a certain sense Lacan stops short of Freud: the feminine could be said to "represent" the masculine as the next or further step in the series of displacements (lack/loss) which constitutes his system. Yet from the perspective of the necessity to alibi for the excluding or losing of women, the homophobic definition of heterosexuality (as the normal) depends from the "factitiousness" of the distinction between "men's *identification* (with men) and their *desire* (for women)" (Sedgwick 1990, 62)—the gordian knot of the psychoanalytic narrative of (Oedipal) development that enforces a certain circularity in the return to castration and an already male-oriented discourse.

Some forms of feminist inquiry tend to reproduce the structure of monogendering. For example, work by feminists on the relevance of sexual difference to epistemology or "ways of knowing" often casts women in the role of the "inside" (connectedness, sympathy, the sensible) as opposed to male abstraction, rationality, and detachment; that is, the male is the prior Subject; the female is "in" discourse (Code 1991, 8–35 and passim). Thus, despite the attempts to introduce a female/male difference that reorients and augments, the female can still be seen as produced by the male. Much of this work is essentializing, that is, proposing a substantive difference of the feminine. The search for the origin establishes firmly that culture is founded on the total exclusion of women. Thus the masculinist bias informs traditional notions of culture—a point that feminists should not forget and indeed continue to unpack. Benign relations between father/son and Subject/subject are fundamental themes in the narratives of reproduction in/of western thought, especially in the sense that the Sophist theory of subjectivity, including the "understanding" about gender, is the core out of which western thought develops.

⟪ 2 ⟫

Foucault and the
Discourse of Subjectivity

T his chapter attempts to confront the issue of a subjectless poststructuralism. Two of the main currents of this "movement" as they concern
the subject correspond readily to the two best-known names, Derrida and
Foucault. Derrida, whom I make no attempt to treat extensively here,
reduces the phenomenological or Enlightenment subject as the origin of
speech/writing, substituting, in a parody of metaphysics, his own origin,
differance—an origin which erases itself yet retains the trace of the replaced
subject and other origins. Foucault in his middle career reproduces the
contingent, shifting discourses and practices which have formed modern
subjectivity—practices whose origin cannot be ascribed to a master subject.
It is this line of desubjectification that I attempt to investigate here.

The chapter follows Foucault through several phases of his interest in
subjectivity. The genealogical and epistemic phases, his most direct attack on
the subject, reveal both an ongoing recuperation and a potential for escaping
the traditional focus of analysis on the subject. The later phase of the second
and third volumes on sexuality marks a reorientation in his thinking: the
recognition that we are historically constituted as self-reflexive and self-
constituting subjects leads him to a genealogy of human self-constitution.
This is not a return to the subject as nature or origin. This latter phase is
analyzed more in detail beginning with chapter 5.

This is first a matter of asking where the subject tends to disappear
in Foucault and his commentators—and where it reappears in this tradition
of poststructural thought and its aftermath. I have taken, as a way of
approaching this question, three critical texts of the late eighties, Paul

Bové's *Intellectuals in Power,* Frank Lentricchia's *Ariel and the Police,* and Paul Smith's *Discerning the Subject.* All three engage the problem of discursive subjectivity and in that sense are representative of the post-age. Also central is their relation to Foucault and their reinvocation of the subject despite that relation. This in turn leads to a reexamination of some of the texts of Foucault, in which a subject that is the origin of power seems to persist. Foucault's concern for "the technologies of the self" in volumes two and three of *The History of Sexuality* is another apparent instance of the return of the subject. The "subjectless" part of Foucault tends toward information theory and invokes through Michel Serres, a historian and philosopher of science, the new ahuman view of science (also evident in Prigogine and others); and of the impossibility of that view without a return of the subject. Bové, Lentricchia, and Smith do invoke Foucault in one way or another; they are about, more specifically, "power-knowledge relations" and, on the one hand, "a subject of knowledge who is or is not free in relation to the power system," and capable of resistance; or, on the other, the subject as a function of power-knowledge (Foucault 1979a, 27–28), that is, produced by discourse.

Bové is closest to Foucault's position, reading Nietzsche, I. A. Richards, Erich Auerbach, and Edward Said as failed attempts to escape or transcend the regime of truth of anthropological humanism. For example, Bové argues that Auerbach's attempt to resuscitate "anthropological or historicist humanism" should be read "as the residual persistence of powerful discursive functions, with all their consequent values and desires, rather than as the self-directed actions of a critical consciousness or subject" (260); and that the important discussions which are critical of Foucault have all been defenses of the "leading intellectual" as a force for social change.

Bové also says, interestingly, that in a close look at the work of Auerbach and Said, "the critic often appears as an originating subject . . . only to disappear as such in order to reappear . . . as a subject who is an inscribed function of discursive and institutional structures" (247–48). This play of priority/posteriority and inside/outside reveals clear connections with the prior western tradition of the transcendental subject, or the subject-as-origin. The texts which attempt to constitute resistance to the hegemonic social formation or to structuralist or Foucauldian "monolithic" discourse (as is sometimes claimed) seem to have few resources to call upon except the traditional conception of the subject. Hence the potential identity: the subject-of-resistance is the originating subject is the bourgeois, Enlightenment subject-of-freedom. And subjectivity begins to appear as the ultimate metaphysical trap.

In Bové, Said becomes the prime example of resistance to hegemonic institutions, discourses, and practices, but one that is reinvested with the assumptions of the discourses it resists and which is ultimately recuperated by them. Lentricchia, in a peculiar and idiosyncratic book (already enacting the subject), resists that "monolithic" discourse of Foucault which refuses to recognize the "personal subject" and its potential for resistance. There is a massive irony in the perception of Foucault's own discourse as the hegemonic discourse of all discourses and practices, but in one sense it is merely the expected reassertion of the repressed subject and in another sense the discontent with the now clearly apparent contradiction between discourse and subject. The latter is what needs to be more clearly focused.

Paul Smith, although attempting to discern a theory of potential resistance in the subject constituted within conflicting discourses, has this in mind; yet he assiduously avoids Foucault except in a long footnote, where he maintains that Foucault submerges the real problematic of the subject in a discussion of power (168). The subject is a dangerous ground. And resistance, if it continues to be thought as grounded in the subject, will always reinvoke the strongest and most pervasive of metaphysical traditions: of the origin which is prior to the play of discourse. If the subject is indeed metaphysics, or metaphysics in deed—making its disappearance necessary—how then are we to speak or to resist? The problematic of the subject and the possibility of an analysis or theory of resistance that escapes metaphysical assumptions about the subject are at issue here.

Vincent Descombes offers a convenient summary of the humanist version of the philosophy of the subject, which

> declares that the only conceivable suppositum of a "properly human" action is the being that identifies itself, not with the empirical person that it is also, but with the autonomous subject. Not the individual, taken up as he is in the tissue of the world, but a being capable of positing itself as *ideally* (or ultimately) different from everything that history has made, from everything that institutions have fixed, from all the futures that past events have already marked or cleared the way for. But also the being that can think of itself, at the end of an infinite effort, as the author of all its worldly determinations. (130)

This is precisely the already doubled subject that threatens to subvert all recourse to subjectivity even in its less ideal and extreme form.

What I hope to have shown in chapter 1 is that the Sophist theory of the Subject/subject provides a useful model within which to pursue the permutations of subjectivity within the modern period and after; the model is also important in that the Subject represents the ultimate recourse to metaphysics, and, more important, that the Subject is never the sole concern of a theory which founds (a) discourse upon this a priori Subject. The theory of the Subject always entails another step: once the system is instituted by its act the absent Subject is paradoxically present within the system as a potential of the subject constituted by the system or discourse. In other words, the subject is always inside/outside discourse; almost every argument about subjectivity of concern here assumes this potential, and if it does, it therefore unconsciously assumes a relation to the Subject and the metaphysics of origin.

"From the 1970s there has been an effort to reconstruct a theory of the subject as agent of change" (Poster 1989, 61). A number of commentators are in general agreement with this statement, although the dates may vary slightly. In France, for example, Foucault's return to the "technologies of the self" in the last two volumes on sexuality published in his last year, 1984, appears to parallel an overall tendency in the eighties to challenge the poststructural attack on the autonomy of the subject in terms of the political dangers of maintaining such a position. This return often ignores the complexities of the poststructural critique (Dews 1987, xii ff.). In Foucault the return is not, however, to metaphysics, but to a "historical ontology."

The generally accepted poststructural wisdom in the United States was that a shift had taken place from the claim that truth could be grounded in the notion of an autonomous subject (as a given) to a notion that the subject was constituted by discourses and/or practices. But that shift, it is now usually argued (as noted above), was also in the process of reversal, at least in part, by the mid-eighties. My argument is that the autonomous subject was never relinquished, not even during the era of the greatest poststructural influence. And further, that such a continual "return" can be conceived in terms of the Sophist theory, that is, relating Subject to subject. In the books by Smith and Lentricchia, subjectivity is the explicit, positive theme; Bové's book is an attack on the recurrence of this subject, and a defense of Foucault along these lines. But when Bové comes to counsel his own forms of resistance, he slides back into a repetition of some of the positions he attacks, notably that of Said. If that is an inevitability, Bové does not address it as such. Foucault's notion of subjectivity is also problematic and to some degree recuperable, and Bové is also partially a victim of that;

the antidote might have been to pursue this dual problem of subjectivity and resistance in Foucault.

Paul Smith and Lentricchia, on the other hand, embrace subjectivity as an important mode of the determination of theoretical relations. They feel the need to theorize a subject of resistance to discourse. Smith enters a detailed critique of marxism and postmarxism in order to situate his own version of resistance of/by the subject formed within discourse. He generally ignores vast tracts of the poststructural: Foucault; Derrida—a short chapter focused on Derrida's skirting of a full definition of the subject and his performance as a subject while ignoring the general theoreticization of subjectivity. Smith bases his own analysis in large part on Lacan and attempts to focus those abstractions concerning the construction of the subject into the historical, actual material existence of individuals.

Lacan provides Smith the openings or discontinuous seams among actual discourses of the Symbolic which, in Lacan, are a concern at the second stage of subjectivity: the narcissistic construction of the seamless self out of a pastiche of discourses, and which, for Smith, provides the space for the construction of perspective and therefore resistance. Yet the analysis, as is Lacan's, is a continuation of theories of the Subject: a subject in discourse which is also outside (for example, constructing itself), and therefore in a position to enact resistance. Smith thus raises the question of the ultimate recuperation of all theories of resistance located in the subject, although part of his problem is his reliance on Lacan, whose work clearly invokes the tradition of the Subject.

From the start Lentricchia assumes resistance and origination as the potential of the individual subject, and, in a series of idiosyncratic or postmodern arguments, represents himself as a subject. He argues that Foucault is deterministic and also develops Foucault's (individual) anarchism; he investigates the Protagorean "interior spontaneity" of William James as political and instrumental, but not ontological, and therefore seriously questions his own argument; his complex, modernist readings of Wallace Stevens suddenly turn into an account of the poet as nothing more than an interpellated bourgeois subject. The book hovers between a pastiche arising from the privileged perspective of the modernist subject and a rhizomatic production, an assemblage, but far this side of Deleuze and Guattari.

Both texts—in fact, all texts—invoke the subject in the form of proper names. They maintain, in other words, a regime based on the subject as locus of invention and interest, as system of reference, and of "personal" ambition. This is something we seem unable to escape. But distinctions can be made. Lentricchia represents the tradition of the return of the subject of the eighties that is a rejection of poststructural problematics. Bové and Smith, however, attempt a careful working through of aspects of poststructuralism in order to recover a resource for agency and resistance, which is important to thinking from the left. If they are recuperated by the traditional notion of an originating subject, as I argue they are, then it is appropriate now to look at the potential within poststructuralism itself to avoid such recuperation. Has the news of "the death of the subject" been greatly exaggerated?

These texts seem to suggest that we now have passed through a relatively short period of theory and criticism which launched and sustained an attack on the notion of autonomous or originary subjectivity ("histories" of this era were already appearing at the end of the eighties). The subject is the locus of philosophic thought from Descartes forward, so any dismissal of that founding notion puts all of modern thought at risk. What is at issue here is the return of the subject during the eighties from its death or, more strategically, the questioning of the poststructural notion of the subject in terms of whether there was the necessity of a "return": whether, in fact, the return was instituted at the very moment of the subject's demise. If we look at the question from the perspective of Sophist subjectivity, we can see that any notion of the subject—even the discursive subject—inevitably replicates the notion of originary Subjectivity. So the return is of a subject which was never completely dispersed. Among the poststructuralists that might be examined in these terms, Foucault and Serres serve as exempla here.

◖◖◉◗◗

Foucault has a great deal to say about the subject and about resistance, although the insights are heteromorphous and ultimately not very coherent. There are a number of forays into the problematics of these two issues, given Foucault's theories of discourse and power, and they come often in the printed interview-essays of the seventies collected in various volumes as well as the texts on punishment and sexuality; most of the essays are relevant because the interviewers push Foucault to reflect on the implications of his thought, although some of these thoughts are tentative.

The best approach to this aspect of Foucault consists in the arguments directed at him: in general that he devises a theory of discourse which doesn't allow for resistance at the social or political level, especially at the level of the subject (Bové 1986, 220–21). Said, for example, says that Foucault fails to develop any theory of resistance at all (221). The structure of discourse may appear to be reductive, coercive, and monolithic (304–5). Lentricchia suspects that Foucault is an "affiliate of a paranoid theory of power so perfectly coercive, so insidiously ingrained at the capillary levels of the social body, that resistance and social change are but figments of fantasy" (1988, 31) and that the "dream of discipline . . . is the extermination of all resistance through total occupation of the space of resistance" (58). All these attacks, including the one omitted by Smith, assume the existence of and a focus on the subject; and Foucault's efforts are precisely to get beyond that kind of analysis.

Foucault's theories of discourse and the carceral society are too well known to require repetition: that there is no position outside discourse or power-knowledge. Foucault is at pains to exclude subjects who might be assumed to have a potential for resistance, even from the "bottom" or margins of the social structure. In *The History of Sexuality,* volume 1, he argues that after the seventeenth century "the fact of living was no longer an inaccessible substrate that only emerged from time to time . . . part of it passed into knowledge's control and power's sphere of intervention" (142). The same might be said of Foucault's relation to subjectivity. Before, the Subject is unlocatable, prior to its discourse or regime of power-knowledge. After the classical age, the subject gets absorbed into knowledge and power.

Foucault reinforces the theme of the "inside" in numerous texts. For example: "It seems to me that power is 'always already there,' that one is never 'outside' it, that there are no 'margins' for those who break with the system to gambol in" (1980b, 141)—and this in answer to a question assuming an "absolutising power" and asking "whom and what does power serve," that is, insisting on a subjective analysis, of both the Subject and the subjected. Further: "power is co-extensive with the social body; there are no spaces of primal liberty between the meshes of its network . . . power is interwoven with other kinds of relations" (142). Foucault reiterates his thesis often: there is no "outside" of power-knowledge; there are no subjects, or rather, no useful analyses which focus on power in subjects, on a Subject prior to discourse, or on "a binary structure with 'dominators' on one side and 'dominated' on the other" (ibid.). It is understandable that Foucault is accused of monolithic determinism.

Although his analysis is usually a concerted attempt to refocus questions normally treated from the given of subjectivity, Foucault occasionally drops into the subjective mode when discussing resistance and related phenomena. In "Truth and Power" he assumes, without interrogation, the (free) choice on the part of the intellectual with respect to "the political and economic demands to which he submits or rebels" (132); he assumes the possibility on the part of the intellectual of constituting "a new politics of truth" or "of detaching the power of truth from the forms of hegemony, social, economic and cultural, within which it operates at the present time" (133). His failure to examine here and in other texts (1977, 208; 1979a, 72; elsewhere) the assumption that the interruption of the prevalent discourse originates with the subject, which is both inside and outside of this discourse, marks his recuperation. This will change with the later volumes on sexuality, to be analyzed in chapter 5.

In general, however, Foucault specifically refuses to empower the subject. This often takes the form, in keeping with his conception of discourse or the regime of truth, of denying the position of the outside: he has a problem with the "theme of the founding subject." This Subject precedes language and forms it to the Subject's (prior) intentions, in just the same way Cicero's great man devises his plan and then uses eloquence to transform humans into civility. This founding subject is conceived, according to Foucault, as "Beyond time" (1972, 227), that is, the one who institutes history but is unlocatable in it. Foucault regularly attacks the subject of knowledge—that is, outside knowledge as its constitution, possession, and control (1970, xiv; 1979a, 27–28, passim). The adaptation in China of a modified form of the bourgeois court (that is, with the army as mediator) poses a danger in that the judge is conceived as outside the struggle of the two parties: for judicial proceedings to be just [according to the bourgeois court] they must be conducted by someone who can remain quite detached, by an expert in the realm of ideas (Foucault 1980b, 30). This subject is almost identical with the "general intellectual," situated historically by Foucault in the nineteenth and early twentieth centuries.

One particular interview, "Confessions of the Flesh," is an attempt by the interviewers to force Foucault to admit the function of "a thinking, willing subject" into his conception of an "apparatus (*dispositif*)," that is, into his conception of the "heterogeneous ensemble consisting of discourses, institutions . . . laws . . . scientific statements" (194) that make up an apparatus or a regime of truth. Foucault argues, against this, that when, for example, imprisonment came to be considered the most efficient and rational method for dealing with criminality, a different kind of criminal was produced; but this "had nothing to do with any kind of strategic ruse on the part of some meta- or trans-historic subject conceiving and willing it" (195).

Foucault repeats this "strategy without a subject" in his discussions of the moralization of the working class, which took form "without it being necessary to attribute it to a subject which makes the law" (204). Foucault makes a double point: there is no Subject but there are subjects. "All sorts of subjects intervened" in "the constitution of a medico-legal apparatus" of degeneracy, especially doctors and magistrates (ibid.). There is pleasure "in the gaze of the surveillants"; "the explosions of hysteria . . . in the psychiatric hospitals of the second half of the nineteenth century" were revolutions of the subjected (1979b: 69). Foucault is saying here that he allows for the recognition of subjects, but concludes that they are not the "essential part" and are not central to his approach; his analysis, in effect, will exclude "the representation of subjects" (70).

We have, then, Foucault's dismissal of the Subject as well as the plan for a history without subjects. The argument might well rest there, except for the fact that there is a Subject in Foucault: a "historical" Subject (a paradox, since the Subject is unlocatable—that is, abstract and ontological) which takes the form of the sovereign, the juridical subject which takes the form of the law, the "general intellectual," and so on. And this conception of the "historical" Subject inevitably affects Foucault's conception of subjectivity— in a way that will refocus the discussion and allow us to see, within his writings, the relation between the Subject/subject in the tradition we have been following.

The attack on the founding subject and the subject of knowledge finds echoes throughout Foucault's work. He argues, for example, that power does not exist in the sense that "there is either located at—or emanating from—a given point something which is a 'power'" (1980b, 198). Rather power means "a more-or-less organised, hierarchical, co-ordinated cluster of relations" (ibid.). To think of power in the traditional way is to think of it as a possession of a free subject, outside of its relations. This is precisely and deliberately how the power of the sovereign during the classical era is conceived in *Discipline and Punish*. The first two chapters of this work provide an outline of the relation of sovereign and subject in the ritual of punishment. And although it is a relation, both sovereign and subject are conceived as existing outside and prior to the relation, at least until the offending subject is fixed by the withering gaze of power of the sovereign. Thus there exists originally the space or separation whose subsequent satu- ration Lentricchia laments as the loss of the space of resistance. Foucault's sovereign marks the prior stage, and this in turn allows for the disappearance of the subject-of-power in the modern age. Foucault is saying that there was a Subject, but that it disappeared into discourse as the mechanism of subjection/subjectivation in the modern age.

The spectacle of the public execution in the era of the Subject is a political ritual: "the crime attacks the sovereign: it attacks him personally, since the law represents the will of the sovereign" (1979a, 47). Public torture is a practice of terror: to make everyone aware, through the body of the criminal, of the unrestrained presence of the sovereign. The public execution did not reestablish justice; it reactivated power (49).

The criminal is "an enemy of the prince" and the annihilation of his or her body attests to the "infinite power of the sovereign" (50). The spectacle of punishment in the classical age is portrayed as a ritual guaranteeing the power possessed by the Subject. This power exercised in the public torture and execution of the criminal represents the presence of the Subject, which is absent. This sovereign-Subject, with its power, exists prior to the relation, initiates that relation, exercises its power, and destroys the offending subject. It is also clear in Foucault that the plebs, in its constant threat of disruption at the scene of the execution, exists in such a way that it is capable of becoming external to the discourse of power authored by the sovereign; thus episodes of rebellion by subjects bear the mark of the originary power of the Subject.

It is interesting that Foucault in *Discipline and Punish* separates this political aspect of punishment from its judicial aspect—secret torture, interrogation, and so forth—as if he meant to emphasize the disymmetry between sovereign and subject and their separation, as well as the "scientific" gaze of the sovereign. Clearly the sovereign is a Subject according to the tradition. The Subject/subject tradition becomes a political theory at least by the classical age—when, incidentally, the practice and theory of imitation was thoroughly revived: when the Subject is conceived as the author of the law, and the law a discourse of prohibition to which no subject can be external, the positive or benign valence of the ancient Subject/subject relation comes to be inverted.

In a slightly later essay, "The Life of Infamous Men," Foucault turns these political and judicial aspects of power into a historical narrative. Here he articulates three relatively distinct stages of the exercise of sovereign power, with the middle stage occurring from about 1660 to 1760 (in France). The first stage is a repetition of the political in *Discipline and Punish:* the sovereign as a prior Subject in sole possession of its power and capable of the objectifying gaze; it possesses the power of the outside. Ordinary subjects are said to be fixed by "the gaze of power and the explosion of its wrath" (1979b, 81). "The discourse of power in the classical age . . . engenders monsters" (83), creates monsters of criminality by means of its separation and perspective.

More interesting is the middle stage, 1660–1760, where Foucault finds a "beginning," or "in any case an important event where political mechanisms and discourse-effects intersect" (82). This period raises the question, in terms of the traditions traced, of the Subject/subject relation, and in this essay that relation is a historical narrative. Foucault identifies the period by the *lettre de cachet* or private letter from the king, which circumvented regular channels. This is not simply another instance of the arbitrary power of the sovereign. Rather, the system Foucault associates with these letters

> didn't ensure the spontaneous erruption of the royal arbitrariness in the most everyday element of life. Rather it ensured its distribution along complex circuits. . . . it was a kind of placing of mechanisms of sovereignty . . . at the disposal of whoever is clever enough to tap them, to divert its effects to their profit. . . . political sovereignty comes to insert itself at the most elementary level of the social body; from subject to subject between members of the same family. (85)

Foucault's narrative produces a historical connection between Subject and subject. Through the mechanism of the *lettre de cachet,* the subject within discourse takes on the arbitrary and external power of the sovereign: the subject in/out of discourse, arrived at here not by a theoretical path but by means of a historical narrative. Further, the Subject/subjected relation, which defined the distance and limit—both being outside—of power relations in the classical age, comes during this period to be a phenomenon within social discourse; that is, the insertion of sovereign power allows the Subject/subject relation to recur within discourse: "everyone . . . can become a terrible and lawless monarch for another: *homo homini rex;* a whole political network comes to lace itself with the web of everyday life" (85–86).

We must remember that when the arbitrary (and therefore free) power of the sovereign is inserted into discourse, the distance of the sovereign-subject relation and the arbitrary power of one subject over another is necessarily repeated. In other words, a repetition without a shift, since the insertion merely reproduces subjects which are external to power relations at another level.

Later Foucault says "A day will dawn" on a new kind of power, that is, the third stage in the narrative process: "it will be made up of a fine, differentiated network in which the diverse institutions of justice, of the police, of medicine, of psychiatry relay one another" (89). This new power is made possible by the insertion of political power into everyday life, the confession adapted for the procurement of secular information, and in general, "the bringing of everyday life into discourse" (84). But here Foucault seems to lose sight of the separation of subject from subject and the consequent hierarchizing of subjects that is the clear result of the insertion of sovereign power. This could lead very easily to the disquieting claim that Foucault must develop, in his analysis of disciplinary society, a recognition of subjects, their definition or identity prior to their relations to power and to other subjects—all implied by the distance of sovereign power before and therefore consequent to its insertion—and in general a traditional analysis of power. Once an analysis adopts the notion of a prior Subject, it is locked into its continual reproduction. Along these lines it would be easy for Foucault to agree with an interviewer who claims there is a fundamental, immutable gulf between those who exercise power and those who undergo it (1980b, 21).

Lentricchia's book is an ironic comment on this aspect of Foucault. Lentricchia laments the closing of the space between Subject and subjected; in Foucault, Lentricchia argues, the subject, on which Lentricchia continues to focus, cannot extricate itself from discursive relations. The irony occurs when Lentricchia insists on the existence of the Subject with power to control yet remain outside the discourse it creates: in Taylorism (1988, 66–67); in "that something else beyond managers" (68, 82) and thus outside the disciplinary apparatus. This is precisely the trap that Foucault falls into when he originates his historical narrative with sovereign power. For Lentricchia it is not a trap but a conservative effort to reinvent the subject. Without noticing Foucault's lapse he sets out to rediscover the Subject. This opens the space of the Subject/subjected relation (there is always a kind of populist paranoia in Lentricchia): if the Subject is outside, so is the subject(ed); the latter exists prior to the operation of power (or withdraws to an internal space of subjectivity while outwardly submitting to the disciplines), and is therefore able to refuse or resist it. There is a certain nostalgia here for the good old bad days.

Foucault's portrayal of the historical sovereign as a Subject—originary, prior, outside—leads us into further complications concerning his notions of subjectivity and resistance. The Subject originates power, and when it is eventually inserted and distributed within the discursive apparatus, the power of the Subject reappears as the power of the subject which is inside the discourse but which uses the power to gain perspective or leverage over other subjects—from the "outside" which is inside. Foucault, by the very use of a narrative, locks himself into a sequence which imitates the traditional model of Subject/subject and, further, conflicts with his claim that power is coextensive with relations within the social body. The Subject model always leaves a residue of the outside, of the existence of subjectivity and power prior to its exercise.

The model of the Subject also conflicts with Foucault's conception of the "indefinite tangled skein" (1979b, 72) of power relations. He argues strongly against the model of state power and against subjective power. He denies that the "father" and the "adult," and so forth, "'represent' a State power which itself 'represents' the interests of a class." "And generally speaking, I believe that power is not constructed on the basis of 'wills' (individual or collective), no more than it is derived from interests" (71). And, further, Foucault usually argues that local relations are prior, although they are often taken up and coordinated into more global strategies (1980b, 122, for example). These local relations, for example, between man and woman or adult and child, are "quite specific relations of domination, which have their own configuration and relative autonomy" (1979b, 70–71). In Foucault we are thus made to approach power from two different directions: from the "top" or sovereign and from the "bottom," leaving us with an unresolved middle. This might not have been a problem for the early Foucault, but it is for the genealogist.

Is absolute sovereign power a historical fact or is it a model drawn from the tradition of the Subject and used by Foucault as the "before" of a power that is inserted into and absorbed by the relations within the social body? In either case we see that it causes some disturbances in his conception of contemporary power relations, yet the *historical* fact of the absolute sovereign, outside and commanding the domain of the exercise of its power, would render the ambiguities more intriguing. But there are in Foucault, as with traditional theories of the Subject, some difficulties in locating the sovereign.

In *Discipline and Punish* Foucault separates the judicial from the political functioning of punishment; only in the latter is the power of the sovereign absolute and perfectly arbitrary, outside the discourse or apparatus. Yet it is clear that the power of the sovereign is also inserted into the judicial apparatus and distributed. In "The Life of Infamous Men" Foucault, as mentioned, makes these into historical stages, but even here it is difficult not to realize that the power of the sovereign is always mediated. Foucault treats the separation between those who exercise and those who undergo power as arising from the institution of monarchy in the Middle Ages: "Sovereign, law and prohibition formed a system of representation of power which was extended during the subsequent era by theories of right" (1980b, 121).

He uses the sovereign as a historical precedent in the above citation, but he is just as likely to mention approvingly the claims of another scholar that "the famous 'absolute' monarchy in reality had nothing absolute about it. In fact, it consisted of a number of islands of dispersed power" (207). But again in *The History of Sexuality*, volume 1, the sovereign of the classical era seems to possess power as a Subject: "power in this instance was essentially a right of seizure: of things, time, bodies, and ultimately life itself" (1980a, 136).

Foucault complains that political theory remains obsessed with the problem of sovereignty, but he himself is also implicated. Like the traditional Subject, the sovereign is unlocatable; it is already mediated at any historical point, yet as an absence it precedes the system into which it is inserted. Foucault treats the Subject as a model sometimes: the "love of the master" is a "way of not posing the problem of power" and this is "due to the insubstantiality of the notion of the master, an empty form haunted only by the various phantoms of the master and his slave, the master and his disciple . . . the master who pronounces law and speaks the truth, the master who censors and forbids" (1980b, 139).

Such a conception of power leads, Foucault says, to a "double 'subjectivisation'": on the one hand "the great absolute Subject" who pronounces interdicts and on the other the subject who yields to or resists power. Both subjects are external to the lines along which power operates; both preexist the power relation as subjects. But Foucault's rejection of the Subject model here merely points to his utilization of it in his narrative of the form of a precedent sovereign power: this is the origin of the genealogy of power that causes such disruption in his conception of power as constituted by and in all relations of the social body. There is a problem because there is no means of transition from the Subject, which remains present as a function—a serious problem for the later Foucault.

That the Subject is used by Foucault as a kind of narrative origin is made clearer by his discussions of the "universal" and "specific" intellectual. The universal or "left" intellectual was, at one point, "acknowledged the right of speaking in the capacity of master of truth and justice" (126); "the intellectual *par excellence* used to be the writer . . . a universal consciousness, a free subject" (127). The specific intellectual emerged after World War II (for example, Oppenheimer) but there were precedents in the nineteenth century (for example, Darwin). The specific intellectual usually bears a "direct and localised relation to scientific knowledge" and engages in local struggles which have larger "political" implications.

The universal intellectual is clearly outside of discourse; like the judge of the bourgeois court, who stands "above" the struggle of the two antagonists, and in touch with justice and truth, the universal intellectual is a subject of knowledge whose function it is to control the discourse, and to modify and rectify it. The connection between this intellectual and the judge locates both as historical—that is, of the bourgeois era—forms. Foucault suggests, in fact, that the general intellectual of the nineteenth century derives from the eighteenth-century "man of justice, man of law, who counterposes to power, despotism and the abuses of wealth the universality of justice and the equity of an ideal law" (128).

Power, despotism, and wealth are representations of the Subject; so is the "man of justice" and the universal intellectual. But historicizing the model of the Subject doesn't help: there is always a prior, ontological model. The Subject gets pushed back in time: there is surely a predecessor to the "man of justice." At the other end, the specific intellectual becomes implicated in its own genealogy: "The intellectual's role is no longer to place himself 'somewhat ahead and to the side' in order to express the stifled truth of the collectivity; rather, it is to struggle against the forms of power that transform him into its object and instrument in the sphere of 'knowledge,' 'truth,' 'consciousness,' and 'discourse'" (1977, 207–8). But to perform this struggle the intellectual would have to be outside the discourse at the same moment he or she was inside: transcendental and empirical. The space and perspective of the Subject is here invested by Foucault as a kind of inheritance in the intellectual within the discourse of power.

The specific intellectual is an important figure today because of the perceived flaw in the traditional forms of representation: the general intellectual's "speaking for" marginalized groups and, as transcendent subject, reintroducing the domination such a "disinterested" positioning was thought to ameliorate. Foucault's notion of the specific intellectual has also opened him up to a number of other criticisms, from pluralism and anarchy to his own form of subjective domination by totalization (Poster 1989, 47–51). Many such arguments against Foucault are based on the reintroduction in the specific intellectual of the "outside," transcendent, objectifying capacity that is the given of the Subject or in this case of the general intellectual.

This brings us back to Foucault's "casual" references to the subject: references in which the subject of resistance is assumed to have a space and a perspective which is necessarily outside the discourse to be resisted. This is a legacy of the tradition of the Subject, and it finds its way into Foucault's work as a consequence of his adaptation of the tradition as historical origin and narrative. There are other instances of the Subject model: the pastor of "The Subject and Power," for example.

◄◎►

To conclude at this point would be to argue that Foucault gets himself recuperated by the very traditions he wishes most to subvert or avoid—those associated with subjectivity. Part of the problem is his shift toward genealogy in the book on punishment, in which there is a historical origin to power—one which consequently allows an ontological notion of autonomous subjectivity to creep in. There are decided virtues in discontinuity, which characterizes his earlier work.

All this is true, but not completely so, for there are important moments in Foucault before his final days when he pushes beyond the analysis of power, discourse, and history focused on subjectivity toward the goal he announces for genealogy, or history without subjects. These attempts take several forms: transforming subjects into functions; traversing or breaking down the traditional unity and interiority of the subject; perceiving an "outside" that is not a reinvocation of the Subject tradition; and generally displacing his analysis beyond the traditional subjective focus. Not incidentally, these attempts also reveal Foucault's notion of resistances to power that are not sited in the subject.

Foucault often uses the structuralist strategy for deemphasizing the traditional humanist subject: he speaks not of individual subjects but of social functions and roles within relationships: parent, child, manager, worker, and so forth. This is obvious enough in such essays as "The Subject and Power" as not to require elaboration. More important are his attempts to break down the subject. In "Confessions of the Flesh," in the face of the interviewers' attempts to insert the subject such as Jacques-Alain Miller's argument that in the "practical" field of actual political struggles "you can't escape the question of the subject," Foucault answers (in specific response to the question of who is opposed to whom in these actual struggles): "it's all against all. There aren't immediately given subjects of the struggle . . . . And there is always within each of us something that fights something else" (1980b, 207).

To Miller's further questioning Foucault answers that the components of the struggle are "individuals, or even sub-individuals" (208). Although he doesn't elaborate, leaving the statement easily recuperable, Foucault is here attempting to get beyond the unity of the subject, and is therefore attempting to deny the self-actualizing quality—the quality consistent with the subject's being outside the discourse (often sited as interiority, as in Lentricchia below) and at the same time within it—that is, in modernist terms, self-reflexive. The subject is being made to disappear even as a function, as when Foucault says that he is interested in "how the relations of power are able to pass materially into the very density of bodies" (1979b, 69–70; 1979a, passim); or when he links the new deployment of sexuality to "an intensification of the body" and its "exploitation as an object of knowledge and an element in the subject as mind or as a mind-body unity."

Lentricchia, responding to another text of Foucault, gives an assessment that appears to make the same point; but it is one which actually depends on an assumption that there exists a unified subject:

> for Foucault undisciplined individuality may be precisely the unintended effect of a system which would produce individuality as an object of its knowledge and power (the disciplinary appropriation of biography) but which instead, and ironically, inside its safe, normalized subject, instigates the move to the under-ground where a deviant selfhood may nurture sullen counterschemes of resistance and revolution. (26)

But "selfhood" is the key to the difference: Lentricchia conceives of a subject occulted within the subject formed and normalized by disciplinary procedures. The interior subject is single and unitary, and actualized by its own interiority—which is its perspective on the disciplinary apparatus, its "outside," or self-reflexivity. Lentricchia correctly perceives the interior, anarchic subject which sometimes appears in Foucault, but he is unwilling to conceive of another analysis that works through and beyond the subject, as Foucault often attempts to do.

One of the clearest expressions of the attempt of Foucault to circumvent subjectivity is the explanation of the shift to bio-power, that is, to a power centering on life and leading to a "normalizing society" as a consequence (1980a, 144). In the classical age, the individual was outside the power of the sovereign until "the line that separates the enemies of the sovereign from his obedient subjects" (ibid.) was crossed. Afterwards the subject is instituted as a norm within the disciplines and regulatory procedures applied to the (anatomical and) biological body: "the mechanisms of power are addressed to the body, to life, to what causes it to proliferate. . . . [Sexuality is] an object and a target" (147)—not the traditional subject. Even the "rights" ultimately asserted to challenge bio-power are supported by the same thing which this power invests, life and living beings (144–45). Resistance is from within power relations.

The attempt by Foucault to conceive an "outside" to power that does not simply reinvoke the Subject is closely related to his traversal of the subject. In "Powers and Strategies" Foucault suggests the existence of a "plebs," a conception obviously drawing on the traditionally unruly populace of Rome but also related to "the people" who are described in *Discipline and Punish* as necessarily present at tortures and executions during the classical age (1979a, 57ff.). These witnesses, Foucault says, could never be completely controlled: "the people . . . drawn to the spectacle intended to terrorize it, could express its rejection of the punitive power and sometimes revolt" (59).

This is another example of the space within the relation of power during that era, or, in other words this is Foucault's model of the "original" configuration of power, with both Subject and subjects outside the relation.

But for Foucault the "plebs" of contemporary times is "not a real sociological entity" (1980, 137) despite the obvious relation to a classical or ancient population which stands potentially outside power. Yet the plebs is still resistance to power: "there is indeed always something in the social body, in classes, groups and individuals themselves which in some sense escapes relations of power . . . a centrifugal movement, an inverse energy." The movement is partly transsubjective and suggestive of an "outside" of power. Foucault continues:

> There is certainly no such thing as "the" plebs; rather there is, as it were, a certain plebian quality or aspect ("*de la plèbe*"). There is plebs in bodies, in souls, in individuals, in the proletariat, in the bourgeoisie, but everywhere in a diversity of forms and extensions, of energies and irreducibilities. The measure of plebs is not so much what stands outside of relations of power as their limit, their underside, their counterstroke, that which responds to every advance of power by a movement of disengagement. Hence it forms the motivation for every new development of power (138).

The plebs as a strategy of resistance is transubjective and subindividual, but as an "outside" it is a much more tricky proposition. Foucault implies here, as in the historical narrative of the insertion of the power of the sovereign into the social body, that there is a historical outside or "underside"—a friction?—to the encroachment of power, or that a potential locus of resistance precedes the further exercise or the extension of power. The original sovereign-plebs relation of power recurs in this outside. But it is a delicate balance: the outside/underside/limit of power is not necessarily sited in the subject. The subject, Foucault maintains, is not necessarily the focus of the analysis of power or resistance.

Foucault adds that the plebs may be incorporated into power by "its stabilising itself through a strategy of resistance" and that this would be "a strategy without a subject." He follows this up later in the interview when he summarizes his views of power: that "power is co-extensive with the social body . . . that relations of power are interwoven with other kinds of relations," and so on. What becomes important here is the contrast between global and local relations: "that dispersed, heteromorphous, localised procedures of power are adapted, re-inforced and transformed by . . . global strategies, all this being accompanied by numerous phenomena of inertia, displacement and resistance" (142; also 1979b, 71). Foucault makes clear that this resistance is a repetition of the plebs when he summarizes further: "there are no relations of power without resistances . . . they are formed right at the point where relations of power are exercised." The "indefinite tangled skein" of power relations creates its own resistance by a kind of reactive conjunction, somewhat like the interference of noise or electrical resistance. And although the specter of the Subject always lurks just beyond the analysis as a consequence of the origin, Foucault here is attempting to move beyond.

In the first volume of *The History of Sexuality* Foucault continues the attack on subject-oriented analyses. He does this by arguing again that relations of power are coextensive with economic, cognitive, sexual, and other types of relationships—all of which constitute subject positions— and by a much more forceful form of his argument that "Power comes from below" (1980a, 94). Reiterating his distinction between " 'local centers' of power-knowledge" (98) and global strategies, Foucault also insists that local and global levels are interdependent: not "discontinuous" but not "homogeneous" either (99–100).

Ultimately Foucault mediates between these two levels by a redefinition of "discourse" as a polyvalent collection of tactical elements from one level, ones which form the potential for more comprehensive strategies— that is, the organized or univocal subdiscourse that disciplines—and hence also the possibility of resistance and opposing strategies internal to the discourse. There is no "outside." The subject disappears as the origin of power or resistance; in its place is an analysis of primary/secondary levels of power relations (which flirts with the materialist parallel: simple or real/constructed, or base/superstructure, but never quite submits to it, especially as a captive or determined relation), with "discourse" as the middle term: the various and unstable tactics gathered into a reservoir available to global strategies.

Such an analysis is not *necessarily* asubjective, except for Foucault's claim that it does traverse or exclude the subject. This argument for the exclusion of intention and agency does open onto a basic materialist doctrine that selection from a multiple potential depends on chance, bringing Foucault closer than before to Deleuze and Guattari. In addition, the conception of discourse as polyvalent (and, later, even of strategy as nonunivocal) opens up the space of the subject-as-origin of power and resistance by and within the discontinuities. This is precisely the maneuver of Paul Smith, and it recalls the manifestos of both Foucault and Bové to intellectuals to work against the power-knowledge regime which results in multiform oppressions—work which could only be performed from "outside," or, here, from within the interstices of discontinuous discourses. Perhaps the conjunction of Smith and Foucault here is an indication of Foucault's renewed matriculation toward organic or political materialism and its conception of the subject (see chapter 4).

These attempts to overcome the legacy of the Subject can be comprehended in one general strategy, which is simply Foucault's intention to displace the analysis of power from its traditional focus on and empowerment of the subject in resistance. In an interview already discussed Foucault readily admits that a subjective analysis is available: that those who practice surveillance are subjects who experience pleasure and that subjected hysteric patients could and did stage resistance; but that a different kind of analysis is more appropriate: "What I am after is to try to show how the relations of power are able to pass materially into the very density of bodies without ever having to be relayed by the representation of subjects. If power gets into the body it isn't because it has been interiorised in people's consciousness to begin with. . . . [There is] a network of bio-power" (1979b, 69–70). This bio-power is anatomic or applied to the performance of the body, and biological, an attempt to control populations through the control of the processes of life. It is power operating not through the Subject/subject, but a power "applied at the level of life itself" (1980a, 143).

The interviewer, Lucette Finas, at this point summarizes Foucault's position for him: "You represent this power, this play of power as producing itself at every moment, at every point, in every relation between one point and another." Correct. But Foucault is further claiming that each "point" is not necessarily the site of representation of the subject. The traditional alternative to Foucault is the analysis which pretends to the scientific gaze, objectifying relations as those of domination and creating subjects as the origin and recipient of that domination. For Foucault the relations of force imply a relation of power as "the instantaneous [cross-]section of the relation of force" (72). Thus his analysis even diverts attention from the initiatory and final positions of the relation, and refocuses on the relational procedure or process.

The claim by James Miller in *The Passion of Michel Foucault* and by others that the second and third volumes on sexuality mark a return to the notion of the subject is an important one. But it is an ironic one: the reinvocation of the subject serves as a means of showing its historical construction, not its metaphysics. Miller's biography, however, in which a "life" is constructed, follows the narrative conventions: coherence (for example, the coalescence of thought and act), growth/crescendo (the "limit-experience"), and significance (the possibility of "thinking differently") are all implemented as the real. The results are excrutiatingly modernist. There are echoes of T. S. Eliot (somewhat transformed, it's true), but what comes to mind most strongly is the Yeats of the Byzantium poems and the desire for self-transformation, although in this case Miller argues that it is precisely through those "bodies and pleasures" (1993, 157) which Yeats seeks ambivalently to transcend that Foucault finds transformation. To attempt to construct oneself as an aesthetic object (Foucault, 1985b, 10–11) is to embrace the modernist project, especially of the "outside" subject made possible by the assumption of self-reflexivity. So Miller's conventional modernist biography incorporates another narrative of self-fabrication as it relates to antiquity in the Mediterranean basin; in fact, Miller's narrative depends on Foucault's for its claim to veracity. And there is certainly no break in the connection with Cartesian self-reflexivity and Kantian enlightenment in Miller's text, however surprisingly implemented. Doesn't Habermas say that the project of modernity has yet to be completed?

Does, then, Foucault return to an ethics of the subject? That is a complex question, but primarily one that demands a modernist context and a focus on the author as central, a strategy not generally identified with Foucault. If we read *The Use of Pleasure* and *The Care of the Self* as a heroic personal quest, as an attempt by Foucault to transform himself and his thinking—in effect, to give himself a positionality "outside" of culture— then the thought and act of the "author" must be taken as identical. For these two Foucault texts provide an analysis of still other texts from antiquity which assume both a self-reflexive stance and a self-transforming *askesis,* that is, practices of the self by which individuals become subjects or subject themselves to a "regimen" in relation to *aphrodisia.*

Foucault's archaeological and genealogical texts, focused on European culture from the sixteenth century onward, present a different kind of subject: these texts refer more to contingent discourses, disciplines, and practices which have little to do with originating subjects and even less with self-reflexivity and self-formation. Subjects are those subjected to and constituted by the disciplines, individuals that become subjects without passing through the stage of self-reflexivity, insight, and choice. This is Foucault's idea of bio-power, which short-circuits free, reflecting subjectivity.

Has Foucault merely shifted from the "other histories" in the genealogy of the modern age to a reading of the "same" in the ancient world? In a sense this is true, but many commentators have noted Foucault's revisionary reading of the modern age in a lecture of 1984 entitled "What Is Enlightenment?" as parallel to the two later volumes on sexuality. The tendency has been to see this return in Foucault to the self-constituted subject as understood "now in historical-social, not in ontological terms" (Poster 1989, 54). Ontological claims are always historically grounded, and that is Foucault's point. The statement that "We must try to proceed with the analysis of ourselves as beings who are historically determined, to a certain extent, by the Enlightenment" (1984a, 43) is in one sense to agree that canonical philosophical texts warrant as much attention as medical, penal, and psychiatric texts, and that the connection had previously been generally ignored. It could be added that this subject "we" is *already* self-reflexive—its mode of contemplating its own partial formation by the historical context of the Enlightenment—or is both inside/outside its historical traditions (that is, discourses). It perceives itself as historically constituted as a self-knowing subject.

What Foucault failed to do in his genealogical period was to reconcile the two "histories" of the modern, the one with and the other without subjects—what the 1984 essay attempts to repair; and that is also a not quite resolved problem in the two later volumes on sexuality. There is a recognition of the relation between the modern philosophic conception of self-reflexive subjectivity and the disciplines which subject the individual to an internal moral self-constraint in *Madness and Civilization;* this has been aptly put as Foucault's attempt "to dissolve the . . . link . . . between consciousness, self-reflection and freedom"—and to substitute "subjection"/"subjectification" for the latter term (Dews 1987, 155–60); in a word, the discourse of self-reflection is the form of subjectification which characterizes modernity. But this form of self-relation is much less foregrounded in the later genealogical works such as *Discipline and Punish,* although it appears briefly in the first sexuality volume in the discussion of the confession (1980b, 58ff., esp. 61).

It is important to see how Foucault frames his reading in the sexuality volumes, since this is literally the foundation of Miller's argument. In the introduction to *The Use of Pleasure* Foucault puts his work on sexuality in the context of his work on knowledge and power. Each demands a "theoretical shift," the third, on sexuality, in terms of the subject in which it is "appropriate to look for the forms and modalities of the relation to self by which the individual constitutes and recognizes himself *qua* subject" (1985b, 6). In his archaeological study of knowledges the subject was the individual who was qualified to speak—that is, able to inhabit the slot constituted by the discourse and its functioning; in the genealogical study of powers, it was the individual which was subjected to and constituted by disciplines and practices; the difference *The Use of Pleasure* introduces is the choice by the individual to constitute itself within an area of freedom beyond the rather rudimentary cultural morality and political ethics that, according to Foucault, obtain in fourth-century B.C.E. Greece, Foucault also introduces a self-reflexivity which cannot be separated from an "inside/outside" subject of knowledge that is also glimpsed in the autopsy in *The Birth of the Clinic* (1973, 124ff.) when he asks of the Greeks "[W]hat were the games of truth by which human beings came to see themselves as desiring individuals?" (1985b, 7).

When Foucault comes to speak of his own motivations for producing this history of sexuality, with all its divergences, what may appear as a personal quest is also the possibility of the self-reflexive subject in general, and even more so. It is a matter of crossing the limits of the conventionally knowable, getting "free of oneself" in order to reach the possibility of thinking differently (8).

As Foucault says in the Introduction to *The Use of Pleasure,* philosophical "activity" or "discourse" has an obligation to get outside itself. This is specifically not a demand that it should position itself outside of humanity or culture in order to dictate truth but that it stand outside itself and implement an "*askesis,* an exercise of oneself [itself?] in the activity of thought" so that "it is entitled to explore what might be changed, in its own thought, through the practice of a knowledge that is foreign to it" (9). Miller the biographer is claiming the real or actual Foucault, while Foucault himself argues that the historically constituted subject, as self-knowing, can use this very constitution as a means to dismantle the strategies of that constitution. The issue of self-reflexivity in the two later volumes on sexuality is reintroduced in chapter 5.

Foucault's notion of subjectivity is complex, sometimes conditioned by the traditional but also sometimes having the effect of making the subject disappear from the analysis. In his "discipline/power" phase, Foucault begins to open up an alternative to subjective analysis, and, in particular, begins to suggest a resistance that is not focused in subjects. Thinking resistance without recourse to the subject is difficult, but if he is sometimes recursive Foucault also works against this "natural" assumption of Lentricchia and Paul Smith that resistance is necessarily subjective. They look backward toward the Subject and humanism. Foucault often looks in quite another direction, toward information theory. The child of twentieth-century mathematics and nineteenth-century thermodynamics, information theory and other related disciplines such as semiotics focus on the probabilities of the message and, like Foucault, tend to fold the origin and destination into the message. There are other notions of information that have been discussed in relation to Foucault, most notably by Mark Poster in *Critical Theory and Poststructuralism*. Poster distinguishes between mathematical, generally quantitative information theory and his notion that electronically transformed media have thrust us into a new epoch of disciplinary power (1989, 121–69). Thus while there might be general agreement that power is coextensive with the relations of information, it may also be useful to pursue information theory in its more scientific form.

((◦))

The sense at the inception of information theory was that the humanist subject is a given, and that it must be accommodated into the generality of information theory. And subjects are dutifully made to appear, although not always as holistic operators. But later developments began to undo the position of the human subject. The applications of information theory in biochemistry and genetics tend to traverse the subject. These applications are merely the intensification of the medical-scientific impulse which is perhaps first evident in the autopsy: the subject as merely a diverse package of systems, the latest form of which happens to be information. Jean Baudrillard marks a clear "before" and "after": the bourgeois body is "an individuated space of pulsion, of desire and phantasies" (49); now "the body has been reduced to a division of surfaces, a proliferation of multiple objects wherein its finitude, its desireable representation . . . are lost" (44), a position not very far from Foucault. It is this tendency in information theory which must be followed out in its more imaginative applications to the human sciences, and then brought back into relation with Foucault.

Michel Serres's use of information theory in order to reorient attitudes toward the subject takes the form of a bracketing of the single organism (his term) within two sets of parameters: the organism as a momentary organization or curl of turbulence in the field of laminar flow; and the organism itself as a series of hierarchical, interlocking levels of information flow: the organism from outside and inside. One of the difficulties here is that Serres's analysis automatically reproduces the unity of the organism, which might not so easily be assumed and which is, in fact, potentially put in question by part of the analysis. We will come back to this later.

The organism exists as a momentary organization within the entropic laminar flow. For example, the downward rain of primordia in Lucretius could be conceived as entropic in the sense that the downward movement continually dissipates the energy and organization of the system

74

as the primordia move further downward—taking the average distance of the primordia from the point of rest as a function of the energy remaining. (Lucretius and other atomists suggest such a center and deny it, leading back to the originary vortex [*diné*] of Leucippus; but that is another issue.) The *clinamen* would create a micro-organization that is negentropic, or moves against the overall entropic flow; this organization is turbulence.

This organization is also "homeorrhetic"; that is, it is an open or "flow-through" system in constant exchange with its environment, always in a state of dynamic imbalance, and which can be maintained only by further interchange; the system is irreversible, subject to increasing entropy. The organism is a "multitemporality": a movement upstream against the increase in entropy because of its organization and increasing complexity, but also subject to decay and above all borne along, as an organization, in the overall entropic flow. "What is an organism? A sheaf of times" (Serres 1982, 75). A discontinuous unity. What Serres produces in this analysis is hardly the human subject of humanism; yet he does create a space for this subject, an opening within the organization thus delimited against the background of universal flux. This brings us to Serres's second view of the organism, the "inside" account.

The organism, once delimited, has the character of a complex set of information flows, a series of "levels of integration." This description follows the tendency mentioned previously to break down the unity and volume of the subject into a myriad of disparate or relational (in Serres) systems. Foucault's attempt to dis-integrate the traditional unity in the conception of the subject when he treats the body as subjected to the disciplines or makes many of his references to subindividual levels, is the same attempt to traverse the subject and to deny it holistic operational status as occurs in Serres, and is a general tendency of information theory.

Serres, however, attempts this traversal while clearly holding on to a notion of the unity of the organism, an attempt ultimately inconsistent with the account. Serres's description of the organic process is as follows: "Consider any level of an interlocking system. It mobilizes information and produces background noise. The next level in the interlocking series receives, manipulates and generally integrates the information-background noise couple that was given off at the preceding level" (77). Serres adds that the position of the receiver of this couple is important: from the point of view of the second or upper level the noise is added to the information—as information: "Its value [i.e., of 'ambiguity,' a function of noise] depends on whether . . . [the observer] is submerged in the first level or whether he examines the whole unit from the next level. In a certain sense, the next level functions as a rectifier . . . of noise. What was once an obstacle to all messages is reversed and added to the information" (77–78).

The "observer" becomes an even more important issue at the higher and final levels of the organism. Serres says that "for our own organic system we are the observer or observers in question" (76). On cellular and molecular levels a "proto-language" functions, and "at the most highly integrated level, a language is still functioning, but now as individuated signals equipped with something like meaning" (79). Serres goes on: "I know who the final observer is: precisely he who utters language" (82). He collapses the subject/object opposition—now a function of position and level—and moves the human organism into universal relations: "a macro-molecule, or any given crystallized solid, or the system of the world, or ultimately what I call 'me'—we are all in the same boat" (ibid.) as complex information systems. The subject is traversed and transcendent at the same moment.

Serres's traversal of the subject, his distribution of it into levels of information, might be a step toward folding the subject out into a communicational network if he did not find a "natural" termination point at the highest interior level of the conscious subject. If the information account is to have value then the boundary between individual organism and its environment must be seen as a traditional one which must be overcome. The account would have to pass through that opposition and dissolve the subject. Serres does just the opposite: he traverses the subject while holding to the holistic account of it. Information levels reach their apogee in the speaking subject. Serres also repeats the unity of the subject at every level: of the "first dispatcher" at the lowest information level he says: "it is an island in an ocean of noise, just like me, no matter where I am" (ibid.)—simply a reinstitution of micro-subjects.

Serres gets closer to a dissolution of the subject when he treats the organism as a homeorrhetic system, a notion that, along with the term, goes back at least to the Hellenistic era. But even here the individual organism is "an almost stable although irreversible" system—Serres calls it a "syrrhesis"—a quasi-stable whole whose limits are predetermined. The aleatory subject remains. Finally, in the global account, the laminar flow/turbulence opposition precisely demarcates the traditional unity of the organism, since there is a discontinuity at the point at which the analysis moves from organism to environment. And Serres's narrative of information, in terms of the position of the ultimate observer or subject, raises even more troubling questions.

In Serres's fable of Descartes and La Fontaine it is the position upstream, the maximization of the perspective which allows for the objective ordering of chaos by means of rationality. This also means that the observer is able to step outside/upstream of the process while remaining in contact with it: the subject as frame or parergon which originates order. Smith and Lentricchia are, on one level, absolutely correct; there seems always to be a subject.

Serres provides a complex example of this scientific gaze. His folding out of the individual organism into levels of information processing preassumes the integrity of the organism; thus he ends his account at that limit. But the analysis must extend beyond that limit, for it must account for the position which Serres occupies, that is, at a level of information external to the typical organism described from that external position. The informational account must flow through the position of the external observer if it is to be an account at all; then, however, there is no organism or limiting envelope and no position "outside"; an "inside" account is not possible. Further, my own account of Serres's dilemma implies an even more external position; and by this time we run into a regress. Simply, Serres's account cannot account for itself.

Once the unity of the organism is dissolved, despite or perhaps because of the regress, Serres's laminar flow/turbulence account comes into question. That opposition allowed for the internal account based on the assumption of the unity of the organism, as turbulence within laminar flow. But the opposition cannot account for the "scientific" observer who sees the border or discontinuity between the two processes, or process and subprocess. It is true that the turbulence forms a peculiar unity, a "sheaf of times." The account of the organism entails different and successive positions of observation. But in place of noncoherence and therefore nonentity, Serres finds a "sheaf," something bound into a discontinuous unity. What he actually finds is a perspective which is able to comprehend the discontinuous positions or bind them. It is the purest motivation of science: extend the gaze.

The external observer is, moreover, necessarily both turbulence and laminar flow. We have, then, a relational opposition constructed by the maximized, external (at whatever level) observer for the purpose of imposing order and an opposition in which the lesser term, turbulence, precedes laminar flow. Culture precedes nature since the latter, the supposed origin, can only be proposed from the perspective of the former. In the same way, the laminar flow/turbulence opposition can only occur within turbulence, that is, within consciousness or at the highest level of information processing. There is also the godlike position totally outside laminar flow/turbulence; in that case the opposition is subverted and overcome by the opposition between observer and cosmos.

The Serrian text is haunted by the Subject and the external scientific gaze. But so are the texts of Baudrillard, of Foucault, of Derrida, of Lyotard (who often seems indulgent in his position), and any others who attempt to reduce the subject. Each one speaks as a Subject: outside, possessed of the objectifying view, reductive of the subject but in that gesture self-replicating. The disappearance of the subject in one place simply marks its appearance in another. It is the space between the two in which we are forced to work, as subjects against subjectivity, and it will always be an uncompleted work. This is appropriate to our historical ontology.

The connection between power relations and information may yet turn out to be useful in producing a potentially desubjectivizing analysis—if it were expanded to include other work such as that of Lyotard, Baudrillard, Deleuze and Guattari, and numerous others. But, again, can a thinking be thought which is not the production of the subject and is not enclosed by the subject at some level of displacement or another? Is there a language which short-circuits the recourse to a subject? Is there a future possibility of reading that does not found-er on the subject? On the other hand, is it possible to read or to construct narrative without a fundamental recourse to the subject? Did the poststructural era in fact change our way of reading narratives? Can we dismantle our own narrative or historical constitution as self-reflexive subjects? Is that mode of self-relation necessary to its deconstitution? Foucault would agree to both.

Gender Studies

Discourse, Subjectivity, Agency, Theory

T his chapter deals with one aspect of Foucault's influence, in this instance on gender theorists of the late eighties and nineties. It focuses on the problems inherent in adapting Foucault to gender study, especially as it relates to his notions of discourse and genealogy. These have been treated in the previous chapter but are here subjected to a more rigorous analysis in terms of the fundamental differences of the two notions. The focus on gender studies has its own justification, but it is also used to facilitate the explanation of this shift in Foucault from discourse to genealogy. Since this is a relatively early shift in Foucault's thinking, the chapter belongs to this part of the overall organization.

I begin briefly with familiar ground: feminism, or more specifically, feminist theory and the conceptual basis of feminist criticism, have experienced two phases since the sixties (and, in fact, since the nineteenth century). The first phase assumed, more or less precisely, a feminine nature usually equal to but different from that of the male. From the perspective of the second phase of feminism, the earlier phase of the movement has come to be seen, and often regretted, as based on the notion of a unifying feminine nature, or even essence, and to have promoted an identity politics. "Nature" is not a precise enough term here. One notion of nature is material: sex is anatomically and physiologically determined, and that sexual nature determines gender. The other notion of nature comes from the humanist tradition: there exists a prior, pregendered subjectivity, from which women have been excluded, but to which they will attain. Beauvoir and Wittig, for example, despite their concern with the body, clearly belong to this latter tradition of contesting male subject privilege (cf. Fuss 1989, 39ff.).

Irigaray, on the other hand, at times bases her argument on the difference of feminine anatomy (1985, esp. 23–33). The feminine "masquerade" prescribed by the masculine symbolic economy "corresponds scarcely at all to woman's desire" (30) or to nature, which is non-identitarian, that is, "not one," or polymorphous and *not* logically ordered. The feminine origin or zero-point is "her body-sex" (29). This position is often called a "strategic use of essentialism" (Fuss 1989, 55; Butler 1990, 30). This must be taken to mean that Irigaray belongs to the second phase of feminism, inventing a "nature" in order to create an outside and to advance the argument against male hegemonic discourse; yet this configuration could also signify a self-reflective recognition of one's anatomical nature as the essential difference which will disrupt the masculine regime.

Under the influence of poststructural thought there is a shift in the eighties from "nature" to "culture" in feminist thought that figures the difference of the two phases. The influence of Foucault is especially strong here: the antifoundationist arguments of others such as Derrida had a profound undermining impact, unsettling the arguments from nature, but Foucauldian genealogy seemed to offer the possibility of reconstituting the experience of women in terms of specific historical/cultural discourses. Central to this shift away from a given nature was the discursive notion that culture precedes nature: that the prior "nature" is generated by the discourse as its justification. The subsequent work on gender formation within culture was necessarily opposed to any notion of natural sexual differentiation. The attack on "nature" opened up further the connections to lesbian and gay studies, and put feminism in fruitful contact with multicultural studies, especially of marginality based on race, ethnicity, or any difference which separated the margin from the hegemonic center.

This shift in feminist theory, the development of gender studies, is a development that has created excitement, interest, and insight in current critical endeavors. Yet there are a number of problematic issues associated with these changes, especially theoretical ones. Primary among these is the notion of agency, which is discussed in chapter 2. The question concerning feminists who exploit Foucault *in discourse* is whether the production of agency from the notion of discourse and discursively produced subjects succeeds in going beyond fractional notions of autonomous subjectivity.

The second, although related theoretical issue is the appropriateness of using a genealogical approach as the basis of an activist and political theory. Foucault the genealogist is also implicated in the activist/objectivist opposition. Specifically, there is the question of the relation of genealogy to structuralism. The latter was in part a reaction to the nineteenth-century search for origins and for historical explanation. But the questions of origin and change are invited back in by genealogy. This is a particularly critical issue in that recourse to a creative or originating subject is no longer a viable strategy.

Foucault struggled with the question of origins and the a priori, and some of his later work—volume 1 of *The History of Sexuality*, "What Is Enlightenment," and the introduction to *Herculine Barbin*—gives evidence of that. This can be situated as a conflict between Foucault and some of the second-phase feminists, who want to distance themselves theoretically from the notion of an origin, material or otherwise—that is, distance themselves from a "nature" which determines the consequent structure or discourse. But they are equally and necessarily concerned with process and change, both of which raise the issue of origins, however displaced it may be. Also to be considered are the poststructural notions of the function of theory—perhaps an activist theory as opposed to the modernist notions of the theoretical Subject as prior to discourse and outside it.

As a means of focusing precisely on the issues mentioned above, I have chosen to concentrate on one text, *Gender Trouble* by Judith Butler. It appeared at the end of the eighties, at the high point of second-phase feminism, where feminist theory becomes gender study and cements its alliance with other groups constituted by naturalized differences usually adduced for the purposes of domination and repression. Butler provides the most articulated reading so far of Foucault's genealogy, clearly going beyond him in many instances, in the service of dismantling any claim that might be made for a gender determination which emanates from a natural sex—whether feminine principle, the anatomical configuration of the body, or physiological process. As forceful and as salutary as this Butlerian imperative is, her "feminist political theorizing" (142) raises the central issues of a poststructural theory: how can discourse be said to produce agency? What kind of theory is appropriate to a political activism which, unlike Kristeva's claim for the semiotic, does not (according to Butler) produce "concrete cultural options" to phallocracy (89–90)? And what is the particular relation of this theory to genealogy? Finally, what is the relation between a poststructural (or even postpoststructural) theory and its more traditional forbears (a question clearly within the province of genealogy)?

Butler's use of genealogical criticism naturally involves an analysis of how Foucault stands on the issues mentioned, especially where Butler uses Foucault against himself in order to stage the crisis of "nature" and agency.

Not every aspect of the issues raised by either can be treated conveniently within the scope of one chapter. Thus I refer the reader to the following chapters: the chapters (7–9) on self-reflexivity, which take up Descartes, Kant, and the tradition of modern philosophy in terms both of the prior history of self-reflexivity and the provenance and importance of this issue (which logically involves agency) in Foucault, Butler, and others; the chapter (4) on materialist theory and the inevitable notions of origin and process necessary to it. This latter chapter begins with an instance of classical materialism, Lucretius, and shows how this tradition is both reinvoked and countered in Foucault, Butler, and other feminists. These chapters should provide some insight into theoretical issues in the (post)poststructural era.

Butler says often that earlier feminist criticism assumes a "doer behind the deed" (1990, 25, 142, passim), that is, a prediscursive subject, which has both ontological and strategic functions within the enterprise. The site of Butler's argument—the second phase of feminism and the appearance of gender studies—is, however, based on the belief that any a priori conception of the "we" as essentializing notions of "female" or "woman" work to the detriment of "feminist political theorizing"; they are an employment of "the imperialist strategies" that feminism must eschew (147), and, most important, they operate as a constraint on "the very 'subject' it [feminist theory] hopes to represent and liberate" (148).

Central to her argument is the means by which discourse produces a sense of agency. In Foucault, genealogy appears as a contingent and arbitrary process of contact/interference/consolidation of specific (that is, historical) discursive structures, whatever their provenance. This method is best exemplified in *Discipline and Punish* and *The History of Sexuality*, volume 1. Genealogy is also, in Foucault's phrase, "history without subjects," and that follows from his notion of discourse as prior to and constituting subjective identity. In opposing the natural sex-gender argument, Butler utilizes Foucault's discursive and genealogical critique of foundationalism in order to demonstrate how current "hierarchical and binary gendered positions of compulsory heterosexuality" can be disrupted—that is, in a way which involves a notion of agency that does not have access to the traditional conception of a prediscursive subject or one predisposed or determined by its prior nature toward a certain kind of identity.

Butler mentions, in the shift toward the utilization of poststructural thought of the second phase of feminist theory, the nagging problematics of the cultural construction of identity for many feminists: this seemed to evoke the discrete binary of "free will vs. determinism" (8, 147), an aporia which seemed to argue that there was no alternative to the founding conception of the humanist subject—in terms of both identity and agency. But according to Butler, "Construction is the necessary scene of agency" (147): agency and (the possibility of) resistance are not assumed as properties of the pregiven subject; the subject constructed by discourse—postdiscursive—has produced in it the capacity and/or positionality for resistance to the constituting discourse. This is Butler's gloss on Foucault's claim that discourses produce their own resistance.

Let it be noted, however, that Butler's notion of "genealogy" differs somewhat from Foucault's. For her, genealogy does not often involve the temporal process of consolidation (and so forth) of specific historical discourses; rather, she uses the term to denote what is generally implied by the term "discourse" as Foucault uses it: the tendency of discourse to cause proliferation rather than merely to prohibit. Specifically, she refers in "genealogy" to the tendency of discourse to generate a prior nature whose control, repression, or distribution becomes the warrant of its own necessary existence: "the operation of this law is justified and consolidated through the construction of a narrative account of its own *genealogy* which effectively masks its own immersion in power relations" (72–73, my italics). Butler thus identifies the discourse's narrativizing of its own provenance as genealogy. This is noted not merely to avoid confusion; it can be shown that this tendency in Butler points to problems in her handling of specific historical discourses temporally (that is, genealogy as "history") as opposed to a kind of universalizing—a tendency which she accuses Lacan and others of in an attempt to distinguish her own mode of argument—that makes of genealogy a more synchronic and theoretical than historical concept.

The most remarkable aspect of Butler's text is not the attack on the natural-sex-gender configuration of earlier feminism but its mode: she launches a two-pronged attack which ingeniously and convincingly dovetails psychoanalytic notions of gender and subject formation with the concept of subject formation deriving from Foucault's notion of discourse. Lacan stands as the major figure in the background of this consolidation, although his tendency is toward a universal notion of subject formation, which Butler rejects. Butler develops the psychoanalytic or "interior" version of gender formation primarily in chapter 2 of *Gender Trouble*. This in itself is a common feature of feminist thought, since psychoanalysis from the late Freud onwards has been a discourse intimately concerned with gender formation, not merely of the subject in general. Utilizing Gayle Rubin to separate the homosexual prohibition implied as prior and requisite to the incest taboo (as the "foundation" of culture), Butler argues the following: 1) using the psychoanalytic notion of "melancholic incorporation," she shows how the external or cultural prohibition against homosexuality generates the loss/rejection of the same-sex desire and object—a *refusal* of both the object and that the desire for it existed—which nonetheless results in an interiorization and walling-off or encrypting of the object and the desire.

Thus homosexual desire is both prohibited and preserved by this process of melancholic incorporation, and it results in "literalizing" and activating the surface of the body as capable of only one kind of desire: "the disavowed homosexual love is preserved through the cultivation of an oppositionally defined gender identity"; "*incorporation* literalizes the loss *on* or *in* the body, and so appears as the facticity of the body, the means by which the body comes to bear 'sex' as its literal truth" (69, 68). It may seem that a homosexual prohibition could only operate in conjunction with an already constituted sexual subject; otherwise, how could the subject, even in the process of becoming-subject, understand the prohibition of same-sex desire?

This is in fact a problem within the psychoanalytic tradition, beginning with Freud himself (Mitchell and Rose 1982, 11ff.; see chapter 1); for the assumption of a determining origin: a nature, a "disposition" or even bisexual tendencies (see Butler 1990, 58ff.). Those same tendencies toward a nature (bisexuality, pre-split, holistic sexual being) remain for Lacan as the constituted origin contained within the Imaginary, or the true origin for which nostalgia and a sense of lack are the only appropriate responses (see, e.g., Fuss 1989, 29ff.; Butler 1990, 55–57). Butler, however, attempts to moot the question of a natural "homosexual" tendency in humans and to avoid the nostalgia of Lacan for a nature limited by its entrance into the Symbolic in the process of subject formation, and she does this precisely by paralleling those interior processes of subject-formation under the pressure of cultural taboos to Foucault's notion of discourse. In other words, homosexual desire can be thought of as not merely preserved but generated. There is no prior homosexual nature which is truncated in these interior processes of subject and gender formation; it comes to be with its prohibition as an excluded potential.

Butler tends to anthropologize psychoanalysis here along the lines set out originally by Lacan. Although she distinguishes her treatment from Lacan's by describing his version as universalized (for example, the paternal law) and her own as historical and specific, she is not consistently successful in sustaining the opposition. But that is the price she pays for attempting to historicize the notoriously abstract processes of subject formation characteristic of psychoanalysis. Her specificity appears in the objective of her attack: the regime of heterosexuality, discrete binary sexual identity, and gender hierarchy generally associated with western culture. This is a historical (group of) discourse(s) which does not emerge from a prior essence or nature but is arbitrary and contingent. There are alternatives to heterosexuality: in fact the interior processes by which modes of desire alternative to the regime of compulsory heterosexuality are constituted, repressed, and preserved represents an interior archive with liberatory potential.

The second aspect of Butler's double attack on compulsory heterosexuality derives from Foucault's elaborate rejection of the repressive (of a fundamental, urgent sexuality) hypothesis in *The History of Sexuality,* volume 1. The "deployment of sexuality" poses itself in this "natural" explanation as necessary in order to control and channel the prior sexual energy along culturally productive lines (reproduction, hygiene, and so forth). Foucault's well-known response to this hypothesis is that the prohibiting or limiting law is in fact productive of the sexuality it claims to regulate. This argument is one version of the general poststructural strategy of inventing and redefining traditional hierarchical binaries—here with the notion that culture always precedes nature and produces it.

In Butler's terms the initial prohibition, law or discourse "produces *both* sanctioned heterosexuality and transgressive homosexuality. Both are indeed *effects,* temporally and ontologically later than the law itself" (74); or "the desire . . . conceived as both original and repressed is the effect of the subjugating law itself" (65). Further, the regime of compulsory heterosexuality requires, for its own cultural intelligibility, an equally intelligible conception of homosexuality, which is also necessarily repressed; what is "unthinkable" and also excluded is already *inside* culture (77). Again, this is in opposition to the notion of a prediscursive and determining nature, whether of sexuality or of gender or subject determination—that is, the assumption of some sort of potentially "subversive" sexuality which existed prior to discourse and which would reemerge at its demise (74).

This description of the process of Butler's argument is useful for isolating what is notable in her work, but primarily here it is necessary as the preliminary to a discussion of her development of a conception of discursive agency. We are already halfway there with the notion of an archive or potential available for disruption, precisely along the lines of Foucault's claim that discourse produces its own resistance. Yet Butler further articulates Foucault: she supplements his account with a psychoanalytic version, as discussed just previously; she shifts Foucault's concern with sexual-subject formation to a more precise focus on gender formation—necessary to all feminists who utilize Foucault. The quotation from Foucault which proves central to Butler's argument is his account of how sexual nature is constituted by discourse: "the notion of 'sex' made it possible to group together, in an artificial unity, anatomical elements, biological functions, conducts, sensations, and pleasures, and it enabled one to make use of this fictitious unity as a causal principle" (Butler 1990, 92).

Butler appropriates Wittig's phrase, "fictive sex," for this constituted sexuality. The binary "ontologies" of male and female sexual nature are the result of the "univocal construction of 'sex,'" which "conceals and artificially unifies a variety of disparate and unrelated sexual functions"; or "sex" "unifies bodily functions and meanings that have no necessary relationship with one another" (94–96). It is important in what follows and in chapter 4, which takes up again the notion of a *material* nature, to note the phrases "disparate and unrelated," "sexual functions," and "no necessary relationship." The question is, ultimately: what is the nature of these prior "parts"? Are they in fact already "sexual" and, if so, why? What is the perspective from which these parts can be characterized as either prior or sexual, given the already accepted notion that discourse itself constitutes what is prior to it and its cause? In addition "necessary" would seem to demand recourse to a foundational positionality from which accurately to distinguish the necessary from the arbitrary.

But what is the origin of discourse, or what exists prior to it? That question will reappear once we arrive at Butler's notion of agency, but it remains the basis for Foucault's double presence in *Gender Trouble*. First, as the theorist of discourse (what Butler calls "genealogy"), he provides the groundwork which opens up into Butler's formidable attack on binary gender formation within the heterosexual regime and, as we will eventually see, argues for a theoretical basis for resistance to that regime. But Butler also considers Foucault guilty of succumbing to what he exposes in *The History of Sexuality*, volume 1, an "unacknowledged emancipatory ideal" (94). In his short introduction to the memoirs of Herculine Barbin, Butler contends, Foucault envisions a "happy dispersal of these various functions, meanings, organs, somatic and physiological processes as well as the proliferation of pleasures outside" heterosexual and binary-sex discourse (96). Foucault is here put in the position of claiming a nature—that is, the "sexual" parts and their potential as parts, unorganized—prior to the discourse of (gendered) "sex," a "primary sexual multiplicity" capable of being released (96). It is also true that in *The History of Sexuality*, volume 1, Foucault proposes as the counter to the deployment of sexuality "bodies and pleasures"

(157). Butler counters this Foucauldian "nature" with the argument that the sexual parts from which "sex" is artificially constructed are themselves constituted—as sexual—by the medico-juridical discourse which is central to the deployment (101); but that answer might be considered merely a displacement of the question of origins. These are the grounds of difference which inform Butler's texts, and they are central to our understanding of both Butler and Foucault. The thorny question of origins in relation to the theory of discourse and genealogy will come up again in this chapter, and in the case of material origins in chapter 4. Clearly for Butler there is no origin, yet that merely makes obvious the question of the provenance of discourse, a problem Foucault may have been attempting to address in the late texts mentioned above.

To return to the question of agency in Butler: sex is not a prior nature or an inner essence which determines gender as its effect. Quite the reverse: gender identity is performance, a repetitive behavior within the limits of discursive gender specifications—in this case a performance of binary and univocal sex/gender within the framework of compulsory heterosexuality. Performance, in turn, creates the impression of a given or interior nature, a natural sexual disposition, which, like a textualized intention, is thought to be expressed in and by the performance. The pre-eighties' argument about gender assumed, according to Butler, a "doer" behind the deed (25, 142). However, the second-phase of gender argument: lacking an origin in nature and/or a prediscursive subject, there exists only a consolidating performance which can signify gender; interiority and priority are produced as alibis for the gender performance mandated by discourse. According to Butler, then, gender as performance repeated over time does not emanate from the prior subject but "must be understood to found and consolidate the subject" (140).

Despite the split between first- and second-phase feminism over the notion of prior subjectivity, it should be noted that Butler draws her notion of performance in part from Beauvoir's opposition between sex and gender (Butler 1990, 112, passim) and Wittig's notion of gender enactment (ibid., 124–25), as well as (primarily) Lacan's split between the real and the symbolic. Butler's notion of the performative (related to Irigaray's mimicry [76 and passim]) is, however, not only more forceful and striking: "the gendered body is performative . . . [and] it has no ontological status apart from the various acts which constitute its reality" (136), although producing in its wake an afternotion that an interior nature is being expressed; but the notion of gender also becomes the keystone in the development of a conception of discursive agency: gender identity becomes a "regulatory fiction," which "conceals gender's performative character and the performative possibilities for proliferating gender configurations outside the restricting frames of masculinist domination and compulsory heterosexuality" (141).

This performative gender opens the possibility of the production of agency. As mentioned, this is a new or poststructural conception of agency. In an example of the shift, Butler mentions that Wittig's notion of gender entails both consolidation and subversion of cultural gender through performance, and it is this "subversion enactment" on which Butler follows through (125); but Wittig assumes a knowing agent which subverts the discourse to which it is *already* external. Butler argues that discursively mandated performance must produce agency from within itself, in the following way: gender as performance over time necessitates repetition; and repetition inevitably involves failure or slippage, which in turn creates a self-reflexive stance; the consequence is a *produced* agency—by the same discursive regulations which produce gendered subjectivity.

Central to this is Butler's paralleling of anthropological (or structural) psychoanalysis's process of gendered subject formation and Foucault's notion of discourse as productive. In each case the forbidden is also produced/preserved, so that it constitutes an archive of potential behavior available to disrupt the binary-sex, compulsory heterosexuality regime. There is no "nature" and no subject prior to discourse, so the archive can never be identified as a natural, polymorphous potential of human beings that has been circumscribed and repressed by culture and that can now break free. Butler does not follow either psychoanalysis or Foucault slavishly. For example, she apparently ignores Foucault's "Rule of the tactical polyvalence of discourses" (1978, 100ff.), which follows from his more general notion that discourse produces its own resistance. Foucault's example of the "polyvalence" is the constitution of homosexuality in the nineteenth century. This led to the social control of this "perversity": "but it also made possible the formation of a 'reverse' discourse: homosexuality began to speak in its own behalf, to demand that its legitimacy or 'naturality' be acknowledged" (101).

The notion of a "reverse" (or an inversion of) discourse has been utilized to explain the use of nineteenth-century and first-wave feminism—as in *Foucault and Feminism*—but it seems to have been excluded by Butler because prohibition/constitution, for example, of the homosexual, seems to imply a self-consciousness—a perspective from which one sees oneself as *described* by or contained within the discourse—rather than to explain how this self-reflexivity is produced.

What then causes the failures or slippages in performance which result in the production of self-consciousness and therefore agency? On this issue Butler's text proliferates almost as much as performance is said to "proliferate" genders. First, the "injunction to be a given gender produces necessary failures"; what is "legitimated performance can't be sustained" (145). If repetition consolidates, it also displaces, for the following variety of reasons: gender is "instituted through acts which are internally discontinuous" (141), so performance engenders an awareness of this; the "occasional *dis*continuity" of the performance: "the abiding gendered self will then be shown to be structured by repeated acts that seek to approximate the ideal of a substantial ground of identity, but which, in their occasional *dis*continuity, reveal the temporal and contingent groundlessness of this 'ground'" (141)—thus the claim that chance, inadvertence, or failure of vigilance causes self-reflexivity.

Also suggested in the same passage is the discursive ideal of a prior nature or disposition which determines gender performance—precisely the alibi of discourse that conceals its operation. These prior natures are "ontological locales [that] are fundamentally uninhabitable" (146) and in light of which failure is inevitable. There are two issues which arise immediately in relation to Butler's claim about a "discursive ideal," one of which may be broached here, and the other of which will come up shortly. The first problem with the notion of a discursive ideal is that it is centralized and extraordinarily strict. That is an assumption Butler makes without following through on it, but it tends to conflict with the type of discursivity she is attempting to manipulate. A binary differential system of gender—one which Butler takes as promoting centralized and fixed gender norms, ones to be overcome by the agency that comes from the inevitable failure to reproduce those norms in performance—would actually allow an extremely large latitude in gender performance.

It is only at the margin that identity becomes problematic: a "woman" can retain the identity of "woman" as long as this subject performs up to the limit or gap between "woman" and "man," but does not cross over into the "other." For example, in the *Cours de linguistique générale*, Saussure says that a "t" can be written in a variety of ways; and that "La seule chose essentielle est que ce signe ne se confonde pas sous sa plume avec celui de *l*, de *d*, etc" (1972, 165). It appears that Butler overestimates the inevitability of failure in performance and thus its potential in producing agency.

Butler is also interested in the possibility of parody for producing agency and, eventually, disruption. She looks explicitly at butch and femme roles among lesbians, which can be said both to consolidate heterosexual roles (in the sense that unauthorized desire repeats the articulation of desire in dominant, heterosexual contexts) but can also serve to "denaturalize" binary heterosexually mandated genders. The object of lesbian-femme desire entails "neither a decontextualized female body nor a discrete yet superimposed male identity, but the destabilization of both terms as they come into erotic interplay" (123). But "parody" implies traditionally both intention and self-consciousness, either of homage to or deliberate destabilization of heterosexual categories. In this sense the perspective necessary for agency or resistance—that of self-reflexivity or of being inside and outside the discourse at once—is already given or assumed. Or there is a Lévi-Straussian moment from which self-consciousness emerges. The most that could be said is that what begins as compulsory parody of heterosexual norms fails and becomes pastiche—literally the falling apart of a prior cohesion—producing in its wake a self-consciousness of the constructed and performative character of gender. Yet even here the performers are *already* positioned *outside* the dominant discourse. Butler also uses drag and cross-dressing as examples of behavior which can produce, even more directly, consciousness-through-performance of the performative nature of gender.

The other possibility for producing a sense of discursive agency derives from the notion of multiple, convergent discourses. This is a route followed by the postmarxist Paul Smith, who develops Lacan's Symbolic as a multiplicity of overdetermining but also often conflicting discourses (think of Elizabeth I as a queen and/or woman, and the conflicting discourses of sovereignty and marriage, the latter requiring the submission of the woman to her spouse—made familiar by Renaissance New Historicists). According to Butler, psychoanalysis allows for multiple and conflicting identifications (67, passim); and she speaks in general about "The very complexity of the discursive map that constructs gender" and that "the very multiplicity of their [sex and gender] construction holds out the possibility of a disruption" (32); but it is not a very developed prong of her attack on binary, fixed gender. Adaptation and consolidation seem to be the contingent teleology of genealogy in Foucault—for example, in *Discipline and Punish*—and that would lead to the convergence, overdetermination, or coherence of specific discourses in a historical culture. Agency would derive only from the conflict which, following Foucault, would arise from chance interference patterns among converging discourses. The argument would be that these conflicts would inevitably surface in the constituted subject as self-consciousness—that is, the discursive subject projected "outside" of either or both discourses by the emergence of the conflict in consciousness as the positionality of agency and resistance.

Ultimately Butler argues that the subject produced in discourse achieves a position *outside* through the discursive instability, an instability which has the multiple causes discussed above. As incisive as her argument is, it also raises a number of problems. She notes a shift from "an epistemo-logical account of identity" associated with Hegel and modern philosophy to an account for which the locus of identity is found in "practices of signifi-cation" and language (144–45). But to say that language is "an open system of signs by which intelligibility [that is, cultural 'objects'] is consistently cre-ated and contested" implies an already determined capacity for contestation and change.

Again, to say that discursive gender mandates the protocol—that is, based on the difference between successful subject formation and a failure of cohesion—and now produces the salutary disruption of dominant discourse is a shaky argument. Failure may be said to lead to self-reflexivity, but what in historical culture has changed so that where once self-awareness of failure led to efforts to reconsolidate one's gendered subjectivity, now failure leads to the political subversion of the dominant discourse?

That is properly a historical question, and as such will be taken up later, but it makes several cracks in Butler's logic clear: there is no necessary causal relation among self-awareness, agency, and resistance—not any more than there is between agency and consolidation; further, the argument that failure produces self-reflexivity cannot be extended beyond a mere claim that this is in fact the case. Failure, as mentioned above, may lead to an intensification of performance based on the self-consciousness of failure, but Butler's claim is that failure thrusts the performance "outside" of the discourse. Self-consciousness becomes self-reflexivity when the subject, constituted within discourse, achieves a perspective from which to see itself as so formed, a perspective from which it is then able to understand the character and operation of discourse.

If there is any doubt that this is an "outside" position, note that it is precisely the position of the scientific subject of modernity, as well as the position of the traditional subject of theory: external to the "object" and in fact constituting the object—or "objectifying." The subject of/in discourse is propelled outward to this traditional critical and creative position, able to objectify discourse (read: able to "understand" the operation of discourse and see it objectively, including its capacity to constitute its own alibi in the narrative of its origin). This objectivity or understanding, according to Butler, opens access to the constituted/forbidden archive, which may then be utilized to disrupt dominant discourse by proliferation of genders and by otherwise manipulating and frustrating the limitations and coherencies imposed by that discourse. But the figure of the agent and its position merely solidify traditional notions of the subject. In contrast, the Foucault of *The History of Sexuality*, volume 1, refuses to locate resistance in the subject.

Butler still does not explain a necessary process from failure in performance to disruption of discourse or how self-reflexive insight is produced. What she does do is the following: argues, as already noted, that feminist wariness about social construction invokes the discrete binary philosopheme of "free will" vs. "determinism" (8, 147); argues that social construction is "the *necessary* scene of agency" (ibid., my italics); finally, overcomes the binary by arguing that the subject is both inside and outside discourse at once. It is constituted in discourse but also achieves a position critical of discourse.

It is important at this point to remember what Butler is arguing against: the conception of a natural configuration of sex which determines gender (or "should," according to the culture) or an a priori or prediscursive "humanist" subject. In both cases, but predominantly the latter, the subject is conceived as "outside" or prior to discourse, culture, or system. The only difference between Butler's conception of "outside" and the notion she attacks is the difference between a temporal, process conception and a spatial, epistemological one (which yet impinges on process), and the difference is not very great: between the absolute origin vs. the in-process subject which is able to divert the process, thereby participating in the originality of the origin. Self-reflexivity or split subjectivity is the identifying mark of modern philosophy and modernism.

《∞》

The argument of the previous section is that agency, realized as a function of the subject, replicates the metaphysics of origin. A dominant inclination of eighties gender study is the reexamination of gender binarism and heterosexuality as historical instead of natural, that is, as specific discourses which, as arbitrary, are open to change; in this context it is also interesting to inquire into the possible complicity of genealogy (as a current theory of historical change) and notions of origination and the a priori.

Genealogy bears a family resemblance to structuralism, and yet structuralism has for a long time been dismissed categorically by feminists and other activist critics as committed to the status quo by its synchronics of totalization. Genealogy actually appears as an attempt to modify the static and universalizing tendencies of structuralism by introducing the notion of a contingent historical process by which specific discursive structures and practices come into contact, merge, and reinforce each other (or the reverse).

The issues which arise when gender study utilizes genealogy (or discursive theory) as a means of its critique of contemporary culture: in general, there is a question of the appropriateness of discursive theory to an activist agenda; specifically, the problem of maintaining that one discursive structure should be broken down, exposed, or replaced by another, this within a context of an arbitrary historical process which is specifically ungrounded, hence without a reference point or origin from which to determine value or appropriateness. What lies behind these issues is the weight given to the binary, the *natural* (the origin, the given term of a necessary or causal link, the foundational) versus the *arbitrary* (the contingent, the unmotivated). Nature in this system has always provided the basis for choice. This theoretical binary in turn raises questions about the relation between theory (universalizing; associated with the natural, the logical, the "law") and specific historical discourses; can, for example, the *theory* of discourse and genealogy be mapped exactly into the *ontological* real (or, more appropriately, the ontological *unreal*) and the historical real? In other words, at what level is a theory of the arbitrary appropriate?

Feminist theory exists in a critical context that has seen an overall shift toward genealogy or, in general, toward history and contingency, and this has promoted analysis of specific discourses (usually of oppression by the dominant culture over its marginal elements) in particular historical periods. Genealogical feminism itself is faced with contesting a specific discourse of male dominance, often incorporated within a binary-gender, heterosexual regime. But at this point there may be a confusion of the universal with the historical. Feminists, in order to mount a resistance to male hegemony, have usually portrayed themselves as having always been victimized or excluded from male privilege, and that, in traditional terms, has given rise to the sense of near-universal dominance that is at the same time historical. This is the common feminist mode of argument, assuming, for example, a prediscursive male conspiracy, but it also makes specific the problematics of feminist discourse theorists: the theoretical privileges the universal explanation, and can easily give rise to claims that male dominance is natural because it is prior; and this conception of theory easily incorporates genealogical and discourse theory, that is, as founded in nature.

On the other hand to dismiss theory altogether, that is, to replace any possible notion of an ontological basis with an alternate notion of the historical real is to be left without a ground for attacking a basically contingent occurrence. Genealogical theory incorporates this paradox of the natural and the arbitrary by maintaining that the process of emergence and consolidation is contingent (although that in itself is a universalizing claim), and so feminists who hope to get beyond the prior notions of a feminine nature and interrupt masculinist discourse by turning to Foucault must contend with a sometimes intractable instrument. Whether discourse feminists such as Butler are able to overcome these intractabilities while dismantling masculinist discourse—without reference to the centrality of the subject—is the issue at hand.

Despite his protests, Foucault's discursive and archaeological theory was the inheritor of structuralism: archaeology represents "history" as a discontinuous succession of deep structures; this succession is marked by gaps similar to the demarcations of time zones, that is, without negotiable transitions. This situation is generally understood to have pushed Foucault into the genealogical or process notion of the historical, which marked the second half of his career—what is, I want to maintain, ultimately a struggle with the notion of an origin. This is despite the fact that Foucault was generally successful in challenging the traditional view that subjects accounted for historical change.

But discursive theory is related to structuralism in its ahistoricity. For the latter there is neither a past nor a (motivated) future, while for discursive theory there exists only a future to be reached by the dismantling of dominant discourses. Foucault's realization that he needed to understand the nature of the process by which discourses merge and supersede one another led to genealogy. Genealogy then provides for a historical process that does not utilize subjectivity as a cause of change—remember that genealogy is curiously not implemented by Butler—and conceives of that process as a contingent one of the intersection of discourses not previously in contact. But that only brings us back to the question of the origins of these separated discourses: does the same "contingent" or "arbitrary" label apply to the emergence of these prediscourses?

Foucault was uncomfortable with being called a "structuralist," primarily because he was a historian, that is, concerned to show historical difference. But his archaeological writings, which represented history as a succession of unmotivated structures only liminally connected by discontinuity, ignored the problems of origin and change in a particularly obtrusive way. "Nietzsche, Genealogy, History" (1977, 139–64), generally taken to mark Foucault's shift from archaeology to genealogy, is a sustained dismissal, through Nietzsche's work, of metaphysical or essentialist history (*Ursprung*) in favor of "emergence" (*Ertstehung*) or descent through specific, complex, unstable and heterogeneous "assemblage[s] of contingent elements." The notion of a continuous and progressive emergence of the essential nature present or potential within the origin gives way to the notion of change as haphazard, the result of the play of contending forces, the eruption of the will to power—all of which deny continuity and coherent identity.

The most representative genealogical texts which result are Foucault's *Discipline and Punish* and *The History of Sexuality*, volume 1; the emergence of a disciplinary society from the classical notion of sovereignty four centuries ago and the emergence in the modern world of a specific "deployment" of sexuality result from a notion of historical process different from that of the archaeological texts. One example of the process in *Discipline and Punish* is the manual of arms, used to order the bodily movements of soldiers when mass conscription and large armies came into being: that discipline became generalized as it was applied to other populations in schools, prisons, and factories. Similarly confession, which arose as a religious practice, came to be applied by civil authorities in order to produce the information concerning sexual proclivities and actions from which the deployment of sexuality was to emerge.

Each discourse came in contact with and reinforced other tendencies—contingently, not by nature or Providence, not by the intentions of authorities, and not in terms of a telos. Foucault, in other words, if pressed on the question of the origins (whether *Ursprung* or *Enstehung*) of these disciplinary or sexual discourses, would reply: other discourses. This is both to echo the synchronic Saussure and to displace rather than undo the notion of an origin: the manual of arms has a military provenance, so there is no necessity to inquire more than cursorily into its origin in that context: only that this discourse was historical, specific, and happened to be available for the purposes of more comprehensive regulation. Current discursive structures are simply the result of accidents which have led to the convergence of prior discourses. Assumed in this notion is that there exist central and marginal locuses of discourses—the central one being defined as the focus of the genealogical text at hand—and this is somewhat unwieldy. But primarily the problematic relation of discourse and origin—and here not *Ursprung* but *Enstehung,* or what was available for convergence at any given time—has simply been displaced to the question of the origin of the prior discourse.

It is this set of problematic issues which feminism is likely to take over along with the adoption of Foucauldian method. Butler's adoption of Foucault's notion of discourse in order to destabilize the current heterosexual regime includes, as noted previously, a collapsing of genealogy into the more abstract conception of how a discourse operates. For example, "the genealogy of the law," which it attempts to conceal, is that it is "productive of the very phenomenon it later claims only to channel or repress" (Butler 1990, 64). The law produces its own genealogy; but this does little to explain the appearance of the discourse as a specific historical phenomenon. Butler, since she is most emphatic about how a discourse "genealogizes" itself, is faced with the issue of the nothing prior to discourse, already mentioned as reinvoking the problematics of structuralism.

But even further, by collapsing the notion of genealogy into discourse Butler removes any possibility of a notion of historical process, genealogical or otherwise, from the agenda. Discourse constitutes its own origin and provenance; there is nothing ontologically prior to discourse, not even other discourses. This is clearly a stance that refuses to distinguish between the ontological and the historical real. There may be no essence of human nature which can justify a discursive structure such as compulsory heterosexuality, but at any point in time human beings are *something*, or have a distinct nature. The naturalized is precisely identical to the natural from a perspective inside a historical discourse; they cannot be distinguished except from a perspective *outside* the discourse and therefore outside of historical process.

Butler's commitments are to theory rather than history and to philosophical arguments that dismiss ontology. Her neglect of history parallels her tendency to universalize, which, though far this side of a structuralist such as Lacan, is always shadowed by notions of the "natural," the "logical," and the order of structure and the law. It is, for example, difficult to ascertain in Butler whether male dominance is part of a specific historical discourse, a historical universal, or a universal; it is, according to her argument, historical and contingent; but we do not have any discussion of the provenance of this hierarchical relation of genders, the contingency of its coming-to-be. Without that, it is easy to see how an explanation of the "natural" disparity of the sexes and genders will reappear.

Butler resists all attempts to determine what exists—or that something does indeed exist—prior to discourse, and that is the same as a refusal of either a general or a genealogical conception of historical process. Thus she rejects, without much inquiry, Gayle Rubin's and Foucault's notions of the prior. Butler, as noted, refuses Rubin's notion of prior full sexuality. In Foucault, what is prior to the discursive notion of sex consists of "anatomical elements, biological functions," and so forth, formed into an "artificial unity."

These elements, functions, sensations, pleasures are very specifically *natural*. They are "parts" of human nature, which, as noted, is always historical. That is, they are determined as human nature by discourses prior to the deployment of sexuality and contingently available to the latter discourse; the "nature" available for deployment by that discourse is, in effect, prior discourses. Butler makes precisely this point, that the heterogeneous elements and functions have already been constituted as such by discourse.

She makes this as a telling argument against Foucault's assumption of a "natural heterogeneity" (101); that is, because her argument does not allow for a genealogical process she must assume that there is only one overarching discourse (universal?). Since to pursue this issue further it is necessary to develop a more theoretical conception of process, I refer the reader to chapter 4 for a continuation of the argument.

Butler and other feminists who utilize Foucault are faced with an inevitable dilemma. The historian Foucault supplies with discourse theory the grounds for making an anti-ontological argument; but that, it seems, must be made in such a way as to deny any possibility of provenance and of process. The anti-ontological argument—not a historical but a theoretical one—is necessary as the basis for overcoming the notion of a nature or disposition which determines cultural structures and positions such as gender and gender hierarchy. The dominant cultural discourse is arbitrary, a quality that the discourse occults by means of the production of the natural tendencies in relation to which discourse claims to have emerged. To say that this discourse is contingent is to recognize a process in which discourses intersect, merge, and consolidate (or otherwise), constituting other discourses in the process, and that is where the difficulty enters. The current discourse of binary sex, compulsory heterosexuality, and male dominance may be ontologically arbitrary, that is, it is not the necessary or even the potential result of natural human tendencies in the way, for example, that Kant relates the structure of knowledge to the natural epistemological character and capacity of human beings. And the argument against ontological determination is necessarily theoretical.

However, the arbitrary and the contingent (that is, involving historical process) discourse is also the historical "real," once it is removed from a conceptual framework. What discourse constitutes as, for example, discrete binary sexual identity is a "nature" or naturalized construction. In a genealogical sense, a discourse whose formation is being scrutinized has as the "nature" the objects, and so forth, constituted by prior processes. As mentioned, the distinction between an ontological and a discursive nature is only possible from the theoretical or objective perspective of traditional thought. Ironically, this is precisely the perspective necessary for agency, which is in turn necessary to resistance in Butler's argument. Hence on two levels an activist feminism which looks to Foucault would seem to assume a theoretical perspective that is neither antifoundational nor focuses on historical specificity and contingency.

Foucault was active in campaigns for social reform, particularly the reform of prisons (Miller 1993), but in his archaeological texts there is no provision for resistance. There is more provision in the genealogical texts, but here resistance can often be traced to displaced (traditional) subjects. Butler clearly marks Foucault's departures from his attack on the repressive hypothesis, that is, when he assumes a "prediscursive libidinal multiplicity," especially in the introduction to the journals of *Herculine Barbin*. This introduction as well as Foucault's argument that the deployment of sexuality can be resisted by "bodies and pleasures" (1980a, 157) in terms of his assumptions concerning a prior nature are discussed in chapter 4.

Butler's discursive perspective reveals Rubin's nostalgia, but at the cost of a return to structuralism in which a culture, more universal than specific and historical, constitutes itself by means of its prohibitions. The structure is also totalizing, Butler's claims for the discursive production of resistive agency notwithstanding, since the self-reflexivity necessary to agency is either a given of the conception of the human subject or constituted by the historical discourse itself as human "nature." Butler's rush to escape from a prior nature, for example, of sex, to discourse, which constitutes its own "causal" nature, in the current genealogical or historical critical context, leaves her with no position on origin and process except to imply, as noted above, that discourse/culture founds itself by means of its own institutions.

This leaves her with little to choose from between Lévi-Strauss and the Sophist theory of origin: of a founding act or event from which the binaries nature/culture, natural/arbitrary, and necessary/contingent emerge. The discourse is an origin, through its constituting prohibitions, which has already been in place; it is both natural, that is, an origin, and entirely arbitrary, since it has no provenance or cause—a founding event without foundation. Butler's insistence on an absolutely discrete distinction between culture and nature (there is no nature, nothing prior to discourse) forces this return to the traditional notion of the self-originating subject which founds discrete categorical oppositions; that is, stands at the prior position of the production of differentiation. Butler needs to develop a sense of specific historical process, but that in turn would force her to reconceive her rejection of the origins of discourse.

Butler's refusal of genealogical process is not merely the uncomfortable consequence of her refusal to countenance any notion of origin; it is suggestive of a threat to genealogy itself. Genealogical theory entails a sense of specific historical process, not of subjects but of discourses. It entails a notion of causality, although a contingent one. And ultimately it too reproduces the question of origins. The explanation of a mediate origin, that is, a shift toward or an emergence of a "new" order deriving from prior, scattered discourses of different provenances—this can never dispense with or be separated theoretically from absolute origin or the notion of process itself.

Foucault's archaeology was a way of avoiding questions both of mediate and absolute origins, especially in terms of the hoped-for marginalization of the subject of knowledge as origin. To restore history as specific process Foucault adapted genealogy from Nietzsche, but that exacted its own price: the prior discourses could only appear as already existent. That is, to speak genealogically means to include origins; but that meant also to displace origins to a scene prior to the current mapping of change. Foucault seems to have faced the implications of this, the second stage of his thinking about history. Later chapters trace this possibility of a third level or stage of Foucault's thinking.

Butler is an activist: she seeks to develop through discursive theory a means of resisting oppression in the particular form of the regime of compulsory heterosexuality. Her distinction of the implications of her own work as contrasted with that of Kristeva is informative. The periodic eruptions of the semiotic within the symbolic fail to provide "concrete cultural options" (89–90), that is, avenues along which the current discourse may be permanently disrupted and transformed. In Kristeva the outburst always marks the beginning of a return to the normal. On the other hand, Rubin's and other feminists' recourse to nature simply replicates the hegemonic discourse's politics of origin as the natural determiner of the regime.

Positing discursive theory as necessary to progress is to argue that discourse is arbitrary and therefore subject to change. But at the same time: 1) discourse, and specifically hegemonic discourse, appears as a totalizing institution more static and universal than historical, and this risks a return to the claim that the discourse is based on nature; 2) genealogy, a process whose "agents" are specific historical discourses (and whose notion of origins is suspect), must be ignored; 3) the notion that there exists no ontological real seems to include the denial of a historical real or that a naturalized nature exists; 4) there is a profound residual respect for nature inherent in the notion that change or progress is only possible when nature is successfully removed from the theoretical agenda; 5) nature seems to return to Butler's discursive theory in the assumed capacity of the subject to stand outside the discourse which produces it (although she does argue that discourse produces the "nature" as well).

Is genealogical theory useful for an activist agenda? The answer might be yes, except that in Butler's case genealogy is simply discursive theory, and that is too static or structural to include the possibility of resistance, disruption, and progress. Also in genealogy the valence of the term "progress" is problematic; further, Foucault's notion in *The History of Sexuality,* volume 1, that discourses produce their own resistance has little to do with individual or group subjects as such. Butler's notion of agency is, on the other hand, retrogressively subjective and individual; and while it can logically be claimed that the discourse in question indeed produces individual subjects, the self-reflexivity necessary for agency in Butler closely reflects the ethos of essentialist humanism. Genealogy may be better than discursive theory for the understanding of change (although not progress), but in the first place Butler does not utilize genealogy, and in the second, genealogy dispenses entirely with the subjective perspective independent of discourse. We may be sure that, to paraphrase the old bumper sticker, "Change happens"; but, genealogically, we have little to do with it. As is the case with Butler and with most of us, we have been both profoundly influenced by the poststructural disappearance of the subject and loathe to relinquish an individual and personal sense of agency.

There is also a problem of a separation of discursive notions of gender and sexual preference from other categories such as race, class, ethnicity, and so forth—all relevant to critical theory today. Much criticism bases itself on a preconceived distinction between dominant and marginal elements in culture. According to discursive theory the prohibited is by definition the marginal, for example, the homosexual subgroups as opposed to the dominant heterosexual group. But what happens when discursive theory is applied to race, for example? Clearly, a dominant discourse constitutes the various "others" as well as its own prior nature: the WASP constitution of itself as the central subject depends on "frogs," "canucks," "niggers," "polacks," "spics," "gooks," "slopes," "chinks," (the names tend to shift rather rapidly). How would a member of a racially "other" group distinguish between Butler's argument and Irigaray's? Might not that racial other prefer the latter, that is, that of a real existence prior to or external to the discourse? There is, of course, a tendency in criticism according to which speakers at the margins replicate central subjectivity, thereby claiming the paradox of power/victimization—that is, the power to speak of victimization. The recuperative possibilities of claiming an originating subjectivity at the margins could force us back toward discursive theory. But if there is nothing prior to discourse—since discourse constitutes the margins—that leaves very sparse room indeed for the now-deemed necessary activist work necessary at the margins. Another reason that we are reluctant to relinquish the humanist subject. Genealogy might provide some middle position in this instance.

《◎》

The problematic of theory in Butler can be focused here on the specific question of male dominance or hegemony, and this results in a paradox of sorts. The issue of masculinist culture is not highly articulated in *Gender Trouble;* instead, it is assumed as an important component of the specific historical discourse of binary gender and compulsory heterosexuality that Butler seeks to disrupt. The paradox derives from the fact that Butler's mode of analysis is theoretical, and this tends to universalize the supposedly specific discourse under attack. And inevitably the universal gives rise to the claim of a prior and determining natural origin of discourse.

Butler answers briefly that the difference of cultures precedes any universal, whose application cross-culturally would then have varying results (1990, 76); but this mediation of the binary of culture/cultures barely begins to address the issues raised. What, in an era committed to the analysis of specific, local historical discourses, does "theory" signify? If theory is significant at all, how does it function, and how does it help promote the activist agenda of many feminists and participants in gender studies? For Butler "feminist political theorizing" leads to the disruption of the heterosexual regime that claims to derive from natural sexual identity, so it is appropriate to focus questions concerning the efficacy of theory on *Gender Trouble.*

The regime of compulsory heterosexuality and binary gender is an arbitrary discourse: this is the foundation, so to speak, of the discursive argument, and the point at which we may begin. Without much discussion of the issue, Butler claims that the incest prohibition "sanctions [that is, institutes] hierarchical and binary gendered positions" (72). Although there seems to be a certain "logic" associated with male dominance—that is, that the determination of two gendered positions indicates a necessarily differential power relation—it could only be argued discursively that male hegemony in any specific discourse, including that of a heterosexual/binary gender regime, is contingent. For example, in Butler gender is not the expression of an inner, natural essence but the result of performance mandated by discourse; the discourse is arbitrary and contingent and so is the mandated gender: "gender is instituted through acts which are internally discontinuous" (141).

Though Butler goes one step further—for example, from what perspective is the determination of discontinuity possible, in relation to what conception of natural, necessary, or logical relation?—her argument derives from the familiar passage in *The History of Sexuality,* volume 1, where Foucault argues that the deployment of sexuality organized "sex" as a "fictitious unity" of disparate parts, functions, behaviors, and feelings (154)—with no natural or necessary relation among them. Once again, it is the discourse which constitutes the "nature." In Foucault there is not the sense, as there is in Butler, of a foundational position from which both the natural and arbitrary can be understood and therefore distinguished; Foucault's position allows him to determine that the parts are not necessarily related, but not the foundational sense of "true" natural relation that would render acts absolutely discontinuous. And there is more to say about Foucault's notion of this "fictitious unity" of sex as a "nature" that will distinguish him from Butler ever further (see chapter 5).

The neglect of genealogy and of a sense of historical process in Butler makes it impossible for her to show how the discourse of male dominance became contingently associated with binary gender and heterosexuality in specific historical eras. Butler's argument in this respect replicates Lévi-Strauss, although his structural notions are always understood to be under attack. The latter's implicit assumptions that humans are naturally heterosexual and that males dominate are institutionalized in the founding of culture by the incest prohibition—and this is repeated in Butler's argument that males were already in control of language when they "figure[d] nature as female," and culture as male. The consequent "binary relation between culture and nature promotes a relationship of hierarchy in which culture freely imposes meaning on nature" for the benefit of males (37). This is in no sense a historical argument about the consequence of male domination but rather a universalizing one; or, alternatively, given that the explicit nature/culture binary becomes operative at a moderately late date in western history, are we to assume that male dominance is historically coextensive with that?

These theorizing and universalizing tendencies allow Butler to ignore genealogy, as I have said, but also the study of specific historical cultures. For example, Foucault's study of the fourth-century B.C.E. Athenian discourse of sexuality joins binary gender and male dominance but not compulsory heterosexuality. Bisexuality is mandated by the discourse: male-male desire, on a primary level, is necessary to a reproductive regime—the reproduction of citizens; opposite-sex desire is necessary only secondarily, for the replication of bodies. Butler's commitment both to discourse as arbitrary and to theoretical universality, together with her failure to consider specific instances such as the above suggests a sense of a yet-to-be-revealed natural connection between compulsory heterosexuality, binary gender, and male hegemony.

There is the related problem of the "reality" of masculine domination or of gender in Butler. Her theoretical approach, which focuses on the arbitrary character of discourse and its production of the "nature" on which it claims to be based, suggests that to be arbitrary is to be inauthentic or unreal. Gender is merely a culturally intelligible performance continuity without a substantial foundation; gender is disrupted in Butler by a series of anti-ontologizing arguments which show that it is not a result of being, not ontologically determined, but arbitrary. But the fact that gender is constituted by an arbitrary and contingent discourse makes it no less historically real. Indeed, from within the discourse there is no difference between the ontological and the historical real—no difference between nature and the naturalized. Whether the subject is gender or male hegemony, the issue of the real is the same.

This theoretical, anti-ontological mode of ontological argument always operates slightly below the surface of Butler's argument, appearing at times as a kind of evanescent foundation from which to dismiss binary gender, compulsory heterosexuality, and male dominance: for to argue against prior being always risks ontological complicity. This is especially disruptive of the current discourse: "to center on—and decenter" the "defining institutions [of] phallogocentrism and compulsory heterosexuality" (ix). She proposes, as the successor to feminist identity politics, "a *feminist genealogy* of the category of women" that will displace essence with a demonstration of how "the juridical subject of feminism" is constituted by discourse, that is, arbitrarily. This sort of emancipatory imperative—the freedom from mandated binary gender especially, but also from heterosexuality—is obviously at odds with the norm of objectivity claimed by traditional theory. If this "old" theory is not appropriate to activism, what kind of theory is? Marxist theory, often associated with revolutionary potential, simply points to structural contradictions in the material order which it claims have or will lead to a new stage in the process. Butler's theoretical demonstration that gender is the locus of contradiction of the natural and the arbitrary may be said to open up disruption and consequent change in the discourse. Yet to take this stance is to demonize binary gender (and the associated male hegemony and heterosexuality).

But if the discourse is contingent, arbitrary, and historical, what is the theoretical ground which warrants its disruption? Is there an implied ground or set of principles, reference to which will allow for the condemnation of the discourse? If for example the discourse is a configuration of oppression, the latter term would suggest a new phase of the Enlightenment, as well as prior subjects (women, racial others, and so forth) who are oppressed by the discourse. This is not to say that women have not been and are not oppressed both by males and the masculinist regime, or that other forms of oppression do not exist. But is a theoretical analysis an appropriate way of identifying these ills, addressing them, and reconstituting ourselves? And since traditional theory seems not to be appropriate to this task, it will be useful to ask whether Butler succeeds in developing a new sense of theory, one which is antifoundational yet instrumental to social change. It is on this question of theory that discursive gender studies stands or falls.

In the last few pages I have used male dominance as a specific question which points to general issues within feminist theory and gender studies that take Foucault seriously, that is, which use some version of discursive theory in order to dismantle the notion of nature and essential identity. Butler's text especially, raises the question of the appropriateness of theory in addressing historical (discursive) questions or, in brief, of a potential opposition between theory and history that cannot be resolved simply by relating an abstract model to empirical processes. Foucault argues that specific, local and contingently but complexly related discourses characterize the emergence of specific cultures such as the disciplinary society in *Discipline and Punish;* and this particular nonsubjective historicizing impulse in turn characterizes literary scholarship today.

The "end of theory" in the eighties may in part mean the return of agency by way of individual or group subjects as part of this new historicism; but it means primarily the end of the ontological argument, of necessity and causality, of universality and the abstract—in effect, the end of the ontologically supported argument against metaphysics that is embodied in the aporetics of deconstruction. In Butler specifically, there is a question of whether theory is in fact at an end, and this takes the implicit form of history (that is, genealogy) vs. theory (that is, discourse)—implicit because Foucault's notion of genealogical emergence is simply absent from the discussion, although the term is not.

The association of the traditional notion of theory with ontology and necessity signifies its foundationalism, and this leads to an opposition between genealogy and agency. For Foucault genealogy is an account of history which does not make primary reference to an initiatory capacity in human subjects—that is, it refuses agency as cause. Agency is ipso facto foundational, as Sophist theory clearly demonstrates. Butler attempts to produce agency discursively or without reference to a prior subject. But the discursive construction of the subject, or the subject "inside" discourse, cannot account for positioning the subject outside of, and potentially critical of, the discourse within which it is produced. Theoretically, to claim the discursive production of agency by means of the inevitable failure of the performance of subjectivity simply reveals the assumption of a prior self-reflexivity that is displaced/revealed/occulted in the positioning of the theorist. This position is of course the ground from which the objective view is possible, the traditional theoretical perspective, and it is utilized by Butler in producing agency from discourse. But she doesn't show how this self-relation is produced historically.

Would it not be simpler to argue genealogically that self-reflexivity is constituted as an essential part of human nature in the specific historical discourse of modern philosophy? The potential for being outside or prior to discourse is not ontologically determined but is historically actual. That is, self-reflexivity is produced as an *essential aspect* of human nature not by the abstract processes of the operation of discourse, but by the very specific discourse which begins with Descartes (see chapter 7). This is Foucault's argument in the late "What Is Enlightenment?" Butler's argument that objective awareness of the arbitrariness of discourse as well as its alibi of a "prior" nature is the necessary product of subjective constitution, reveals her theoretical commitment and her failure or refusal to appreciate Foucault's genealogy.

Butler, for example, fails to account for the historical shift from the anxiety of performance to performance as disruption. Theoretically the shift defines the parameters of the production of agency and is thereby justified; but if this is an actual shift in attitude (toward suspicion about "natural" sexual identity, and so forth) then we are faced with a complex genealogical question whose answer would be enormously useful to our understanding both of history and ourselves. The historical capacity for self-reflection would be of little use here, since it could be equally productive of anxiety or disruption. The "genealogy" of Butler's own argument about the production of resistive agency is relevant here: in effect, she inverts Lacan. Lacan's theory is one of the universalized processes of subjectification (including gender subjectification) in which the being prior to injection into the Symbolic is both constituted and rendered unavailable by subjectification itself. This prior being is inaccessible except as a source of anxiety based on a "cognizance" of its loss or of lack; this failure of subjectification clearly implies an assumed or produced self-reflexivity, directed against the self.

Lacan's "romance of failure," as Butler labels it (56–57), that is, locating the central fact of humanness in failure, is reproduced in Butler's sense of the inevitable failure of gender performance, now as a narrative of agency, resistance, and emancipation from the binary-gender/heterosexual discourse.

As noted earlier, Lacan and Butler together forget what constitutes identity in a negative differential system (x remains x as long as it is not-y) and substitute a severely constricted range of identity, thereby rendering failure overwhelmingly certain. Butler even mentions a discursive "ideal." Failure is for one the ultimate identity and for the other the means for disrupting hegemonic discourse. Butler rejects Lacan's structuralist universalization of gender subjectification in favor of discursive theory in order to engage the specific or historical discourse of compulsory heterosexuality. But discursive theory, if detached from genealogy, is static, and can only envisage discourses as abstract mechanisms of domination. It is totally incapable of representing the historical shift from gender anxiety to gender disruption—if, as it seems, such a shift has indeed occurred. How does, in other words, the shift from the natural to the naturalized in notions of gender take place historically?

The primary issue for Butler is opposition to feminist identity politics, since it ultimately entails recourse to the conception of a prior female substance which ontologically determines gender. Thus she confronts the claim to an ontological reality with the discursive notion of the arbitrary and contingent, and hence the *merely* historically actual. The "real" and the "actual": "As the effects of a subtle and politically enforced performativity, gender is an 'act.' . . . [subject to failure and 'subversive repetition'] that . . . reveals its fundamentally phantasmatic status" (146–47). The adjective may be justified from a theoretical, "outside," or ontological perspective: gender is a performance which is neither the necessary consequence of nor the external expression of a prior or interior essence. But discursively the performance is actual gender; it is, in effect, the "real"—the *historical real*.

Even further, in discursive terms, natural gender and the naturalized performance that is identified with gender within a specific discourse are indistinguishable. Rather, the difference between the natural and the naturalized appears only from the theoretical/agential perspective external to the constituting/naturalizing discourse—the very position Butler argues is produced by the "movement" of understanding between the two. Also, Butler says that for feminists to utilize the conception of a prior subject ("a doer behind the deed") is to risk the "imperialist strategies that feminism ought to criticize" (147); yet the supposed production within discourse of this objectifying subject is similarly recuperative. To argue along with Foucault that a "fictive sex" is produced in discourse by combining not-necessarily sexual "parts," would necessitate knowledge of a prior or foundational necessary/arbitrary binary distinction. In other words, it is impossible to know that the coherence of "sex" is arbitrary without some privileged insight into what is natural—again an external, objective perspective. Butler says, for example, that gender is "instituted through acts which are internally discontinuous" (141), acts which promote a notion that gender is substantial. But how to identify discontinuity without a solid conception of continuity (or natural coherence)? There are several ways to argue the arbitrary without a prior conception of the natural, one by way of traditional materialist theory (see chapter 4) and the other by means of a discursive conception of self-reflexivity (see chapter 7); Foucault utilized both in his genealogy; Butler, however, finds in the Foucault a failure to maintain his own discursive insights into "nature."

The basis of an activist theory is necessarily evaluative, or even moral: resistance as a good necessitates the conception of a specific discourse as instituting domination, oppression, or harmful constraint. Resistance liberates the polymorphous sexual potential (Rubin) or the constituted/prohibited alternatives to strict binary gender (Butler); but in both cases the sense is of a repetition of the Enlightenment narrative of human emancipation, only now including gender and possibly marginal groups in general. On the other hand, discourses determine the cultural (as the "natural") and thereby determine what is approved and prohibited—in other words, provide the basis for evaluation. This argument is similar to the above: only the theoretical perspective, beyond discourse, provides for a determinate evaluative basis—the return of the Subject as the origin, or to what Foucault calls the universal intellectual.

Butler is specific about a new sense of the "political," now no longer the representation of the interests of a group whose identity is predetermined. Politics is thus non-objective; power and the political operate "within signifying practice" (148), that is, arbitrarily, within discursive practices. Since discourse constitutes both subjects (individual or group) and practices, and since the specific heterosexual discourse Butler confronts constitutes binary and hierarchical gender, we once again need an external perspective in order to characterize discourse as political: male hegemony as arbitrary (and oppressive) can only be determined from this position of the investigative or theoretical subject.

Gender studies of the last few years has undermined the notion of the natural underpinnings of gender. Butler represents the attempt to use theory to focus on how discourse legitimates itself by means of the alibi of essence or nature. I have tried to show how at many points this specifically theoretical discourse is compromised and recuperated by the traditional notions of the universal, the ontological, and the (male) position prior to/outside of the discourse. In other words, I have taken a traditional theoretical perspective from which to evaluate Butler's argument. What is immediately recognizable here is the deconstructive matrix, which is a poststructural cliché; that the attempt to elide metaphysics, to un-found it, is always from within its discourse; deconstruction is thus a continuous, unachieved project, a process. Deconstructors careless enough to look back always find something gaining on them. My reading of gender studies through Butler simply repeats the cliché, but that may be useful for considering whether or how theory has changed in the post-age. In other words, can there be any basis for claiming that a poststructural utilization of theory would not automatically condemn such a theorist to recuperation?

But suppose we, following Foucault, consider theory as a historical archive. In other words, just as a "fictive sex" is constituted by the deployment of sexuality from a contingent archive of available "parts"—anatomies, physiological processes, feelings, pleasures, pains—so theory is a "natural" instrument of the constitution of the discourse of modern philosophy. Theory, in other words, is a nature that reveals itself as naturalized. Every attempt to attack poststructuralists is a reference to this historical archive as nature, foundation, truth; every demonstration in which poststructuralists leave themselves open to recuperation is a recourse to this archive. But what is arbitrarily constituted is open to deconstitution or dispersal; hence the post-age cliché of recuperation transforms instantaneously into the divisive play of and in the archive.

The contention between Butler and Foucault is double, and both parts are relevant here. Foucault gets accused of a retrogressive slip into the metaphysics of the prior in the case of Herculine Barbin. According to Butler, the notion of Barbin's "happy limbo of a non-identity" suggests "the release of a primary sexual multiplicity" (91–96). Indeed, in *The History of Sexuality,* volume 1, as well, Foucault recommends "bodies and pleasures" as resistance to the deployment of sexuality (157)—the dispersal or scrambling of parts which as an associated network constitute the cultural matrix of intelligibility of sex and sexuality. Butler's understanding is that Foucault means the constituted, nonnecessary unity is of naturally sexual parts, and her answer is that the dispersed parts are already constituted as sexual by the discourse itself; they do not constitute a prior natural foundation. But what Butler misses here depends on her exclusion of genealogy: the "naturally" sexual parts emerge from a prior discourse; so naturalized, they become the prior "nature" from which further discursive organization emerges (see chapter 4). This point is applicable to the more general notion of theory.

The first experience of poststructuralism in the United States was the collapsing of traditional binaries, speech/writing particularly but also nature/culture and others. Apart from the inevitable recuperation which, incidentally, rendered it more heroic, deconstruction can be understood as a new discourse whose specific project was the dispersal of the natural unity of the prior discourse of modern philosophy. Recuperation augurs a belief in the residual natural power of this prior discursive unity, theory, and/or metaphysics. In one sense, then, Butler is a step beyond Derrida. Her new sense of theory operates specifically as a dispersal of theory; it is, in effect, deliberately contradictory; it dismembers and re-members the parts of the prior unity; it is a logic that insists on its own paralogical character.

The contradictions are not something Butler could have failed to notice. Her claim, for example, that gender is constituted by a set of performatives which are internally incoherent (141) or, along with Foucault, her notion of a "fictitious unity" of sex are contradictory because they depend on a prior, foundational notion of nature and order, and a position external to discourse which would allow access to this prior ground. Butler's new theorist, like the agency which gets produced, stands at a remove from the traditional archive of theory, able to scramble notions of logics, subjects, origins, and so on without being restrained, as most of us seem to be (there was always a sense of illicitness in deconstruction), by even a residual loyalty to that prior nature of theory.

But that prior discursive unity is the naturalized ground of the subsequent as well. Butler, for example, maintains the externality of the agential or theoretical subject while rejecting the prior or originating Subject. In western philosophical discourse that is a paralogical stance, but it is one she maintains consciously. The opposition between the universal and the historical is equally cheerfully collapsed; that is, the regime of compulsory heterosexuality appears in her text as universal-historical. She neglects genealogy while claiming it. The relation between origin and nature is easily disrupted: discourse is both arbitrary and an origin; it is a primal event, historical and universal at once, which institutes its own prior nature arbitrarily. In this new configuration theory is politics, is politics without a preexistent constituency, is objective in that it understands discourse, and is antifoundational in advocacy. Butler projects and predicts a disruption of gender, through performance, but she performs the disruption and re-creation of the theoretical enterprise. This is an important shift in feminist theory from the earlier feminist association of theory with politics—for example, Louise Turcotte's introduction to Wittig, which conceives "theory" in traditional terms (the "outside" perspective) in relation to a "politics" constituted by the actions of a group Subject (Wittig 1992, xi–xii).

There are, however, other ways to skin theory. Historical study can often reveal the paralogical as already instituted in western thought. This is the inheritance of Derrida who, despite his tendency to universalize (about writing, for example), deals with historically situated texts historically, and my own suggestions about the traditional outside/inside character of subjectivity follow in this line. Then, too, Butler seems too hard on Foucault, even though the stakes are high. Genealogy contains an implicit notion of the exchange between naturalization and the natural which seems to be drawn from materialist conceptions of process that might well be investigated and clarified. Yet Butler's is a bolder and more provocative strategy. Her argument is a failure in the sense that it can be recuperated; but it is also a challenge thrown at the apparatus of modern philosophy that constitutes the archive of recuperation.

❧ 4 ❧

Foucault and Materialist Reasoning

History and historicality have in recent years become issues of central critical importance. In fact they are so inscribed within our critical operations that we no longer wonder at the confrontation of history and metaphysics that has recently formed the horizon of critical thought. Foucault is in part responsible for the critical shift toward historicism, one that has led, for example, to cultural studies, and to the questioning of transcendental or a priori notions of human nature—or what has been characteristic of philosophy since Descartes. Questions of the naturality of sex/gender, race, class, ethnicity, sexual orientation, for example, seem possible only within a historicist, non-essentializing perspective that allows for the consideration of the subject as constituted within and by the cultural discourse of a particular age. We all know the drill by now.

Butler's ahistoricism suggests that it may be worthwhile to look for Foucauldian continuities in which historical processes are inscribed, specifically the possibility of a material substratum. If Butler is correct about Foucault's return to a sexual nature, and to some degree she is, then we need to ask whether there are not two but three levels in Foucault's analysis which warrant attention: discourse, the discursively constructed nature, and a material substratum which is prior to the construction by discourse—a kind of proto-nature. Butler indicates as much but assumes the "libidinal multiplicity" is an identity, which Foucault explicitly denies. Non-identity is in fact the claim Foucault makes about Herculine Barbin in the introduction to his/her memoirs (xiii). That is the crux of the disagreement. Butler's version of discursive theory is not calibrated to deal with origins, and certainly not with a material origin. This aspect of Foucault's analysis warrants further inquiry.

Foucault's middle-late texts, primarily *The History of Sexuality*, volume 1, exhibit a materialist logic. In these works he often criticizes marxist dialectics and the conclusions deriving from them. Yet there is a strong sense in which Foucault's readings of history invoke the methods of ancient, non-dialectical materialists, in the specification of a material minimum and of the processes which emerge from that material basis. It is not that marxism bears no relation to ancient materialism. Marx, after all, completed a dissertation on Epicurus and other ancient materialists, establishing a position from which to confront Hegel.

The relation of Foucault to marxism in the context of ancient materialism is actually a very complex matter that can only come into focus here from time to time. One clear connection is the inscription within materialism of history: materialist theory of any sort is inseparable from a conception of process, and from process as temporal and emergent/declining. For this reason it is more direct to read Foucault through the lens of ancient materialism. Marxism has traditionally provided a historicist mode of thought, and although it has influenced Foucault in an important way, he is never comfortable with its dialectics. The important difference here relates to agency or subjectivity, which traditional marxists usually make central to the production of historical consciousness. Foucault constructs a genealogical analysis, which he often calls "history without subjects," and so attempts to bypass marxism. In later texts he does of course return to his own versions of self, self-relation, and historical consciousness (see chapters 5, 6, and 7).

What is staged in the relation of Butler to Foucault is, at the first level, the confrontation of discursive theory and genealogy; the theater of this opposition is that of origins. Ignoring origins and historical process, except in the present moment of transformation, Butler pushes toward a pure structural synchronics. Genealogy makes the gesture toward origins, without, however, being able to fulfill that promise: it seeks to explain the contingent process by which a discourse or even episteme is constituted, but it can do no more than refer to strategies or discourses at a prior stage. To paraphrase Saussure: the discourse at any one stage emerges, contingently, from a prior discourse; there is no prediscursive origin.

What gets staged in *The History of Sexuality*, volume 1, and related texts is more complex: epistemics (the two deployments); genealogy (for example, the journey of the technique of confession); and beneath these a material substratum, an origin. Foucault's simplest phrase for this substratum is "bodies and their materiality," and it is repeated in many variations.

Can this be read as a prior nature—that is, that which discursive theory is calculated to deny? It seems so. Does, then, this nature predetermine discourse in the sense that the material determines in advance the forms that it may take? Foucault's central notion of contingent process would be threatened by such an assumption, but on the other hand the presence of a material substratum would have the advantage of diminishing the importance of human agency in history. I propose to address the questions arising in Foucault from his clear articulation of a material substratum of "bodies and their materiality," and I propose to do this by first placing the inquiry within the frame of ancient atomism, its methods and the problematics which constrain its explanatory potential.

In the following two sections I analyze parallel notions in Foucault of a material substratum, and of emergent and diachronic process. The ultimate question arises as part of a meditation on Foucault, here during his genealogical "period." This is not a question about materialism per se, but about genealogy: the kind of historical process it envisions, its possibilities, and its limitations.

《◎》

The major atomists of antiquity, Leucippus, Democritus, Epicurus, and Lucretius, differ in a variety of ways. I will exploit these differences, focusing primarily on Lucretius because his notion of the *clinamen* or swerve indicates precisely the unexpected problematics of origin in material systems. But at other levels the systems of the various materialists are all similar. In classical materialism there is always a minimum material entity, the atom, *primordium, eidolon,* and so forth, which is unseen but in combination constitutes the reality we do apprehend. Hence a two-level structure that, in Democritus's case (we have only fragments) produced the fundamental opposition between the real (atoms) and the apparent. He was fond of saying that "truth is as deep as a well." The earlier Leucippus is reported to have said that there exist only atoms and void. A strong sense of process is an inevitable part of materialism, as well as a strong notion of causality: the combination and recombination of atoms (as well as the reverse) determines a process constituted by the successive stages of secondary or apparent reality characteristically related by terms such as "growth" or "emergence" (also of declination). Everything is in motion; everything changes; the potential for change at any one stage of the process is vested in the material entities which underlie that stage of the process, and which determine a further combinatory potential.

113

For Lucretius the two levels constitute a double reality. For example, "corporibus caecis igitur natura gerit res" [nature produces reality from unseen bodies] (1963, 1.328). The secondary level is most strikingly represented by Lucretius as "quod in summis fluitare videmus / rebus" [what we see floating on the surface of things] (2.1011–12), or what we see flowing or in process on the surface of things; this secondary level is otherwise presented as: what appears "ante oculos" [before the eyes] (1.342); "res apertae" [things open (to the view)] (4.467); "hoc in promptu manifestumque videmus" [what we see manifestly and ready to hand] (2.246); "quod cernere possis" [what you are able to perceive] (2.248). One of the primary tasks of book 1 of the *De rerum natura* is to argue that there must exist beings prior to or beneath the perceived reality.

The relation of levels in materialism is in general sequential and determinate. What appears at the secondary level is determined by the primary material—the *primordia* in Lucretius—and their relative configuration, which in turn depends on their innate qualities such as weight or mass, their surface configuration, and the prior stage of their interaction, which Lucretius refers to in general as the resultant of "plagae," blows. This primary-level/secondary-level hierarchical or vertical relation has a recognizable parallel in the base-superstructure relation (if we ignore the problematic of contradictory relation) or the notion of material representation.

Classical materialism is naturalist or organic, not dialectical, and this is apparent in the relation of levels: the secondary level necessarily emerges from the primary level. Even in Marx the contradiction of the real or material conditions of production and their representation appears only against a background of the past or the hoped-for or future organic relation of levels. In addition, the earlier materialists are specifically atomists, that is, concerned primarily to explain the material nature of the universe, and admitting human agency as little more than chance or as part of the normal interplay of atoms. Aside from Epicurus and Lucretius, there are few humanist concerns; but of course the surviving writings of these two far outweigh the literary remains of Leucippus and Democritus and so our knowledge may be skewed.

The relation of levels is usually thought of as synchronic, thus opening a space of contradiction between, for example, the real means of production and the institutions of a society. But material relations in atomism are also lateralized: emergence operates diachronically in a process constituted of a series of stages of the material configuration of *primordia*. Each stage may be read as a primary/secondary double-leveled existence, but the temporal process-relation shifts the focus away from this in order to concentrate on each stage of the diachronic process as the effect of a prior stage and the cause of the subsequent one, which necessarily emerges. In other words, the material potential at any one state—the particular characteristics of the entrained *primordia*, their state of interaction and combination—determines, within limits, the actualization which makes up the consequent stage. Incidentally, contradictions are usually said to arise when the shift from stage 1 to stage 2 occurs without a corresponding shift in representation, at the secondary level.

Materialist process is thus always successive and it is usually progressive or pre-entropic. If the potential at any stage determines further actualization in process, it also serves as a limitation; a certain stage has the potential to result in a very restricted number of possible further stages. Also, conceptually, "progressive" means the same as "degenerative," since whatever the "direction" of the process—for example, the addition to or deletion from the available fund of *primordia*—the relation among the stages is the same.

Can Foucault's mode of historical analysis have anything to do with this determinate material process? Perhaps not, or not so far. But the materialists do provide a model structure of diachronic process that is nonsubjective, and would therefore lend itself to genealogy. Keep in mind that "emergent" does not imply a value. Although some ancient materialists equated positive material growth with progress, there is no theoretical basis for preferring one stage over another. Contingency remains a problem, and to address that we need to move on to other aspects of ancient materialism.

Materialism appears at first to have little difficulty dealing with origin. Yet the notion of the origin constitutes a crisis in all philosophies, and in materialism as well. The origin is the material minimum or the *primordium;* being is beings, an indefinite supply of them, and this is the given or the origin. Among materialists, Democritus's fragmentary writings display no concern for the origination of process. Leucippus had possibly anticipated the problem, and solved it for Democritus as well as himself, by claiming that the original condition of atoms in the void is the *diné* or swirl: the atoms were already in motion and interaction because of the curvilinear motion. In other words, material process is not subject to a critical moment of origination.

Epicurus, the most humanistic of the atomists, has little concern for the absolute material origin, but considerably more for human origination, the positioning of the subject within physical space and materiality. For example, the centralizing perspective of the subject determines "up" and "down" as directions (Diogenes Laertius 1925, 10.60). Humans thus enter into the ongoing material process by orienting it in terms of their own positionality. This is a particularization of what has long been said about the Hellenistic era in general and Epicurus and the Cyrenaics specifically: that they had no interest in natural science beyond its contribution to an undisturbed or pleasurable life—in Epicurus's case *ataraxia*. Yet Epicurus also wrote a long treatise entitled *Peri physeos*, which remains only in tantalizing fragments.

Lucretius occupies a peculiar position in materialist theory because of his notion of the *clinamen* or swerve. Materialism was regularly derided in antiquity because the swerve was a nonmaterially motivated origin within a materialist system (e.g., Cicero 1925, 1:4; 1933, 1:19–20).

The swerve unlocks the material potential of the *primordia* for combination and accumulation into perceptible bodies. At the same time it unlocks a multipotentialed process. Originally *primordia* move downward into the void because of their mass, then begin to interact according to their material potentials because of the swerve. Hence the notion of multiple potential that is necessary for Lucretius's conception of combinative material process: at any given stage of the material process there are multiple ways in which the given fund of *primordia* is able to combine into a larger whole (or disintegrate). There is, in effect, slippage in the process: the potential is multiple but the actualization determinate. The swerve thus interrupts a thoroughly determinate system—the downward rain of *primordia;* as itself a chance motion, the swerve introduces chance into the system of exact, step-by-step determinism. Lucretius's version of this is the "fati foedera" (1963, 2.254), the law of fate.

If it is true, as is sometimes claimed, that Lucretius works retrogressively from evident free will in living creatures to the philosophic necessity of instituting the *clinamen*, the results are not particularly satisfactory from a human perspective. The swerve may resemble the Sophist Subject in its capacity for origination; this is certainly evident in Cicero's attempt to set the Epicureans straight by insisting that the swerve be translated into a human act (1975, *De fato*, 18–23). But ultimately in Lucretius free will is merely a species of chance: within the limits determined by the potential of the *primordia* for combination, free will amounts to contingency—the impossibility of explicit determination or of predicting which of the multiple potentials at any one stage will be actualized.

This last statement is complicated by the assumption of an external or scientific observer—a subject—the significance of which ancient materialists generally attempt to ignore. It could be argued then that the system these materialists develop fails to take account of or include the theorist, and so are incomplete (Gödel). Ancient materialism nonetheless tends to exclude human agency as origination, or they include it as a part of the overall material process. Lucretius does on occasion use human agency as intervention in natural processes in the later books of the *De rerum natura*, but it is the general nonsubjectivity and the contingency of the method here that draws Foucault in this direction. Explicit influence of the materialists on Foucault is a matter of debate, but multiple potentiality is central to Foucault's epistemic and genealogical arguments in *The History of Sexuality*, volume 1.

The materialist presumed to have resolved the *aporia* of origins: at the primary, unseen level there exist minimum material beings. Yet the atom as a separate entity is not pure materiality—the supposed origin—but formed or configured matter, even if the material is thought to determine the form it takes. The primary level of pure materiality does not exist. It has already, like the Sophist Subject which has already disappeared into the culture which it originates, been assimilated into material forms, or into the system which it now claims to have originated.

The atomists were particular about claiming that the atom was the minimum material being, but the law of mathematical divisibility enters here. Materiality necessarily implies extension and a companion set of divisibilities (for example, any determinate weight can be halved, progressively). Infinite divisibility of material is implied, and the possibility of minimum beings negated.

The other origin, of process, that is, of motion and interaction, holds no interest for most materialists except Lucretius, and even he begins with the *primordia* in downward motion. In general, any "original" stage of the process results from a yet more prior stage for the materialists. Given the added complexity of the notion of appearances/presentations (*Vorstellungen*), we can say that Kant uses precisely these terms to describe "*The Universal Law of Natural Necessity*" (1949, A538/B566ff.). There is no possibility in this *enchainment* of an originating act or event (A543/B571), according to Kant, who seeks to contrast this originless process with the transcendental idea of freedom or human agency as an origin—that is, prior to or external to the *enchainment*. Ultimately the materialists are unable to resolve the crisis of the origin as the minimum or as the beginning of process. The materialist Foucault has precisely the same issues of method to resolve, but he never addresses them at the theoretical level. That is entirely characteristic of Foucault, but the problematics arising in his text as a result of the general materialist method are interesting because they help define the limits of Foucault's text as historical explanation.

Materialism suggests another way to situate the confrontation about a prior sexual nature between Butler and Foucault taken up in chapter 3: the difference of the two positions can be seen as a space of negotiation. Butler's claim that nothing exists prior to discourse means that the possibilities for constructions of prior natures by discourse are unlimited, if apparently contingent. If Foucault's material substratum is determinate, it is (a) nature; and that nature would determine the identity of the emergent discourse or culture. This is the very notion that Butler's Foucauldian-discursive argument attempts to deny. If, however, Foucault's substratum lacks identity—if, for example, the material is infinitely malleable or divisible—then the position of the materialist Foucault *comes to* the same thing as Butler's position. Non-existence and infinite malleability are asymptotically equivalent. Butler's and Foucault's positions are then equivalent but not identical. But Foucault's prior material substratum is in fact not infinitely malleable and therefore does impose some limits on what can be constructed from it; the limitation operates along the lines set out by the ancient materialists.

The explicit context for scrutinizing the role of the material substratum in Foucault's argument includes the following: 1) the deployment of sexuality, a historical discourse (using the term generically) or overall strategy; this deployment constructs the fictitious unity or "imaginary element" sex, and "the desire for sex," as "one of its most essential operating principles" (1980a, 156); 2) this constructed "notion of sex brought about a fundamental reversal" or inversion, so that sex came to be understood as nature, that is, "as being rooted in a specific and irreducible urgency which power tries as best it can to dominate" (155); 3) the substratum appears when Foucault says that the "fictitious unity" of sex is an artificial configuration based on "anatomical elements, biological functions, conducts, sensations, and pleasures" (154, 155; see also, 67, 152, and passim). Foucault means not the body as a concept but actual material bodies and their material aspects and functions. "Material" in Foucault is limited to the human body, not extended to all the world.

There are then three levels in Foucault's argument: discourse or, in the above quotations, the specific, historical deployment of sexuality; the constructed sex as the prior nature, which alibis the deployment; and the actual material substratum from which, necessarily, sex is constructed. This is the crux of the matter for Butler: the substratum imposes a limit on consequent constructions of identities, and from her perspective this limit might be used to dehistoricize masculinist culture, making it inevitable. This is somewhat ironic: Butler's attempt to combat gender essentialism results in a forgetting of history; Foucault, who claims a prior material substratum, uses this notion to support his historicism. The overall argument turns on the issues of origin and of limit, and ultimately on the substratum as either an identity or not.

Foucault addresses directly the question of the prior or the natural at the end of *The History of Sexuality,* volume 1. This is framed as a response to an imagined opponent who argues for "the biologically established existence of sexual functions" (150–51) as foundational or as nature. Foucault's response has two phases, the first of which addresses the question of whether the analysis of sexuality elides the materiality of bodies, that is, whether the construction of sex has anything to do with the material body or derives from it. The description here of the material substratum is close to the previously cited ones: "bodies, functions, physiological processes, sensations and pleasures" (152); and Foucault conceives of his analysis as opening access to "a 'history of bodies' and the manner in which what is most material and most vital in them has been invested" or constructed as an identity.

This would also be a history in which the biological is not prior to the historical (as nature to discourse); in this Foucault is making clear that the biological, "the modern technologies of power that take life as their objective" is the nature constructed by discourse or, specifically, by the deployment of sexuality, as its origin. Foucault thus brackets sex and the biological between a prior material manifold and the specific historical deployment; in the construction of this middle term, sex, "one sees the elaboration of this idea that there exists something other than bodies, organs, somatic localizations, functions, anatomo-physiological systems, sensations, and pleasures" (152–53)—that is, the same list, representing the material substratum or what exists prior to deployment and the construction of sex—an atomic level, so to speak.

This material origin surfaces once more in Foucault when there is a question of resistance to the deployment of sexuality:

> It is the agency of sex that we must break away from, if we aim—through a tactical reversal of the various mechanics of sexuality—to counter the grips of power with the claims of bodies, pleasures, and knowledges, in their multiplicity and their possibility of resistance. The rallying point for the counterattack against the deployment of sexuality ought not to be sex-desire [that is, the constructed "sex"], but bodies and pleasures. (157)

The first thing to note, although it is incidental to the question of the substratum, is the necessity of self-relation to resistance: the knowledge that one is constituted as a subject or identity within the deployment, along with the perspective external to that discourse that this knowledge requires; this in turn allows for some sort of return to the prior material substratum as a means of resistance. The issue of this simultaneously inside/outside subject, which is also prominent in Butler, as noted in chapter 3, and the overall problematics of self-relation are reserved for chapter 5 and subsequent chapters.

Even here there is no return to the prior or to nature. The material substratum is always already deployed. To return to "bodies and pleasures" is to scramble the current deployment—that is, the explicit current configuration of the material substratum—in order to produce a new deployment that is resistant to the current one (see, e.g., 1987, 15, and Bernauer 1992, 271). In Foucault's terms, it is to penetrate the deployment or overall strategy in order to reverse, tactically, the discursive elements that constitute it. In his discussion of power in *The History of Sexuality*, volume 1, Foucault argues that discourses as tactical elements are polyvalent, and hence reversible (1980a, 100–101). Butler's claim is in effect that this is a return to a nature that is already deployed, or not a nature at all. Foucault agrees that the substratum is not a nature, although it is prior and is the material fund from which identities such as sex are constructed. The substratum is pre-identity.

The distinction between the prior as either substratum or nature is based on this notion of identity. Sex is an identity, or a set of them, and "bodies and their materiality" are not. One of the most notable aspects of *The History of Sexuality*, volume 1, is the construction of identities, normal as well as perverse and pathological. The onanistic child is one such identity, constructed by "using these tenuous pleasures as a prop" (42; see also 27ff.). The "pleasures" are not otherwise characterized beyond the subsequent label "onanism," but they are nonetheless clearly recognizable and specifically related to material bodies. The sexual molester of children is similarly invented (31–32) as well as the homosexual (43) and other perverse identities, all of which are the result of a focus on some tenuous pleasures, activities, experiences, and so on that are in turn transformed into identities that are then "implanted in bodies" (44). Each of the four "great strategies" of the deployment of sexuality constitutes a sexual identity, although Foucault is often less than clear in this respect (e.g., 152–54); under each of the four strategies sexual identities can be multiplied.

"Bodies and their materiality" do not constitute an identity in the above sense. The phrase rather points to a fund of material which has the potential for being constructed in a variety of ways, as identities, such as the entity "sex" or, in an earlier age, "blood." This notion is a discursive version of the Lucretian claim that a given fund of *primordia* has a multiple potential for actualization. This material manifold is, in a sense, an accumulative totality or an excess, since the identities constructed from that substratum all represent a selection and a set of emphases. This is in effect a "choice" from a range of possibilities without there being a subject that can be construed as initiating that choice. There is no nature which precedes and determines discourse: this formulation always assumes that nature is an identity and is therefore capable of determining or controlling the consequent process of construction. But Foucault's substratum is a simple materiality awaiting a form. On the other hand, the material substratum always constitutes a relative limit on the stages of development, without completely determining those stages, although Foucault makes little of this. To make such a claim, however, is to recall the founding paradox of materialism: the notion of a pure materiality as an impossible but necessary conception. The atom or *primordium* is already an identity. From a discursive perspective, Butler makes the similar claim that Foucault's lists of bodies and pleasures do not describe a material substratum but already sexualized parts (101). They are already identities.

This is sufficient as a first step, that is, to show that Foucault utilizes some of the arguments, as well as the potential *aporias* of the ancient materialists: there exists a prior material substratum, a disparate collection of "parts" and experiences rather than discrete minimum particles, and this serves as the potential for construction by various and successive deployments. But the substratum can always be recuperated as an identity. At this point genealogy and historical contingency enter in. The Foucauldian minimum or substratum is usually denoted by a long list of anatomical parts, physiological and biological functions, activities (connected to the body), and sensible/mental affects or responses to the environment, including other bodies—all governed by the phrase "bodies and their materiality." *The History of Sexuality*, volume 1, seems to be the text in which Foucault's materialist reasoning is most prominent; as mentioned, the notion of self-relation tends to diminish the need for much of the former method of reasoning in the last two volumes on sexuality. These remain for later chapters.

《◎》

The relation between Foucault and the early materialists is by no means a simple one. His explanation of historical shifts and their causes results rather from a complex technique of layering of materialist process conceptions;

its result is a kind of pastiche. Also, as argued above, there is a similarity between a material substratum of bodies and pleasures and one of atoms, but also a great difference between the two notions of the level at which the "minimum" is perceived. Ancient materialism had as its goal a clear, replicable, almost scientific quality of explanation, although what it proposes as explanation is *ipso facto* beyond knowledge. Such self-deconstructing features are now regularly recognized as characteristic of all systems. It is true that an explanation in Foucault often produces a sense that it is not replicable, that it is a fiction or fabrication, as he himself labels his texts. We might question his representations in terms of how they emerge from the material available for explanation; that is, the data has a multiple potential for serving as explanation. But Foucault's complication of materialist method does not cut him off from one of its central benefits: the tendency to disparage or dismiss human subjective agency as the cause of change and history; except for the early materialists, this subjective mode of explanation has until recently been central to western thought. And Foucault follows an even stricter nonsubjective trajectory than Lucretius.

We have bodies and deployments: "deployments of power are directly connected to the body," producing sex as the "most internal element" in the current deployment of sexuality (151–52). Sex is the ground constituted by the deployment so that it serves to justify the latter, of course. Resistance is the countering of the deployment or the configuration of the primary level, "bodies and pleasures" (157), in order to produce a new configuration. But Foucault manipulates this schema of two levels in a complex manner. To realize this, one need only look at his explanation of the origin of the repressive theory by way of illustrating the distribution of the deployment of sexuality along class lines (127ff.).

The complexity is also evident in Foucault's argument that "power comes from below," which utilizes the emergent structure and also complicates and questions it. At the primary level are "the manifold relations of force that take shape and come into play" in production, families, work, and so forth (94). These force relations are the basis of larger structures which "run through the body as a whole" as power: discourse, deployment, and so on. Nondialectical materialists, especially atomists, usually envision a fixed structure and a unilateral emergence from primary to secondary level. Foucault first of all specifically denies the dialectical "binary and all-encompassing opposition between rulers and ruled" that is usually read down through all social relations. Power emerges at the level of the social totality from countless primary force relations, as noted, and, further, there is a reciprocal relation between levels: the force relations emerge in larger "hegemonic effects" and those in turn "bring about redistributions, realignments," and so on in force relations. Foucault's system is extraordinarily mobile. It should be noted that in this instance of power the relation of levels is analogical to that of the materialists, with the origin displaced. In other words, single force relations are not atomic identities, but the displaced relation of levels here is equivalent to the model of the two-level structure.

Foucault's conception of the double-leveled structure is notable for its localizations, its contingency, and its historical dynamics. This is particularly evident in his parallel argument about resistance. Resistances to power are multiple and, in an echo of Lucretius, unpredictable, "distributed in irregular fashion: the points, knots, or focuses of resistance are spread over time and space at varying densities" (96; see also, 92–93), only occasionally linking up or emerging in "radical ruptures" or revolutionary divisions (see, also, 1987, 3). Most important is the contingent movement: "one is dealing with mobile and transitory points of resistance, producing cleavages in a society that shift about, fracturing unities and effecting regroupings, furrowing across individuals themselves." Under Foucault's "Rule of Double Conditioning," local force relations "enter into an over-all strategy," which in turn must be supported by "precise and tenuous relations" at the local level (99).

When Foucault says two distinct levels don't exist, nor homogeneity from bottom to top, we must remember that we are not considering the primary level of material bodies but force relations, which already have an identity in terms of themselves (92). The ratio of primary to secondary persists. But there is never a simple level-to-level unilateral relation in Foucault, or a material that is given form at the secondary level. For him there is no ultimate stability: all emergent processes are multiple, fragmented, reversible. Even the method is unstable, since there exists no absolute level of pure materiality. Of course there is no such level in the ancient atomists either, so the fact that Foucault begins at the less-than-reductive level of force relations seems less than significant. Whether he sees this as a problem to be overcome or welcomes it into his method is not clear.

If we add Foucault's rule of "The Tactical Polyvalence of Discourse" we get the same primary/secondary distinction without the same distribution: multiple discontinuous "discursive elements" which may combine, either negatively or positively, into various larger strategies within a "complex and unstable" process (100–101). Discursive elements are like atoms in that they are the building blocks of strategies; in addition, they have no identity (as strategies or parts of them) until they begin to form part of a tactics that will surface in a strategy. In Foucault in general, then, we can say that what emerges at the secondary or visible level of the strategies is a complex function of the material at the primary level—with this being also reversible. The absolute materiality of the primary level is not at issue here; what matters is its potential to serve as material for what emerges at a higher level. Neither local force relations nor "bodies and pleasures" could pose as pure material; nor could the atom. Foucault tends to operate with a transposable or metaphorical sense of the relation of levels; his conception is removed from, related to, and somewhat more complex than the relation of levels in ancient materialism.

Foucault's is a contingent materialism. This is posed against the sense of absolute determination often suggested by materialists and often used against them. Even Lucretius makes determination a central issue by arguing against it. "Contingent" signifies the fluidity, mobility, and multiple potential at the primary level: among the "elements" the possibility of mutual support, linkages, convergence (94), but also oppositions, disjunctions and reversals, even loss of material from the complex, according to the ancient materialists. Classical materialists allow for both growth and decay, but the processes of most interest to them are those of accumulation and maximization in diachronic process. Foucault's historicism accommodates both equally, and ultimately his sense of the contingent is located precisely at the juncture of levels where exact determination becomes a multi-faceted "cause-effect-cause" relation. Polyvalence of discursive elements—as when part of the medical discourse constructing homosexuality as a perversion is reversed to become the basis for the positive claim for such an identity as natural (101)—is another form of this contingency. This multiplicity and contingency will eventually lead us back to Lucretian materialism.

The synchronic relation of levels already is taking on a diachronic dimension in this discussion. When local force relations emerge as universal strategies for a particular society or in "major dominations," this can be read as: emergence as representation, appearance, abstraction and so on; and as a diachronic development, that is, as the second stage or the effect of material causation at the prior stage. The shift from one stage to another is prominent in *The History of Sexuality*, volume 1, in the epistemic shift from the deployment of alliance to the deployment of sexuality. The general notion of history is, of course, almost identical with the notion of temporal process; in Foucault the epistemic transformation over time is enormously complex and is also contingent. While the earlier Foucault might have allowed a simple discontinuity to separate epistemes, now the shift toward the deployment of sexuality had its beginning in the seventeenth and eighteenth centuries, took on steam in the nineteenth, and may someday be complete (106).

The shift is not merely temporal, but spatio-temporal, given a certain prior mapping of cultural space: witness the peregrinations of confession from the religious domain to the secular. Again, the epistemic shift appears to have been the result of an external causality within the given cultural space: the deployment of alliance "lost some of its importance as economic processes and political structures could no longer rely on it as an adequate instrument or sufficient support" (ibid.). There is in Foucault's text continuous reference to a prior shift as the cause of a current one; "prior" here means "out of play" or not to be explained, for the moment at least, by even more prior causes. The deployment of sexuality is constituted of four "strategic unities" that are not necessarily integrated.

One further complexity: the epistemic shift can be represented as a new strategy superimposed on the prior one (ibid.); far from one deployment "supplant[ing]" the other, "it was around and on the basis of the deployment of alliance that the deployment of sexuality was constructed" (107); "the deployments of alliance and sexuality were involved in a slow process that had them turning about one another until, more than three centuries later, their positions were reversed" (113). A set of metaphors or a method? It is in fact a method that fills in the opening between the two epistemes; if the great epistemic shift is from blood to sex, then the analysis of the transformation of techniques such as confession from its religious context to secular and scientific ones, of the appearance of discourses and strategies focused on sex, and in general of movement of discourses across cultural space over the course of three hundred years—this is the genealogical component.

From the perspective of Foucault's materialist inclinations, the genealogical aspect of his thought is the most interesting because it is closely related to ancient materialist conceptions of process. This argument allows for, at any given stage of process, a certain fund of material already configured. In atomic materialisms the material is always in motion; hence the given configuration is already potentially unstable and there is the further possibility of the addition to or subtraction from the fund of material—from the external environment. Localization and contingency are important here: the configured material at a given stage has the potential, with or without external interference, to develop further, to be transformed into a further stage of the process.

Constant process, growth and decay, are the hallmark of materialist systematics, and hence they may easily be adapted to historicist methods, literally or otherwise. Foucault's more general way of identifying the material substratum, plus the fact that to articulate the material is to configure it, means that the potential at any stage to become a consequent stage or configuration is never measurable. In one way Foucault here comes close to the Hegelian marxist Irigaray, for whom material is always material-for-representation. Atomism historically takes two paths, toward science and toward history. Marx, in the nineteenth century wanted to take both. Foucault, however, is not in the business of prediction, except to say that there will be a future and that it will be different from the present. In addition, for Foucault the material substratum for a history of sexuality is relatively stable; outside interference is always a configuration or form, not merely an addition of matter. Yet this interference takes on enormous importance in Foucault.

The stage-to-stage process is central to *The History of Sexuality,* volume 1: the prior stage, both material and configuration, represents the material or potential to be actualized at the subsequent stage, and is itself the actualization of the potential at a prior stage. Foucault is interested primarily in two deployments in this text, but his investment in materialist process always raises further questions: what precedes the deployment of alliance? what caused the economic and political shifts which could not then depend on the deployment of alliance for support (106)? If we follow Foucault, we must be content to enter history at a given stage, or focus on a specific discourse or technique; but we aren't able to trace these back to their origins (as if there were a point at which process itself began) or even to a prior stage. Without an origin, there is no return to a pure material potential, merely the myth of a presence which cannot be represented—except in a written articulation.

Foucault makes clear the complexities of the relation of the two deployments or stages of the history of ———— ("sexuality" is not the term; the space remains to be filled in, perhaps; to say "a history of bodies" means a history of configurations of the material; we don't have a term that governs blood, sex, and other configurations in terms of some underlying materiality). In effect Foucault's text is only about the transition to the deployment of sexuality from the deployment of alliance. But there are within this scope many specific instances that define Foucault's notion of the stage-to-stage process relation. He refers to his analysis of aspects of the transition as "the genealogy of all these techniques, with their mutations, their shifts, their continuities and ruptures" (119).

Foucault refers here in part to "the opening up of the great medico-psychological domain of the 'perversions,' which was destined to take over from the old moral categories of debauchery and excess"; but he also notes that the "new technology of sex" was superimposed on the prior religio-moral code: escaping the "ecclesiastical institution," becoming secular, but not avoiding the "thematics of sin" (116). The new technology does not displace the old systematics: the licit/illicit schema is still present within the distinction between the normal and the aberrant. Confession is an even more obvious example. It functioned during the earlier deployment as a religious and civil technique for the production of truth; in the deployment of sexuality its instrumentality shifted: it took on a new form and produced a new kind of truth (58ff., esp. 65–67). Confession did not disappear, but a new form was imposed on the old function. Again, the family, an entity which functioned in an important way in the deployment of alliance—as a constituent of alliance itself—did not dissolve; new forms were imposed in it.

Foucault approaches the specifics of the transitional process between the two deployments in a number of ways and with various methodological implications. In one instance he gives his characteristic description of the prior regime in which power takes the form of law under the representation of "the juridical monarchy" (89). He argues further that this representation persists, leading to a contradiction (rather in marxist fashion here):

> For while many of its forms have persisted to the present, it has gradually been penetrated by quite new mechanisms of power that are probably irreducible to the representation of law. . . . [The old representation of power] is utterly incongruous with the new methods of power whose operation is not insured by right but by technique, not by law but by normalization, not by punishment but by control. (89)

During the shift from the deployment of alliance to the deployment of sexuality, which Foucault here subordinates to an overall shift between the two stages of the operation of power, the juridical becomes "increasingly incapable of coding power, of serving as its system of representation." We have, as Foucault says, "not [yet] cut off the head of the king."

Here, at his most marxist moment, Foucault utilizes the level-to-level relation within a stage-to-stage process relation. There is, in other words, a historical monarchial period in which the representation of power as law and right emerged from the primary articulation of power (87–88). The material operation of power emerged in the at least minimally accurate representation of the legal monarch; even criticisms of the monarchy, rationalist or marxist, adopted the same kind of representation. But a gradual shift in the actual operation of power since the eighteenth century, as noted by the above quotation, has failed to produce a new representation, or secondary level. Hence the increasing contradiction between the primary and secondary levels in the state-to-stage shift in the strategy of power. Foucault's new representation of the technology of power and sex is meant to resolve the contradiction, or to bring the secondary level in line with the primary one.

It is important to note that Foucault's notion of the forms or mechanisms of power already entails a double level of material/configuration—as in the power operating on and forming "men as living bodies," or bio-power. But, once combined, this can be read as how power actually operates in a historical period or as the real in contrast to its representation at the discursive or textual level. In other words Foucault's analysis involves a double level-to-level reading that is typical of the complex overlay that results from his utilization of materialist methods. It should also be noted that the shift from the first stage to the following stage of the actual operation of power is ultimately unexplained. A literal materialist would argue that a shift in the material (already in motion) which serves as a potential, along with outside interference, causes the further stage to develop.

In Foucault's derived materialism this is a crucial point: the question of how the lines are drawn between inside and outside of process so that a clear representation of the shift in the strategies of power is possible becomes critical. There is a tendency to leave outside of the process what is shifting and to treat it as a cause of the new form of power. This is the case when, as mentioned earlier, Foucault says alliance was weakened as a deployment by economic and political changes. This isolation of an entrained process, typical of the atomists, becomes an arbitrary strategy, unless it is argued that the process is the totality; this is impossible from the perspective of analysis. The ancient materialists have fundamental but unmentioned difficulties isolating an entrained process within the totalized reality of atoms and the void. Lucretius cannot make an argument for free will unless he can guarantee (or assume) that each successive stage is part of the same process. In other words the notion of process in materialism keeps running up against its limit in the arbitrary opposition of included/excluded, that is, in the arbitrary method by which a process is constructed as a discrete process. And this is also something to keep an eye on in Foucault.

Foucault makes his analysis of the shift from blood to sex even more complex in other parts of the text. For example, "the passage from one [deployment] to the other did not come about (any more than did these powers themselves) without overlappings, interactions, and echoes," and he mentions two important "interferences" (149). There was late-nineteenth-

and twentieth-century eugenic racism, which often utilized the myth of the purity of the blood. And psychoanalysis sought "to ground sexuality in the law—the law of alliance, tabooed consanguinity, and the Sovereign-Father" (150). The question of whether the blood or law is a rhetorical alibi or "fake" representation for new forms of power is not at issue in Foucault, since it would entail an external agency manipulating the system to its advantage. He simply refers to each as a "retro-version" that may be seen as similar to the persisting representation of power as law long after it is accurate to do so. Elsewhere Foucault says that psychoanalysis, although it was focused on the sexuality of individuals, "rediscovered" alliance: the family, marriage, incest. This has kept the old deployment "coupled" with the new (112–13); the deployment of sexuality based itself on alliance and reconfigured that, but came in turn "to prop up the old deployment" (ibid.). The analysis in all these instances is a complex procedure involving superimposition of new forms on old ones, displacement, recoding, and revitalization and reinvestment evident in representations. What unites these explanations is the assumption that the prior deployment serves as a material—in that it can be de-configured into its material components—for a new configuration.

There are further complexities of historical process in Foucault. The exclusionary strategy of materialist attempts to construct a notion of a discrete or separable process has been noted. That is an issue in Foucault as well, but his idea of process is often larger and more amorphous because temporal shifts also occur across cultural space (although what defines or limits "cultural space" as a prior existence is never defined by Foucault). In fact, genealogy usually refers the origins of any particular discourse to temporally prior discourses that often arise at the margins of the cultural space and gradually become more centralized. For example, the disciplinary society begins at the margins or in limited spaces—in monasticism, confession, and spiritual discipline; in the army: the manual of arms, marching techniques and so on; in workshops: the rationalization of production (1979a, 135–37). Or the shift is from one institution to a set of other institutions.

In *The History of Sexuality*, volume 1, Foucault says briefly that "the deployment of sexuality which first developed on the fringes of familial institutions (in the direction of conscience and pedagogy, for example) gradually became focused on the family" (110). The same is true of the particular science of psychoanalysis, as noted earlier. There is also the complex itinerary of confession, which spread from the medieval monastery as a "technology of the 'flesh'" (113) to the religious populace in general in the seventeenth century as it became intensified as a practice (20, 116).

By the eighteenth century it was adapted into secular cultural space (23ff., 58ff.). Such a claim raises problematic issues about the more general shift from a religious to a secular culture that is prior or simultaneous to the travels of confession. There is always the question of how the limits of a process isolated for analysis are conceived, both by the materialists and by Foucault. If establishing limits involves an unacknowledged agency, so much the worse for Foucault, or at least until he comes to the history of self-relation. In any case, processes are necessarily constructions—limitations of a larger totality.

Confession, Foucault says, "[f]or a long time . . . remained firmly entrenched in the practice of penance"; but, given other changes, "it gradu-ally lost its ritualistic and exclusive localization; it spread" (63). Confession's relation to these other changes (Protestantism, the Counter Reformation, the emergence of pedagogy and medicine) raises important questions of method. Although confession is a technique relevant to both deployments, Foucault's isolation, as noted above, of its shift from one area of cultural space to another against the background of the transformation of the space itself—that is a bit problematic. But remember that genealogy is just such an isolation of the itinerary of a technique.

The same confusion occurs in Foucault's illustration of the move-ment of the deployment of sexuality within the cultural space now defined by the distinction between the bourgeoisie and the proletariat (119ff.). He argues that the bourgeois class first applied the technologies characteristic of the deployment of sexuality to itself; then, under certain changed cir-cumstances, these technologies spread to the "lower classes," from which the bourgeoisie had then to distinguish itself by adherence to a notion of unmentionable sexuality. But he stages this shift against a space already clearly defined by distinct classes, when in fact these new classes were in the process of being produced. Is this an inadequacy of Foucault's analysis? a complexity? one of the limits that any such method inevitably encounters? all of these?

The spread from margin to center or class to class is closely related to Foucault's notion of the local-(cultural) universal relation, mentioned earlier in terms of the relation of primary/secondary levels. The emergent, hierarchical connection between local force relations and cultural domina-tions forms a template for reading the spread of the deployment of sexuality within cultural space, without, however, the emphasis on reciprocal action in the diachronic that Foucault propounds in the emergent process. One tendency in Foucault's genealogy is the search for the origins or the local relations which eventually take over, contingently of course, the center of the culture. This is a process of what Foucault calls normalization in reference to the deployment of sexuality; the same term would apply to the disciplines which appear in modern society; there would perhaps be a parallel process of legalization which takes place in alliance. The point is that in strategic instances the two conceptions of process, hierarchical and diachronic, tend to merge.

But there remain those instances in which Foucault maintains historical complexity by keeping the two kinds of process conception separate. The already noted problem of the antiquated conception of power as right and law is based on the fact that actual relations of power have gradually become divorced from their representation at the secondary level. That is, a diachronic process involving a succession of stages allows as well for thinking each stage as a relation between a primary and a secondary level. Aside from complicating linear conceptions of process, the primary/secondary level notion sets up Foucault's return to primary materiality. If the stage-stage conception of the process understands the prior stage as the already configured material potential from which the subsequent stage develops, the level/level conception allows Foucault to attempt to return to the "bodies and their materiality" that are absolutely but not actually prior to configuration or form. The return to materiality is the recommended mode of resistance as well as the basis for understanding that both deployments construct this basic materiality as either blood or sex.

That is one "return to origin" that founds Foucault's analysis and at the same time confounds it: there is no apparent lower limit to the division of the material, or it always already has a form. And the problematic consequences of genealogical analysis are equally severe. The shifts that take place over time such as between deployments or from religious confession to its secular manifestation are analyzed and accounted for by reference to a temporally prior stage that entails localized or marginalized practices. Genealogy explains current configurations in terms of prior forms; explanations operate retrogressively, with a particular stage the result of the prior stage (complex, multiple, and so forth); but the prior stage or the stages prior to that are never accounted for. There is only an immediately prior origin. It is striking that genealogical analysis reaches the same impasse as structuralism did. For the latter there always existed structure, and this position allowed structuralists to ignore questions of origin and structure generally. Genealogy counters with its own claim, but merely succeeds in pronouncing its own limit as history.

Consider, for example, the focal points of the history of confession: its emergence during the monastic movement, then its use for "the development of procedures of direction and examination of conscience" (119) in the sixteenth century and its extension to all Christians. What are the context and genealogy of these two moments in the history of a technique prior to its transformation to an instrument of the deployment of sexuality? More important is the question of how one can isolate a "linear" process—that is, confession—from the context or background against which the process can be made to appear. Abstraction, and the consequent notion of a separable and identifiable stage-by-stage process, depend on the construction of an analytical framework. That of course *is* genealogy.

The reference to "bodies and their materiality" makes it clear that Foucault envisions a material substratum. The substratum is malleable, that is, able to take different forms according to the dictates of different deployments. But if Foucault follows materialist reasoning, the material also poses limits on its construction (the paradox remains that if the material has absolutely no form, then it is infinitely malleable; but certainly the ancient materialists had no such idea in mind). In general the same material substratum is prior to both deployments as their material or their primary level. In the stage-stage conception of process the latter deployment would have as its material something already configured by the prior deployment, which it would in general have to deconfigure and reconfigure. The deployment of alliance governs blood as passion/desire for joining of bodies within the genital, heterosexual marital relation, blood as a structure of inheritance, and so forth, within family relations, constructing and limiting bodies and pleasures by an elaborate system based on the opposition between the licit and the illicit, and between rights and obligations. The *telos* is continuity or persistence. In alliance the body was the locus of rights and privileges in terms of the distribution of class and other relations, and also a locus of punishment.

Later the body became "life," and in consequence "sex," the locus of technologies and a subject (in both senses) of knowledge of its desires and instincts that in turn determined its identity. Within the deployment of sexuality bodies and pleasures tend to be divided along the axis of the normal and the perverse on the basis of the produced knowledge of identities; and the notion of blood as familial is replaced by an individualized sex. My point is not to describe the configuration of each deployment here—Foucault does pretty well at that—but to reiterate that the material substratum of bodies and their various functions underlies both deployments. It does so as a potential, not as an identity.

The change in the scope of confession as it became more universal in the seventeenth century is an example of the shift in the configuration of the substratum. The expansion of the confession of the flesh was a shift from an examination of sexual acts primarily, along the obligatory/permitted/forbidden axis to an attempt at "reconstructing, in and around the act, the thoughts that recapitulated it, the obsessions that accompanied it, the images, desires, modulations and quality of the pleasure that animated it" (63; see also, 19–20). After some time the act fades in significance. Sexuality is now not simply the perhaps illicit coupling or encounter but the interior theater of the consciousness of the individual. Descartes, self-reflexivity, the isolated thinker engaged in self-examination in order to arrive at the ground of truth constitute an epistemic parallel (60). Each constitution of the body and its pleasures, as act or as thought, represents a different configuration of that material. A later chapter will take up the issue of the invention of interiority.

The multiple potentiality of the substratum in Foucault brings us directly back to Lucretius, in whose system the *clinamen* opens up the multiple potentiality implicit in material processes. Lucretius uses multiple potential to guarantee human choice, but for Foucault this notion guarantees contingency in the historical process.

Foucault's analysis of power on the primary and secondary levels is one example of his utilization of the notion of multiple potential as it relates to contingency and the instability of discourse. At the first level there is "the multiplicity of force relations immanent in the sphere in which they operate and which constitute their own organization" (92). Note that the primary level here is not the material substratum but is already configured or has a series of identities. These "manifold relationships" constitute a "moving substrate" of "unbalanced, heterogeneous, unstable and tense force relations" (94, 93). Power is related to these force relations as "the process which, through ceaseless struggles and confrontations, transforms, strengthens, or reverses them" (92). The overall power relation that emerges, whether stable or not, is clearly a matter of contingency, a matter of how the force relations happen to line up or fail to do so: the emergence of a cultural universal or multiple disjunctions, contradictory discourses and resistances. As mentioned earlier, Foucault goes the materialists one better by also setting up the reciprocal action between levels and the constant mobility of general distributions of power (94, 99).

The argument from multiple potential is even more evident in Foucault's discussion of the "tactical polyvalence" of discourses, in which he treats discourses as discontinuous segments "with unstable tactical and strategic functions" (100). He conceives of a discourse as a potential part of a larger discourse or strategy; the multiple potentiality derives from his claim that the discursive element is reversible: his example is the production of homosexuality as a perversion and its later reversal as the means of producing positive homosexual identity. Such a discourse is not part of the material substratum but is already configured. Yet its parallelism to the substratum is evident: multiple potentially suffuses the system from the base to the top because it is assumed to be existent at the substratum level. Foucault usually stages his arguments for instability, contingency, or multiple potentiality at the level of the already configured; but these qualities of the material necessarily "begin" at the level of the substratum, in the construction of identities.

For Lucretius multiple potential frustrates determination if the swerve engages other potentials of the *primordia* than that which makes them move straight downward. After the swerve the potential at a given stage limits what emerges at the subsequent stage: material causation relates potential to actualization. Yet causality is not determination because the potential at the prior stage is greater than what can be actualized at the subsequent one. Choice in Lucretius simply means the incommensurability of potential and actualization at every step of the diachronic process.

In Foucault the contingency of the historical process represents his implementation of the multiple potential of the substratum. He says at one point that he is only interested in "a 'history of bodies' and the manner in which what is most material and most vital in them has been invested" by contingent strategies and deployments. Everything he discusses are actualized potentials of the substratum, whether the sexual instinct constructed as nature during the nineteenth century, the bourgeois body, the onanistic body, the hysterical body, or perverse ones. But all the potential has not been exploited. In this way multiple potential is as surely built into Foucault's system as it is in Lucretius's, in the former case to ensure the notion of instability of process.

There is another peculiarity in the relation between ancient materialism and Foucault. It is the tendency of the former to privilege growth and maximization instead of its equally logical opposite, decay or deconstruction. Foucault tends to utilize this tendency as his central counter to the notion of repression as characterizing the modern age in Europe. "There was rather a perpetual inventiveness, a steady growth of methods and procedures" which characterizes the deployment of sexuality (119). But if the same is not true of the deployment of alliance, whose goal is stability, then perhaps the connection is only incidental.

Foucault's notion of multiple potential also has relevance at the level of his own discourse. His famous insistence that everything he has written is "fiction" of course means that his explanations are constructions; but it could also imply a recognition that the materials or data available as or for explanation or construction have more explanatory potential than could be utilized by any one view. Further, Foucault tends to create layers of multiple explanation within his own discourse within a single text, and certainly from text to text. In *The History of Sexuality* volume 1, the stage-to-stage shift from alliance to sexuality makes explicit reference to an already configured material (alliance) available as a potential for the subsequent deployment. Hence the sense of a twice-configured material or stage built upon stage. On the other hand, there is always the sense in Foucault that resistance, which will inevitably lead to a new configuration, occurs as a return to the material substratum: the new configuration occurs precisely as a reorganization of the substratum, an intervention inserted beneath the current deployment.

((◎))

Identity is the ultimate issue. Foucault's line between nonidentity and identity is a tenuous one, as it is generally in materialist thinking. The ancients called the atom the minimum entity, but that doesn't solve the problem: the minimum entity exists in the impossible moment before the final splitting reduces it to pure materiality, which is unrepresentable. It is ironic, as noted earlier, that materialisms founder on the notion on which they are founded, pure materiality. Materialists have the alternative of *instituting*, as Lucretius does the swerve, the minimum material being, of attempting to point vaguely "down there" beneath appearance to some material substratum that has been configured—what Deleuze calls a thought minimum. Foucault's tenuous line attempts to separate this lower level of underlying material from the level of identities.

Further, the moment this substratum is articulated in Foucault's own discourse, it takes on an identity. The material substratum is represented, meaning that it becomes part of discourse and part of knowledge. Butler doesn't hesitate to press the case: the substratum has existence only as constructed within discourse as its origin, and hence materiality itself becomes just another discursive alibi. In effect the substratum can serve to limit discourse or configuration only if it "exists" prior to configuration and identity; it has being only if it is prior to being. And if it does exist, it is represented; this means it is part of discourse, not prior to it, so it cannot serve as the potential and limit of contingent discursive formations.

Foucault's answer to this would be that the substratum operates in precisely this way, but there exists no moment in which it appears (impossibly) as a prior materiality; it is always already configured or deployed—as blood, for example, prior to its construction as sex.

Self-relation becomes an explicit issue in the Foucault of the last two volumes on sexuality. Here, in the first volume, self-relation is contingent on the materialist analysis. The text is ipso facto self-reflexive: the perspective allows for the comprehension, from outside the discourse, of the deployment within which the observing subject is constituted. This is the general paradox generated when poststructuralism departs from modernism and the Enlightenment. The self-reflexivity is also apparent in his call for a return to "bodies and their pleasures" as the mode of resistance. The return is not to nature or the substratum literally but a scrambling of the "fictitious entity" of sex so that a different configuration may emerge; and, having finished reading Foucault's analysis, the subject is in a "position" to be able to do this. Foucault, the advocate for the notion of contingent historical process, despite the virtual presence of agential subjects in the treatment of resistance, could not predict the succeeding deployment: but that gender differentiation would dissolve and the heterosexual norm would disappear is clearly within the potential of the substratum.

Yet the question of self-reflexivity persists: is the existence of the self-reflexive capacity ontological or historical? Foucault argues the latter, if we remember from genealogy that a historical era such as the Enlightenment generates ontological arguments about human nature. This is an issue for a later chapter. Butler argues that performance produces self-reflexivity, but her argument presupposes self-reflexivity. The ultimate question remains: is this a historical or ontological potential, or, on what level and what stage does the potential exist?

Foucault's text also points to the complexities of historiographical representation. The epistemic-genealogical analysis underwritten by materialist assumptions about emergent and diachronic process is one thing, but the actual texture of the representation is overdetermined, replete with "overlappings, intersections, echoes, interferences." The continuous layering, though limited by method, results in a complex and seemingly irreplicable fabrication of representation. It is, however, a collage that is quite unlike Butler's pastiche of methods.

What are the limits of Foucault's version of historiographical representation? Not surprisingly, there are several. The first has to do with the notion of historical process itself. Foucault produces an epistemic analysis of successive deployments, but he views discourses and subprocesses as so mobile, so unstable and reversible, that his method is a continual exchange between the epistemic and genealogical attempt to represent a multiplicity of changes, shifts, and emergences within processes. The limit of genealogical analysis appears at the moment it begins to operate. When, for example, he writes of the shift in the technique of confession from the spiritual to the secular, he argues that the shift was "supported and relayed by other mechanisms"; "for reasons that will have to be examined" confession came to be a technique for the compilation of data on sex (23). And, as noted before, alliance is said to have been weakened by what occurred external to it.

In other words, genealogical analysis must begin at a specific historical point that is not the origin of the assumed ongoing process. Analysis of confession as a technique of the *scientia sexualis* may begin with pastoral confession, but what produced pastoral confession and its later universalization is unsaid—at least, not beyond a reference to the medieval monastery. Genealogical analysis does not and cannot get to the origin of process. Like Saussure, who argued that langue is always an inheritance from a prior generation, Foucault in effect maintains that there always exist prior stages of process unavailable to genealogical analysis; the analysis is always and necessarily incomplete.

Beyond origins there is the question about the identity of any process. Is it to be assumed that one can enter or envision a process that has *not* been produced or constituted by a prior analysis? In *Discipline and Punish* Foucault sees the manual of arms as an important technique: it was developed to discipline a new kind of army made up of conscripts. From the distinct and separate social space of the military the technique was adapted to apply to other populations, of the factory, the school, the prison, and so on. But to situate this genealogy one needs to know the prior of the prior. What caused the changes in armies in the seventeenth century? What sort of structure of analysis is already in place which identifies the military against a background of distinct and separated social spaces? Foucault's analysis of the bourgeois and repression has already been mentioned in this regard. No matter how retrogressive genealogical analysis becomes, there is always a point at which it must assume an already structured space. That langue is an inheritance is not a limit to the synchronic part of Saussure's analysis; but in historical representation it is. It is a large assumption that history is, or that there exists, a continuous if contingent set of processes.

There is another limit to historiographical representation. In *The History of Sexuality*, volume 1, and in general in writings of this period, Foucault says that power emerges from below: power is a configuration of the most basic level, "relationships of force"; they are manifold and they occur in all the various social spaces; they merge, contingently, to form unstable larger strategies. The notion of "the local" is almost as popular a Foucauldian cliché as the invention of the homosexual; but it is not representable for genealogical analysis except schematically and as a theoretical "position." "History," even in Foucault, simply does not descend to that level of representation. The closest one comes to it is the anecdote, such as the one concerning Charles-Jean Jouy of Lapcourt in Lorraine in 1867—Foucault's illustrative example of the invention of the sexual molester of children (31–32). The anecdotal technique has been adopted by major scholars such as Stephen Greenblatt, but it falls short of an accurate or total representation of the local.

Finally, Foucault has little to say about gender, and that may be seen as an instance of the limitedness of his analysis. But historically gender was not the important issue in 1976 that it is now. Both alliance and sexuality construct gender, gender differentiation, and gender hierarchy. If, as Butler implies, there is only one discourse, that of masculinist domination, then gender would not surface in Foucault's epistemic analysis. Yet gender is different in the different deployments. Gender is identity in the deployment of sexuality and, at least until the era of poststructuralism, an identity that emerges from one's interior. Identity in the prior deployment, however, tends to be external and relational. Hence clothes are much more likely to be thought of as conferring identity, as the Renaissance antitheatricalists insist: they claim that young males who play the parts of women on stage become effeminate through cross-dressing. Gender is not nearly so essential to identity except in relations: whether Viola in *Twelfth Night* is male or female is simply a practical matter of who winds up with whom in the final scene—provided they are in legally viable relationships. New Historicists often fail to note the differences between epistemes. Gender is beneath the generality of Foucault's specification of deployments; but his analysis can be suggestive about it.

One final note: when Foucault comes to the last two volumes on sexuality and self-relation he "forgets" his materialist leanings—except that "self-relation" names the genealogical task of opening up western thought in order to tease out a thread of the current fabric of our being. And that fabric is always understood as a configuration of "bodies and pleasures."

❦ 5 ❧

Foucault, Historical Self-Relation, and the Ancients

We come in this chapter to the later Foucault of *The Use of Pleasure* and *The Care of the Self*, the last two volumes of his history of sexuality. More specifically, the concern here is with his "historical ontology" of human self-relation developed in the two texts. This, in turn, is preliminary to an inquiry into self-relation in the Renaissance and seventeenth century and after: the shift between the two centuries that makes Descartes a central figure, and the overall self-reflexive regime that typifies the era of the Enlightenment and the modern considered in its historical particularity. This is taken up in chapters 6 and 7.

Specifically, this chapter focuses on the shift in Foucault's thinking that resulted in the final two volumes on sexuality. I discuss at length his explicit reintroduction of the subject, now as the historically constituted modern self-reflexive subject of knowledge. This subject becomes the "foundation" of Foucault's new genealogy of self-relation in these last two works. After that I turn to *The Use of Pleasure* and then *The Care of the Self*, his analyses first of self-relation in fourth century B.C.E. Greece and then of the Hellenistic and Roman period through two centuries of the common era. Within the context of these analyses, I structure my own analysis as a focus on the absences in Foucault's text. The first is a documentable epistemic shift from exteriority to interiority as a locus of inquiry, and this is locatable in the early Hellenistic period and later in post-Augustan Rome. Set against this is Foucault's leveling normalization of the period from the death of Alexander to Marcus Aurelius and Epictetus in *The Care of the Self*. He incorrectly characterizes fully five hundred years by the phrase of this title;

instead he should have argued that this form of self-relation applies only to writers of the post-Augustan period.

My analysis thus supplies a critical and revisionary reading of these two volumes on sexuality, but particularly of *The Care of the Self.* The section on Epicurus and the early Hellenistic period along with the section on Seneca argue for the importance of understanding the periodic epistemic shifts toward analysis focused on interiority and how that focus heavily influences the subsequent form of self-relation. These forms are, however, different in Epictetus and Seneca. Ultimately, then, my task is to show how Foucault's thinking changes, how that change is manifest in his subsequent work, how his analyses of antiquity can be articulated toward a more precise understanding, and how, finally, these various issues of self-relation are taken up later in western thought.

A more explicit part of the task entails the reconciliation of the oppositions Foucault exploits in *The History of Sexuality*, volume 1, with those of the latter two volumes in terms of the return of the regime of self-reference from the seventeenth century onward: the relation of confession as a technique for the production of interiority and a specific form of self-knowledge as articulated in the former text in connection with Foucault's "prediction" in the last two texts that the arts of the self would be transformed into the "decipherment" of the secrets of desire of the soul as the hallmark of European Christianity (1986, 142–43, 239); and the development of the human sciences and institutional knowledge in the centuries following the seventeenth—what he has called "the invention of man" (1970, 5)—entailing in part the secularization of the technique of Christian confession (1980a, 18–20, 58–67, 116).

Prior to the last two volumes of the history of sexuality, individuals were to be thought of as subjected to the deployment of alliance in the classical era; then, from the eighteenth century onward, they became subjects of sexuality; they were continually individualized according to their interior or "natural" (that is, naturalized) sexual character, inclination, and "being."

The shift in Foucault's thinking announced in *The Use of Pleasure* is well known. James Bernauer, among many others, has articulated the shifts in Foucault's writings in a useful way, particularly the final shift noted here (1987, 48ff.; see also Racevskis 1987, 23ff., and Gillan 1987, 36ff.). Against the background of his prior mode of analysis, Foucault says, he now intends to look at how historical discourses allow for the notion of an individual that is prior to cultural discourse or occupies a position from which to choose its mode of relation to that discourse. This notion bears some resemblance to the Sophist conception of the prior Subject, or what is often called the "sovereign subject"; but there is no sense in which this can be read as Foucault's admitting to the existence of a sovereign subject, as some scholars think (1988, 252, 253). Rather, as Foucault says about the shift in his thinking during a late interview,

> I would say that if now I am interested, in fact, in the way in which the subject constitutes himself in an active fashion, by the practices of self, these practices are nevertheless not something that the individual invents by himself. They are patterns that he finds in his culture and which are proposed, suggested and imposed on him by his culture, his society and his social group. (1987, 11; see also Foucault and Sennett 1982, 10; Flynn 1987, 115; Rochlitz 1992, 248–58, who is critical of Foucault's shift in the final two volumes on sexuality; and Bernauer 1992, 261ff.)

Foucault is simply isolating the theme of ethics or the technologies of the self—that is, he argues that the arts of the self constitute a panhistorical theme in western thought: "subjectivization [as] the procedure by which one obtains the constitution of . . . a subjectivity which is of course only one of the given possibilities of organization of a self-consciousness" (1988, 253). In general, however, he is interested "to know how the reflexivity of the subject and the discourse of truth are linked" in different eras (38). He is particularly interested in the fourth century B.C.E. in Greece, as well as with the first two centuries of the common era, and, by way of generally undetailed allusions in the two volumes covering the two periods mentioned, the Christian era in Europe that was to follow the Greco-Roman period. A further volume dealing with Christianity was promised in 1984, *The Confessions of the Flesh* (*Les Aveux de la chair*) (1986, 12 and elsewhere). It might have cleared up many of the problems resulting from the historical lacuna between the end of the period of *The Care of the Self* and that of *The History of Sexuality*, volume 1. At issue is how self-inquiry produced a new relation to truth: "I am working on the history, at a given moment, of the way reflexivity of self upon self is established, and the discourse of truth that is linked to it." Not the least problem is how self-reflexivity reemerges in the seventeenth century, and in what form, after fourteen hundred years.

Foucault is thus interested in how historical (that is, cultural) discourses propose the individual as prior to culture and how these discourses understand the intricacies of the process by which this individual is subjected to or subjects itself to culture. This is a genealogical inquiry still, but one which exhibits less interest in the contingent discourses which impinge on and cause shifts in another cultural discourse; the emphasis is on the shifting historical ontologies of human nature (1988, 253). In positioning himself in relation to twentieth-century thought, Foucault says: "I have tried to get away from the philosophy of the subject, through a genealogy of the modern subject as a historical and cultural reality" (Foucault and Sennett 1982, 9). These ontologies are, however, no less real. If, for example, the Enlightenment constitutes human nature as self-reflexive—that is, able to position itself outside itself as objectified (a cultural object) and as a subject of knowledge—then that is human ontology within that era (see, e.g., Frank 1995, 197ff. and esp. 181, where he describes consciousness as "something whose being consists in being-familiar-with-itself"). This point is central to Foucault's thinking.

Foucault utilizes this Enlightenment truth of the subject to warrant the function of genealogy, which is ipso facto self-reflexive, an examination of how we are constituted today (including the perspective which is entailed by that sort of objectification) and the genealogy or history of that constitution. Self-reflexivity is problematically implied but not argued in *The History of Sexuality*, volume 1. From the perspective of the later texts self-reflexivity is a given; that is, it is part of the *historical* constitution of human "nature" in the modern period. Selecting or isolating a process—a problematic issue in chapter 4, from the perspective of materialist analysis—is now the form of the self-aware subject's intention to understand the historical processes by which it was constituted as self-reflexive. Now the seemingly arbitrary isolation of process becomes essential to self-knowledge, which is, incidentally, the key aspect of the historical ontology of the modern subject.

In the first volume on sexuality, the genealogy of the subject of sexuality leads to the possibility of resistance to cultural discourse from within discourse, in "bodies and pleasures." In *The Use of Pleasure*, "[t]he object was to learn to what extent the effort to think one's own history can free thought from what it silently thinks, and so enable it to think differently" (1985b, 9). This thinking differently is the contemporary function of philosophy (1988, 330); John Rachman says that "in the history of philosophy, Foucault does not attach himself to a tradition . . . but seeks out events—the sort of event from which there is no return, and which transforms us forever. It is this conception of relationship to self as *ethos*, or as philosophical mode of being, which is the main concern of Foucault's attempt to rethink traditions which we call ethical" (217); and this thought is self-reflexive. In each case Foucault accepts the Enlightenment ontology of "man," as the capacity for objective self-examination; but he attempts to push that to the limit of understanding the genealogy of that ontology, as opposed to recourse to any notion of transcendence. There is in fact no alternative to this if he remains a historian searching for the historicality of truth.

⟨⟨◉◉⟩⟩

At one level the possibility of thinking differently is the basis for the latter two volumes on sexuality, which focus on subjectivation; but the possibility of thinking and acting differently arises as the end, after we have understood how we have been formed as cultural subjects. In Foucault's earlier texts, as I have noted, discourse (discursive practices, disciplines, deployments, and so forth) is prior to the individual and subjectivation is necessary and, so to speak, automatic—at least until the advent of genealogy and its hoped-for effects which, as with Butler, depend on a recourse to a self-reflexivity which is silently imported and is contradictory to the notion of a subject of discourse. Foucault's shift to a concern with the subject leads to a genealogy of the "forms and modalities of the relation to self by which the individual constitutes and recognizes himself qua subject" (1985b, 6)—that is, the way in which historical discourses conceive of the individual as prior and how that individual chooses to or must fashion itself as a cultural subject (cf. Rochlitz 1992, 255).

In terms of method, Foucault utilizes the opposition between individual and cultural discourse as this opposition is articulated with a series of specific historical discourses (see, e.g., 1987, 2). Further oppositions are recursive and hence reinforcing: the opposition of an aesthetics or art of existence ("ethics") to an explicit code of licit/illicit behaviors allows Foucault to pose the freedom of the upper-class male of the fourth century B.C.E. in Greece to fashion or produce himself as a subject against the authority of a later Christian code that would demand self-formation by way of complete submission (see, e.g., 1986, 165, 180–81; 1988, 49, 69–70).

Further, Foucault notes in general that codes prior to later Christianity were relatively stable, and this enables him to expand the other side of the opposition into a "complex field of historicity in the way the individual is summoned to recognize himself as an ethical subject of sexual conduct"—from classical Greece to the "Christian doctrine . . . [of] the flesh" (1985b, 32). The fundamental opposition remains within this theme of self-subjectivation. There is no code, Foucault suggests, so explicit that it excludes choice: "there will be many ways, even within such a rigid frame [of requiring conjugal fidelity] to practice that austerity, many ways to be faithful" (1985b, 26). And once subjectivation becomes the theme, it can be subdivided: ethical substance (or that "part" or aspect of the individual and its behavior which will be the concern of a sexual morality); mode of subjection ("how the individual establishes its relation to the rule"); ethical work or ascesis (the individual's training or practice, taken on to form itself as an ethical subject); and *telos* (the end at which the individual aims) (1985b, 26–28).

A terminological note: "individual" is used in translations of Foucault to denote a state prior to discursive subjectivity, but in the texts written before the shift to a concern with the process of self-subjectivation the term is not very significant; afterwards the term becomes more central. In the chapters prior to this one I have used the opposition Subject/subject, or the Subject prior to discourse versus the discursive subject. Foucault as a genealogist is less concerned with the notion of a sovereign origin as it pervades western discourse, whereas my distinction goes back to the Sophists and echoes the ancient distinction between *subjectum* (foundation) and *subjectus* (brought under the control of), the Subject which institutes discourse and the subject formed within it, the Sophist master and his acolyte.

In *The Use of Pleasure* the individual is never conceived as temporally prior to culture, nor is it the inventor of culture. But understood as existing within but also in relation to a particular historical discourse—that is close to what "individual" means for Foucault. Sometimes this is misconstrued as Foucault's return to a notion of a founding subject (e.g., McNay 1992, 157). Foucault, at the inception of his last two texts, is able to think the reorientation of his own work and to choose the thematic of self-subjectivation as the possibility of thinking differently from a self-reflexive perspective. This gives him the opportunity to look at his prior work differently, "to see what I had done from a new vantage point. . . . Sure of having traveled far, one finds that one is looking down on oneself from above" (1985b, 7).

Again, this is the Enlightenment ontology of the self-reflexive subject of knowledge. Specifically for Foucault, the perspective on himself allows him to ask: "what are the games of truth by which man proposes to think his own nature when he perceives himself to be mad; when he considers himself to be ill; when he conceives of himself as a living, speaking, laboring being . . . as a criminal. . . . as desiring individual?" (ibid.).

This kind of external or abstracted positionality is a signal that Foucault is still within modernity, and this is essentially correct. Consider Foucault's theme, or, more specifically, how that theme is constructed. The notion of historical variation within the thematic of self-reference or self-relation raises complex issues of assemblage, coherence, and, most of all, selection. It is also a question of abstraction, an argument that certain facts, events, and statements are instances of the "same."

In the chapter on Foucault's materialism, there are similar issues of determining which entities are part of a process, that is, subject to a genealogy, and which are context; further, what crosses the horizon separating process from nonprocess, or what impinges contingently on the core process from outside it to cause permutations? The Enlightenment and modernity are founded in part on this capacity to see local or experiential differences as essentially identical: philosophers like Cassirer make central to the intellectual project this capacity to move among levels of abstraction in order to construct themes and principles.

The shift of Foucault to issues of the individual and subjectivation would seem even more to suggest that he is an Enlightenment subject, but in fact Foucault's positioning remains the same throughout his work. And it never seems that he invokes the modernist subject of knowledge purely and simply to undermine it. Consider the alternative, however: if Foucault were to claim to be outside of his own historical ontology as an Enlightenment subject, then he would have to abandon his own argument. As an Enlightenment subject, on the other hand, he can position himself as a self-reflexive subject of knowledge—that is, inside but outside cultural discourse at the same moment. This subject of knowledge appears *within* a historical discourse.

Modern philosophy initiates a historical discourse that represents humans as self-analyzing and self-knowing, and gives rise, on the more abstract level, to the self-reflexive "invention of man" in the modern era, producing at the same time the scientific observer. It is precisely during this historical period that the self-inquiry into who and what we are—what constitutes collective and individual human identity—has become the central issue. That is, as Enlightenment subjects we are constituted as individuals positioned in a self-inquiring space that allows us to investigate exactly how we have been constituted as subjects of discourse. This understanding allows us perhaps to resist discourses which constitute us (1980a, 157) and to think differently (1985b, 11).

Foucault is even more ironic than Derrida: his genealogy is the means to discover his own historical nature; and that in turn positions him—inside history—to counter the historical discourse that determines his being. He uses the truth of the Enlightenment against itself in order to open the possibility of an alternative—though always historical—being. Derrida would never admit to being outside history; he insists that metaphysics must be undermined from within its own language or discourse. But he doesn't ultimately produce the consciousness of historical ontology that Foucault does.

The impulse which stands behind genealogy itself follows the same pattern as that of Foucault's positioning of himself as an Enlightenment subject. In a lecture on Kant and "Enlightenment" in 1983 he is able to begin to trace the genealogy of his conception of the contemporary task of philosophy, which is self-reflexive. Kant's text asks "the question of the present": "What precisely, then, is this present to which I belong?" (1988, 87–88). It is self-reflexive in that the philosopher who questions is part of the process of the present.

Genealogy now has a new foundation in the historical present; it begins with our present historical being and then seeks to discover/construct the process (genealogy) by which we have become what we are. At once the problems noted in the materialist analysis of the previous chapter, of the justification for process construction as well as the origin of process, are founded in the newly articulated historical subject of modernity.

This has been the case since *Discipline and Punish*, but it took Foucault much longer to ground the analysis. Thus everything begins with the question of the present time—in this case Foucault's present—but it is a question produced by the historical ontology of the philosopher of the Enlightenment. In another place Foucault clearly positions genealogy in the present as a form of potential resistance. There he argues that "history serves to show how that-which-is has not always been," that "the things which seem most evident to us"—or what thought "silently thinks"—all are formed in the contingent confluence of historical discourses. In a more particular statement: "What reason perceives as its necessity, or rather, what different forms of rationality offer as their necessary being, can perfectly well be shown to have a history; and the network of contingencies from which it emerges can be traced" (1988, 35–36).

In a late seventies essay entitled "The Dangerous Individual" Foucault performs a model genealogy of the penetration of psychiatry into legal proceedings. He begins with a contemporary criminal case, which suggests to him that judiciary proceeding is not merely a question of crime, determination of guilt, and punishment according to statute; "Beyond admission, there must be confession, self-examination, explanation of oneself, revelation of what one is" (1988, 125ff.). Genealogy, then, begins in the present and is the ongoing legacy of the Enlightenment, used here by Foucault to point out that the Enlightenment's claim of essentiality is "merely" historical being—an ontology which both determines us and allows us to confront our own historicity.

In *The Use of Pleasure,* in which self-subjectivation first becomes a central issue, Foucault's task is specifically limited. The analysis of the "problematizations through which being offers itself to be necessarily thought" is restricted to a genealogy of "'desiring man'" (1985b, 5) or to the moral problematization of "sexual activity and sexual pleasures" in their relation to "practices of the self" (12). The restriction to sexual issues allows Foucault to narrow his task to a certain manageable focus, but this focus is primarily determined in reference to our constitution as subjects according to the current deployment of sexuality, in which identity is conferred by the interiority of our sexual inclination. Foucault is quite explicit about the emergence of the inquiry of *The Use of Pleasure* from his prior work (5)—according to the genealogical imperative.

The differences of ethical substance, mode of subjection, ascesis, and *telos* of self-relation allow for the construction of a genealogy of the practices of the self. Even explicit Christian codes would, as noted, leave a certain degree of choice or freedom to the individual. This individual, free to style itself in relation to cultural discourse, is a near parallel to the Enlightenment subject. This would seem perfectly logical, given the fact that genealogy always originates in contemporary concerns and is thus directed by those concerns. The modern subject (or "individual") is different to some degree: it is now a self-reflexive subject of knowledge, able to stand outside itself and to constitute its own identity as well as its subjection to cultural discourse. And that subjective conception leads directly to a genealogy focused on the thematic of self-relation.

There are a number of crucial issues which emerge from Foucault's later texts. The absence of *The Confessions of the Flesh* produces a serious gap in the genealogy of self-relation (cf. Bernauer 1987, 50ff., and 1992, 267; and Racevskis 1987, 29ff.). Coincidentally, it is precisely the same period that is traditionally called the Dark Ages, or Europe waiting for a Renaissance (see, e.g., Rochlitz 1992, 251). Further, in the references to Christianity there is a serious problem of coherence. There seems to be a relatively static Christian age continuing from the end of the Greco-Roman period until the seventeenth century. But the problem of coherence arises when we attempt to fit the references to Christianity in the two later volumes with the Christianity and the deployment of alliance of the first volume on sexuality. Foucault's death left a number of unanswered questions: the issues emerging from the various texts are not necessarily unreconcilable, but they certainly haven't been.

Another issue here is the important historical opposition between interiority and exteriority, which demands development beyond Foucault, especially in his own terms of a genealogy of self-relation. That issue will be taken up shortly. By means of the foregoing analysis of Foucault's method we can say that self-reference is a theme chosen by Foucault, on the basis of which he can construct a genealogy, or a carefully organized process with clearly determined margins, a process defined in terms of the variations in the form of self-relation in western thought. This history is a "fabrication," but it is at the same time a "true" history—true because it emerges from the positioning of the subject of knowledge in Enlightenment thought; hence the necessity to know, from its present configuration, the succession of this "true" nature.

One of the issues in *The Use of Pleasure* is freedom. In writing about fourth-century B.C.E. texts from Xenophon and Isocrates down to the Hellenistic period, Foucault, as mentioned, produces an ethics-code opposition as the relation of the a priori individual to the moral structure of the culture, whether in the form of general principles or an explicit code. Foucault's claim is, of course, that in ancient Greece there existed a high degree of freedom within which the individual was able to produce itself as a cultural subject. This is not a simple claim, but one fraught with subsidiary problematizations.

The freedom or authority of the free Greek male to fashion himself as a moral subject leads directly to the second of the important issues in Foucault's analysis, that of the relation between sexual activity and power. The latter emerges from the same general issue of authority, but here it is rendered in terms of the relation between specifically sexual activity and morals in the context of the genealogy of self-relation.

This authority is present in Foucault's argument that sexual relations are part of the larger sociopolitical relations in a hierarchical society—what he calls the "isomorphism between sexual relations and social relations" (1985b, 215); or, as he says elsewhere, the "sexual ethics" of the free adult male "was problematized in thought as the relationship, for a free man, between the exercise of his freedom, the forms of his power, and his access to truth" (1985b, 253). The act of sex is understood specifically as penetration, perpetrated by one who is active and dominating on another, who is perforce passive and yielding. The sexual relation is "of the same type as the relationship between a superior and a subordinate" (1985b, 215); the sexual and political relations were isomorphic.

Such a conception of sexual activity is based, Foucault says, on a "harsh system of inequalities" articulated within the society at large. But the power to rule others is never separate from the recommendation that the free male exercise control over himself, or self-mastery, and that he thereby achieve moderation and self-restraint. For Isocrates on Niccocles self-mastery regulates by moderation "the use the prince makes of the power he exercises over others" (1985b, 173). Similarly, marital fidelity, when it occurred, was assumed to be based on the husband's authority over his spouse, and his self-restraint in the use of that authority (151, 167, and passim), or a "part of an ethics of self-delimiting domination" (184).

Power-sex connects with the foundational analogy between self-mastery and the rule over others; Foucault gives this relation signal importance in his characterization of fourth-century B.C.E. Greece and "the relation to truth" in this era: "the exercise of political power required, as its own principle of internal regulation, power over oneself. Moderation, understood as an aspect of domination over the self . . . was a virtue that qualified a man to exercise his mastery over others" (81; also 80, 83, 172–74, 212, 221, and passim).

This relation is important because it enables Foucault to distinguish self-mastery in ancient Greece from the modern notion of this term. Modern self-mastery bears a closer relation to Christian self-decipherment, self-expurgation of the emotions, and the self-production of an objective self— that is, the subject of knowledge. But it is different in another prominent respect: in Greece self-mastery has an exteriorized character which is defined in the individual's relation to others, while in Christianity and perhaps in modernity as well that is not necessarily the case. During Christianity self-decipherment seems, according to Foucault, to be an interiorized mental activity (see, e.g., Bernauer 1987, 52ff.).

In two essays, "The Battle for Chastity" and "Sexuality and Solitude" (the latter with Richard Sennett), Foucault argues that with Augustine and the monastic movement (for example, Cassian) "[t]he main question of sexual ethics has moved . . . to the relation to oneself and to the erection problem" (Foucault and Sennett 1982, 16), and that this self-relation was concerned primarily with the (self-) analysis of one's thoughts, images, dreams, and so forth (15–16; see also 1985a, 20–24, on Cassian). While this kind of analysis was done in the presence of the priest within the penitential system, confession in modern times takes place both under the pressure of authority—medical personnel, for example—but also in isolation; that is, confession secularized, is monitored or private or both. Self-mastery in fourth-century B.C.E. Greece is an externalized performance, the "theater of Power," so to speak.

Self-mastery in this earlier era does involve knowledge and thought, but it is not conceived as acquired by a process of self-decipherment or a self-inquiry into one's interiority. The knowledge was already institutionalized, cultural, scientific, philosophical: of human nature, that is, of the passions, of the violent physiology of orgasm, of the natural difference of genders, the nature of desire, and so on. It was this framework within which self-mastery had to be achieved. This self-mastery, for example, demanded, beyond this knowledge, an ascesis, that is, a practice or mode of behavior; it was the product of *enkrateia* (1985b, 63ff.)—the term referring to the struggle, the activity of dominating, limiting, and controlling desires and their promised pleasures.

And although Foucault characterizes the experience of *aphrodisia*—the Greek "ethical substance"—as a dynamics of act, desire, and pleasure, there is no sense of the individual as characterizing itself by producing its interiority. The Greeks envisioned a political management of the self. For them,

> *ethos* was the deportment and the way to behave. It was the subject's mode of being and a certain manner of acting visible to others. . . . *Ethos* implies also a relation with others to the extent that the care for the self renders one competent to occupy a place in the city, in the community or in interindividual relationships which are proper—whether it be to exercise a magistracy or to have friendly relationships. (1987, 6, 7)

This absence of interiority is important to Foucault's reading of Greek ethics and, as partially indicated here, later eras.

In *The History of Sexuality*, volume 1, Foucault traces the genealogy of the Christian "confession of the flesh." In *The Use of Pleasure* the technique of confession does not play a large part in the periodic references to Christianity; these later references are used primarily to give point to the differences of self-relation in Greece and Christian Europe. But confession is virtually present in these references. Foucault's characterization of Christian morality in this later volume is double: this morality called for self-analysis or self-decipherment on the individual's part; this was to be carried out against the background of a specific codification of licit and illicit behavior, with the goal of discovering hidden desires, renouncing them and achieving purity and submission to code under the aegis of pastoral authority. The Christian individual produces itself as a subject by self-inquiry and subjects itself to code.

In *The History of Sexuality*, volume 1, discourse coerces or produces the individual as a subject of confession. The subject is produced as an interiority. Foucault makes confession important in his genealogy of the emergence of the deployment of sexuality, within which identities are produced according to internal and often hidden inclinations, especially sexual (in a general sense) ones. Confession in its modified secular form comes to provide the "data base" for the construction of the various human sciences. The subject produced is a subject of knowledge: self-inquiry and confession in the modern era always lead to knowledge, both in the local, individualizing form and larger institutional forms. But once these institutions are constituted, individual confession, as in the psychoanalytic session, tends to be read in terms of institutional knowledge, and identities are assigned to patients.

Confession produces interiority as a new kind of identity. But the term "interiority" needs to be defined more particularly. Foucault characterizes self-relation in ancient Greece as a performance, or as an activity of the self producing itself as a subject parallel to the ruler's active management of the subjects of his realm. Self-decipherment is also an activity performed on the self by the self, and this is why we need a notion of exteriorized, observable or even textualized behavior as a distinguishing mark. But this still leads to an incomplete opposition: the exterior-interior opposition doesn't have an a priori, abstract existence, but is produced within and by history. And it is a certain enigma of Foucault's historical reading that will be the issue here.

Foucault mentions this opposition once in *The Use of Pleasure* in referring to the traditional way of distinguishing Christian from pagan morality. He uses "exteriorizing" phrases to characterize this traditional view of Greek morality, concerned, for example, with "acts only in their concrete realization, in their visible and manifest form" (1985b, 63). But Foucault is ultimately convinced that this opposition alone does little to make the genealogy of self-relation clear: Christian interiority is simply a different, that is, "a particular mode of relationship with oneself" (ibid.). But if we admit both modes as forms of self-relation, we are left with a clear distinction of interior-exterior within that.

The underlying issue turns up in a much more interesting part of this volume: here Foucault gives a brief narrative of the breakdown in antiquity of the tight, explicit relation between self-mastery and political domination.

This relation is central to the fourth century B.C.E.; then, "it would not be long before this ascetics [of self-formation as a moral subject] would begin to have an independent status"; "the time would come when the art of the self would assume its own shape" (1985b, 77). In the third volume on sexuality, concerned with the Hellenistic period up through the first two centuries of the common era, he argues that an opposition emerges between identity based on power over others and "the sovereignty that one exercises over oneself" (1986, 85).

In the same place in *The Care of the Self* Foucault challenges the traditional reading of the Hellenistic period as an age marked by the decline of civic and political responsibility on the part of the citizen and a consequent turning inward of the now somewhat isolated individual (see, e.g., Guthrie 1967, 1:16; Sambursky 1956, 123–26; Bailey 1928, 300–309, 337, 356). In another text Foucault does not clearly reject this traditional view (1988, 45–246); but he does reorient it to some degree. The questioning of political behavior, Foucault says, appears within the context of changing principles of the relation to self (1986, 86); those changes remain related, however, to actual political transformations. Foucault thus frustrates the attempt to make a too easy identification of the active life with political responsibility: the relation to self is also an active pursuit, and it is in the later period the basis of one's determination of the proper relations with the outside world (41–42, 81, 85). Yet there are some problems here concerning Foucault's perspective.

Foucault's point is clear: the "active" part is a necessary concomitant to the theme of self-relation; certainly domination is necessary to self-mastery and rule over others in the fourth century B.C.E. in Greece. Yet the problems that arise are as conceptual as they are historical. The Hellenistic period is usually assumed to begin with the death of Alexander. From that point to the close of the second century of the common era is half a millennium.

It is difficult enough to discover the central thematics of freedom and self-mastery in texts as diverse as those of Plato, Aristotle, Xenophon, Isocrates, and the Hippocratean medical tradition, but over a period of five hundred years regularities can disappear altogether. This is not to question the theme of self-mastery or Foucault's overall genealogical impulse; but themes are abstract concepts that may always be used to produce a history. And beyond that it may be relevant to ask if Foucault's comprehensive view may be subject to the scrutiny of other texts of the era.

The conceptual problem of Foucault's analysis relates to the exteriority-interiority opposition. As noted, Foucault mentions this opposition and to a degree dismisses it by mapping it onto the active-passive opposition. He uses the latter to resolve the former opposition: exteriorized activity is essentially identical to interior function. In his narrative of the eventual split between the art of self-mastery and political rule, "it would not be long before . . ." refers to the five hundred years beginning with the Hellenistic period. But Foucault leaps over the details of this split and the consequent transformation; moreover, it is a transformation which occurs in terms of a technical and explicit notion of interiority.

The half-millennium which Foucault attempts to cover in *The Care of the Self* should suggest caution about his conclusions, as well as the fact that writers like Cicero, a dominant intellectual figure during the middle of this period, doesn't appear in the analysis at all. However, the issue of interiority, which is the key, crops up most clearly in Foucault's treatment of the shift in self-relation that occurs between classical Greece and the first two centuries of the common era.

As mentioned just previously, self-domination becomes a separate issue from politics after the end of the fourth century B.C.E. There is a much more explicit self-positioning than in the earlier era: the self of the first few centuries of the common era, according to Foucault, is conceived of as fundamentally isolated, individual, and beset by external dangers (1986, 67). Sexual activity is increasingly pathologized during this period, being associated with epilepsy, for example (113ff., passim); and in general the self is in a vulnerable position, with respect to which the only remedy appears to be an intense self-preoccupation and an *ascesis* which works toward the realization of an ethics of self-enjoyment or pleasure within oneself (65–66, 238–39).

Foucault gives several specific ways in which the self turns actively inward toward the self during this period, and these render the positioning of the self in relation to the self more explicitly still. One of the forms of the *cura sui* or *epimeleia heautou* is the "necessity of a labor of thought with itself as object. . . . it should have the form of a steady screening of representations: examining them, monitoring them, sorting them out. . . . [this is] a constant attitude that one must take toward oneself" (1986, 62–63). Foucault draws this primarily from Epictetus; it suggests that the self, as objective observer, stands outside the self as the (interior) process of consciousness. The consciousness registers impressions—that is, external and internal sensation, feeling, and so forth. "The soul is like a dish of water, and the impressions (phantasiai?) like the rays of light which strike the water" (Epictetus 1928, 3:3). We will return to Epictetus in more detail later on.

It is precisely in terms of this self-positioning that the ethics of self-control of *The Care of the Self* differs from the self-mastery of the classical era in Greece; further, it involves a specific *telos* of pleasure, *hédoné* or *voluptas:* "the relation to self . . . is defined as a concrete relationship enabling one to delight in oneself, as a thing one both possesses and has before one's eyes" (1986, 65). Moreover, the end of this self-reflexive and self-knowing process of self-control is "an enjoyment without desire and without disturbance" (68)—*ataraxia* in Greek and *tranquillitas* in Latin, a state of pleasure defined by absence of pain, fear, and even active pleasure. In other words, the *telos* is a specific state of interiority. And the self-reflexive positioning is precise: the agential or "outside" self which comes to know its own interiority and to exert control over it toward the production of the ultimate state of stable inner tranquility.

In this way Foucault raises the issue which demands to be investigated further in its relation to his historical thematics of self-relation. This is the technical focus on interiority in epistemological and ethical thought which occurs as an epistemic shift during the early Hellenistic period and then seems to recur in a similar form in the first two centuries of the common era. Whereas self-relation is usually only implied and nonspecific in the fourth century B.C.E., in the early Hellenistic period and later one begins by examining mental impressions and presentations, by verifying (or not) the truth of these presentations in relation to external reality; one ends by designating the appropriate inner state of knowledge and feeling.

In other words, in the latter eras self-relation takes the explicit form of the self-as-observer taking account of and managing itself in terms of its interior processes. Foucault's analyses in *The Care of the Self* seem conscious of the similarity of the early Hellenistic period and the first two centuries of the common era; but he focuses on the latter almost exclusively while treating the half-millennium from the beginning of the third century B.C.E. as homogenous or, worse, in the process of developing more explicit forms of intense self-cultivation. This explains his neglect of Cicero and the republican age.

We need to be much more precise in understanding the connection of self-relation and its historical forms with epistemic (or even genealogical) transformations in the general manner in which philosophical questions are framed. I am suggesting here that in certain eras an "epistemological" framing of issues occurs: that is, a focus on the contents and process of consciousness and its relation to an "external" reality. There is a tendency in these eras to isolate the individual and also a tendency toward developing an ethics of thought and feeling; but this is not a necessary consequence. It is important to understand what influences the specific type of self-relation recommended during any era; we can also remember that Descartes invokes roughly the same kind of self-reflexive positioning as the writers of the early Hellenistic period and the first two centuries of the common era. Thus the understanding of the relation of interiority and self-relation in antiquity might well contribute to a more precise understanding of modern self-relation.

꩜

Epicurus was an Athenian. Although he grew up in the eastern colonies he apparently studied philosophy at Athens and returned there at the end of the fourth century B.C.E. (c. 307–306) to set up a school of philosophy (Diogenes Laertius 1925, 10.2). His philosophic doctrines are a clear example of the breakdown of the relation between self-mastery and the art of ruling others that Foucault makes the sign of the Hellenic period; he has always also served as a prime example of the traditional view that Hellenism marks a turning away from politics and civic affairs toward individual well being— "the care of the self." Ignore for the moment the general negativism of this latter view, one which Foucault's notion of activity attempts to correct. If Epicurus's philosophy is an example of these shifts, then they occurred quickly. Epicurus was dead by about 275 B.C.E., within fifty years of the death of Aristotle.

Epicurus's philosophy does indeed argue for a relatively complete rejection of political activity. The Epicurean Garden was apparently comprised of a group of intimate friends and it was distant from the central districts of the Athens of the time. Friendship marked the outer limits of social relations and the distance from the city marked the separation from civic affairs. But there is a political structure within Epicureanism: master and learner. It is not merely that Lucretius manipulates his hexameters to proclaim the glory of the Master; far more important are the details of this kind of relation between master and pupil in the extant writings of Epicurus.

Epicurus's writings are for the most part preserved by Diogenes Laertius, who quotes in full three rather lengthy *Letters* (to Herodotus, to Pythocles, and to Menoeceus). Of the forty works plus correspondence which Diogenes says that Epicurus wrote, these are what remain, along with a few fragmentary texts. One of these is the fragmentary *On Nature* (*Peri physeos*) in thirty-seven books (10.27), apparently a comprehensive treatise on physics. A copy of this work was discovered among the ruins at Herculaneum, but the papyrus scrolls disintegrated into mostly unreadable fragments when unrolled (for the text, see Epicurus 1973, 190ff.). In the *Letter to Herodotus* Epicurus begins by mentioning his voluminous works on physics and then says the *Letter* is intended as an epitomé for those not acquainted with the larger works. These are clearly followers of Epicurus who are beginners or those content with an abbreviated version of his thought.

For these learners Epicurus says he has prepared an epitomé of the principal treatises "to enable [them] to keep the whole of the systems of opinions present within memory" (Diogenes Laertius 1925, 10.35). *Doxai* is usually translated as "principles" or "principal doctrines," but to some degree this translation misses the point: a more accurate term is "opinion." Philosophers have never been accustomed to refer to their work as opinions, at least until recently; but Epicurus does because *doxai*, deriving from the verb *dokeo*, refers to what exists in consciousness (cf. Foucault 1986, 135–36, 139). In the first person the verb frequently functions in terms of the speaker's reference to its own thought or attitude; nouns deriving from the verb refer to opinion, belief, thought, even vision or apparitions. The master-learner relation established in the *Letter to Herodotus* and the other letters—and even more so in the "Master Opinions" (*kuriai doxai*) concluding the final letter—bears directly on an intriguing aspect of Epicurus's thought: that the relation is not an explicit power relation but one of sharing of knowledge between the one who knows and those who seek to know. A very un-Foucauldian notion. But what is more important is the way this relation and the consequent structure of the Epicurean texts bear on the notion of interiority: they, *doxai*, are "opinions" that are to be taken into consciousness and held there for a specific purpose.

Some scholars acknowledge the focus on interiority in Epicurus. For example, "Epicurus meant his . . . [*kuriai doxai*] to be impressed in the minds of his disciples so that they would endure as stable rhythmic movements of soul atoms which could not be confused or drastically altered by the incursion of new *eidola* and impressions from without" (Clay 1973, 276). Clay argues that Epicurus proposes a stability of consciousness that is maintained, at least in part, by the presence of the *doxai* and by the recipient's holding them ready in memory for use toward countering disturbing influences entering through the senses from the external world.

At the close of the *Letter to Herodotus* it is evident that Epicurus's *telos* for the individual is this stable, undisturbed process of consciousness: *ataraxia* or *galenismos* (Diogenes Laertius 1925, 10.80–83). The first term indicates the absence of mental disturbance or disorder and the second indicates calmness, usually associated with the stable undulations of the sea. Usual translations such as "mental tranquility" or "imperturbability," while generally accurate, don't convey the sense that consciousness is an ongoing process; there is no way short of death to cut oneself off from the intrusions of external and internal sensation.

Herodotus, an epitomé of physics, ends with this focus on conscious process: "we must pay attention to present feelings and sensations" and also to knowledge produced by means of these "criteria" of truth (10.82); this is, specifically, knowledge produced by these criteria of truth such as that contained in the first two *Letters:* knowledge of the natural world, physics and, in *Pythocles,* of meteorology. In the latter case, for example, knowledge of the true natural causes of an eclipse would form a *doxa* in the mind of the individual, who would no longer be subject to the mental disturbance traditionally deriving from witnessing an eclipse—the fear of the wrath of the gods.

One of the functions of Epicurean natural philosophy was the sweeping away of superstition, especially religion, yet the important point is that this end is always subordinate to the *telos* of *ataraxia* in the individual consciousness. In the meteorological text Epicurus says, "First of all remember that, as with other sciences . . . knowledge of celestial phenomena has no other end than stable consciousness [*ataraxia*] and certainty" (10.84). Epicurus's natural science has always been a cause for disdain—his multiple-cause reasoning and analogical reasoning (usually near-at-hand/distant)—but that is part of the point. For example, after giving several possible causes of thunder in *Pythocles,* he concludes with the following: "Exclusion of myth is the sole condition necessary" (10.104). Natural causes are to be pursued in order to eliminate certain popular beliefs, for example, that the cause of eclipses is the anger of the gods. The elimination of fear on a cosmic scale opens the way to an undisturbed consciousness. The Epicurean becomes a subject of knowledge to the degree that knowledge contributes to ethical stability.

Since Epicurus is more concerned with well-being than physics, and since well-being is defined individually, his philosophy marks the shift away from the relation between politics and individual ethics. More important, however, is the fact that his philosophy takes as its primary focus the processes of consciousness. His end is to constitute a stable interior process. He doesn't exclude the external world and knowledge of it, but it is to be known and adapted in terms of how externality, as it enters consciousness, either aids or hinders *ataraxia.* Self-mastery becomes in Epicurus the self-management of one's conscious processes, and it is focused on internal sensations such as needs and desires as well as on interference from outside.

But the question for an encounter with Foucault is: how much can this specifically philosophic shift account for the transformation of "the use of pleasure" to "the care of the self" at the beginning of the Hellenistic period?

Another key to the interior focus of Epicurus's philosophy is the place of canonic within the structure of knowledge. Diogenes Laertius says that for Epicurus canonic is prior, providing the necessary access to the rest of the system, that is, physics and ethics (Diogenes Laertius 1925, 10.29–30). Canonic has to do with the criteria of truth or its foundation (*peri kriterion kai arches* [ibid.]). The criteria are sensations, feelings, and prolepses (10.31). This means that the initial problem of Epicurus's philosophy is the determination of the relation between the interior, which is known, and the exterior, between consciousness and external being. The focus is epistemological: can we know? how can we know? what is the relation between sensations, feelings, and other occurrences within consciousness and the (supposed) external world? This was the subject of Epicurus's *The Canon,* according to Diogenes—that is, how the individual is constituted as a subject of knowledge—but the work is not extant. There are traces of canonic in the beginning of the *Letter to Herodotus,* in which Epicurus says that sensations, feelings, and other interior criteria of knowledge are necessarily assumed to be true prior to developing natural philosophy.

Epicurus is a materialist, but primarily he seeks to know how the world and astronomical bodies operate so that he may constitute a limit to their potential for creating pain and anxiety in the human consciousness. Epicurus alone might be enough to show that Foucault ignores this technical shift toward interiority in the third century B.C.E. But in fact it is not difficult to demonstrate that other philosophical schools of the same general era exhibited a similar shift in focus. The Cyrenaics, following Aristippus, were generally skeptical about the possibility of knowledge and gave up on physics entirely: "They affirm that feelings (*pathé*) can be known, but not the objects from which they come, and they abandoned the study of nature because of its apparent uncertainty" (2.92; see also Sextus Empiricus 1905, *Adv. Math.,* vii, 191ff., 199f.).

Events within consciousness—feelings, in this instance—constitute the primary reality: they are known to exist. The model is of the individual "knower" with immediate access to its own conscious processes, but cut off from exteriority by the unreliable mediation of consciousness itself. Accordingly, the Cyrenaics gave themselves over to an ethics of pleasure (*hédoné*) that is different from the Epicurean notion of *hédoné* as absence of disturbance but nonetheless located in interiority. Similarly Pyrrho, a contemporary of Epicurus, and the Skeptics promoted the doctrine of the suspension of judgment (*epoché*)—in effect an argument, laid out typically in the ten "modes of perplexity," citing models of the noncoincidence of external being with appearances or presentations within consciousness. This is another epistemological approach to the problem of canonic (Diogenes Laertius 1925, 9.61, 70, 79–88, 93, 95, 103; Sextus Empiricus 1905, *Pyrr. Hyp.*, 1:36, 40, and passim). The Stoics, like Epicurus but unlike the Skeptics and Cyrenaics, resolved the epistemological skepticism which always haunted canonic: "The Stoics resolved to place the question of appearances (*phantasiai*) first, since the criteria for the existence of external reality are the kinds of appearances [or presentations]" (Diogenes Laertius 1925, 7.49).

The presentation is a forming (*tuposis*) of the soul, the shape that whatever enters through the senses gives to the process of consciousness at any given moment. In all Stoic thought (up to the time of Chrysippus) the seal-wax metaphor always follows the claim to have shown the interior-exterior relation: a "compelling" appearance (*kataleptiké phantasia*), one that gives a precise, articulated shape to consciousness, is to be accepted as a criterion of real existence external to mind (7.45, 46; Sextus Empiricus 1905, *Adv. Math.*, vii, 228, 229ff., 236; *Stoicorum Veterum Fragmenta* [hereafter, *SVF*] 1903, 1:58; see also Rist 1978, 265).

In Epicurus, canonic is only nominally self-reflexive, perhaps because the surviving references to the criteria are slight. But in the other early Hellenistic philosophers, the pursuit of philosophy begins in epistemological self-inquiry: the individual observes its own interiority, that is, actual presentations within consciousness, in order to attempt to determine the possibility of their relation to the external world. The conclusions of the various philosophical schools are various, but the similarity of this self-relation to Descartes—along with other rather large differences—raises interesting questions for a genealogy that considers only self-constitution as a moral agent, as Foucault does. Can epistemological self-relation always be separated from moral self-constitution? Or what relation does the latter have with the individual's relation to the objectivity of the external world? In Epicurus knowledge of the world is prior and necessary to *ataraxia*, but is subordinate to it. Again, what particular part do periods in which the focus of philosophical inquiry is on interiority play in the genealogy of self-relation?

There is no sign of canonic in these same philosophical schools later in the Hellenistic period. In fact canonic is specifically pushed to third place in the structure of sciences, and considered as logic. There is no indication of problems of canonic in Philodemus and Lucretius, the Roman "representatives" of Epicureanism, or in the historian of philosophy, Cicero. Philosophy seems to have taken another shift, again unrecorded by Foucault. And is it an accident that the Greco-Roman period is represented by Foucault by a few references to early Hellenistic period writers such as Epicurus, but primarily by writers who for the most part come well after Cicero and the Augustan age? It would be interesting to see whether thought undergoes another "interiorizing" during the era of Seneca, Plutarch, Epictetus, and Marcus Aurelius.

Foucault is content to rely on his activity-passivity opposition to mask his limited view of the Roman era. Indeed, the shift toward interiority suggests passivity or "passion": the model is of a consciousness under the pressure of sensation and, in general, of potential causes of stimulus penetrating into consciousness. This is precisely Epicurus's argument: because sensation is inevitable, the Epicurean must acquire and hold in consciousness the *doxai* that will ward off the potential harm to *ataraxia* they may cause. Passivity is the condition of being placed in nature. But the remainder is active, and even a prime example of self-management and the art of the self. The only difference is that now self-relation means one's focus on one's interior processes, which constitute the identity of the self.

The various aspects of self-management in Epicurus cover a large range: the isolation from the city and politics in the Garden as a limitation of potentially disturbing stimuli; surrounding oneself with friends, who are so similar in nature and outlook as to minimize disturbance; the understanding of nature, from its constituents, atoms and void, to celestial phenomena to knowledge of human consciousness, human nature (Epicurus, for example, distinguishes between natural needs which are necessary or not, sexual desire being natural but its fulfillment unnecessary), death, religious superstition (eliminated by understanding the material causes of phenomena, including the gods), and so on. These are the various levels of understanding directed toward the ethical end, the self-management that results in a stable state of consciousness identified as *hédoné* or absence of disturbance.

The fourth-century B.C.E. Greek had to overcome a potentially explosive and harmful physiology. This notion is present in Epicurus as well, in the refusal of unnecessarily fulfilled needs related to sexual activity and the recommendation that individuals avoid the "elaboration" of necessary needs (for example, a feast, when barley bread and water would satisfy hunger just as well—although Epicurus was not opposed to an occasional diversion). What is prominent in Epicurus and not in prior thought is the need to manage the threat to the tranquility of the individual from incoming stimuli—in short to manage the exterior world and heavens in terms of its potential for disturbing consciousness. This is the ultimate breaking away of the arts of the self from the self-mastery which is tied to politics, the city, the world: these are now in opposition to the self-management focused on interiority.

◁◁◦◦◦◦▷▷

The figures who represent the thought of the first two centuries of the common era in *The Care of the Self* are Seneca, Plutarch, Epictetus, and Marcus Aurelius, all of whom are either Stoics or are related to Stoicism by opposition. Seneca, on whom I wish to focus here, was in some senses a typical post-Augustan moral philosopher; he was educated by Stoics, grew prominent in Rome, and was important enough in imperial circles to be accused of an affair with an emperor's sister and exiled for eight years; afterwards he was recalled to become the tutor of Nero, but in 62 he left Rome because of Nero to travel and to write. He committed suicide in 65, in apparent anticipation of Nero's condemnation.

But Seneca is not of interest here because of his politics. Rather, it is a question of whether he represents a return to a focus on interiority typical of the early Hellenistic period. And if there is a return, how similar and how different is this interiority from that of Epicurus and his contemporaries and also from the kind of philosophic focus characteristic of the age of Cicero? Finally, and most important, does the presumed focus on interiority determine the peculiar character of self-relation developed in Seneca? Indeed, the return to interiority and the subsequent form of self-relation are at the core of Seneca's thought, and that is the primary subject here.

Considering that Seneca was a Stoic, his relation to Epicurus and his representation of the latter's thought is striking. Seneca quotes Epicurus favorably in many of the first thirty of the *Letters to Lucilius,* written near the end of his life. The quotations, however, are general maxims about the conduct of life of the type which Seneca also produced in volume, not statements of a precise philosophic position (see Hadot 1992, 228). Seneca makes something like the notion of *ataraxia,* which he renders as *tranquillitas,* prominent in his own thought; he even gave one of his dialogues the title of *De tranquillitate animi* and speaks of tranquility frequently (e.g., 1925, 66.45–48). In one letter he even provides a version of Epicurus's notion of *doxai,* arguing that certain notions (*notitiae*) must be learned and held in memory and "ready to hand" (*in promptu*) (1925, 94.2, 39.1; cf. 33.7).

161

But in more central and extended passages Seneca also attacks the Epicurean notion of *hédoné* or pleasure in certain fundamental ways. Seneca's work is not precisely philosophic: his texts are full of moral exhortation and diatribes against the abusive nature of contemporary social habits and practices (e.g., 1925, 108). Although he explains Stoic philosophic notions from time to time, he is often vague, redundant, and not particularly analytic (e.g., 1925, 45; Sandbach 1975, 152, 162). Thus the possibility of recovering a strong sense of systematicity from his texts is considerably lessened. But his attacks on Epicurean thought serve well enough to distinguish his own general philosophic commitments. His notion of interiority—to be discussed in detail in the following pages—differs from that of Epicurus in substantive ways. He distinguishes between sensible and intelligible functions in humans, assigning pleasure (*voluptas*) to the former and situating the latter within the mind (*animus* or *mens*) in which the true choice (*iudicium* or *adsensio*) of good is to occur through reason. Thus Seneca is much more a candidate for Richard Rorty's claim that the ancients considered mind as coextensive with reason than is Epicurus (1973, 38ff.).

Epicurus had devised a system in which *ataraxia* was equated with pleasure, a state of well-being from which fear and pain were necessarily absent. The *summum bonum* was this state of undisturbedness. *Voluptas* in Roman thought is a considerably more active engagement and, according to Seneca, one likely to lead to increased, passionate, and corrupt desires and a subsequent dangerous connection to the external world. He substitutes, in Stoic fashion, a state of *gaudium*, a kind of inner joy that is removed from pleasure. Pierre Hadot argues: "[I]f the Stoics set store by the word *gaudium* . . . this was precisely because they refused to introduce the principle of pleasure into moral life" (1992, 226). Thus in the *De vita beata* Seneca rejoins the attack on Epicurean thought by refusing to countenance a suggested joining of virtue and pleasure. Here he specifically associates tranquility of mind with pleasure in Epicurean fashion, but treats this as secondary or an adjunct to the *summum bonum* of the individual, which should be primarily concerned with virtue and the honorable (*honestum*).

The form of self-relation is subsequently distinct. In fact, Seneca's sense of the individual self is much stronger than that of his predecessors. This is a tendency of Stoic thought, but the notion of self ultimately bears the stamp of the Roman Seneca and his successors (see Rist 1978, 265 and passim). Of the other traditions: what is implicit in Epicurus concerning self-relation and self-management comes clearly to the forefront in Seneca: the self is the primary focus, along with its relation to itself, or in brief, the *sui cura,* the necessary attention paid to the self by the self. For example, Seneca argues that happiness is impossible without *felicitatis intellectus,* the self-awareness that one is happy (1994b, 5); this is built upon the traditional Stoic notion of a lower form of self-awareness in animals (ibid., *Letters,* 121 and passim; Sandbach 1975, 32–33). Few pre-Augustan texts exhibit such an intensive notion of self-focus as those of Seneca.

In Cicero, self-relation is often potentially negative. In the *De finibus* the argument often centers around pleasure—not merely the well-being sought by Epicurus but the sense of active accomplishment of desire or even titillation (Seneca uses the verb *titilare;* cf. Stokes 1995, 145–70). In a discussion with and about the ancestors of the Epicurean Torquatus: concerning their noble deeds and the motivations for them, even the descendant is unable to argue that they fought bravely in battle for pleasure. Utility or self-benefit must be substituted as a possible motivation, to be countered by Cicero's claim that *honestum* is the only legitimate basis for action (1925, 1:33–34, 2:45, and passim).

Honestum, that peculiar Roman virtue of honor, is important in Seneca as well. In the *De finibus* the focus is on the action, the intention of *honestum* or *utilitas* supplying the means to characterize the act or to determine its meaning; for Seneca, however, *honestum* is a state of mind, prior to and detached from any subsequent act in the sense that a certain state of mind is the end in itself, whether or not action eventuates. *Honestum* in Cicero may imply self-relation to a degree, but the alternative motivation of the *De finibus* clearly situates the individual as recognizing that an activity is to his or her own benefit; thus the more the motivation indicates *sui cura,* the less it is legitimate.

This brings us back to issues raised earlier. If the *sui cura* is typical of Epicurus—if only implicitly—and Seneca and his successors, what of the era of Cicero that stands between? Foucault doesn't enlighten here: he treats the five hundred years or so from Epicurus to Marcus Aurelius as relatively homogeneous, leaving Cicero and his contemporaries out of the reckoning. Clearly the care of the self is not a Ciceronian issue; but what takes its place? Foucault's neglect of Cicero masks another question: why the *return* to interiority in Seneca, although in a different form? The traditional explanation of the earlier, Hellenistic turn toward interiority as caused by political changes might be attempted here, even if it has not stood up to scrutiny for the earlier period: certainly periods of first-century Rome could prove a nightmare for any person involved in the affairs of state. Seneca was importantly involved in Roman imperial state business, and he was twice burned. Yet politics or even Seneca's supposed attitude cannot explain totally the turn toward interiority; and perhaps the question can't be answered more theoretically either.

One thing is certain: the focus on interiority determines the *sui cura*, and most explicitly in Seneca. Also explicit is the notion of the individual, even isolated, self whose only recourse is to turn to its own resources as a means of establishing a stable and independent existence. This notion of the self is where Seneca "begins," in a sense. Where that leads is to the important issue of how self-relation and the focus on interiority are mutually shaped.

The opposition between the individual self and the world external to it is central to Seneca's thought. This in part allows for the increased and explicit focus on the self: the world is potentially harmful to the integrity of the self, so the latter must be resisted and held at bay.

> Let him have a household of attractive slaves, a beautiful home, a large plantation, and earn a fortune in interest; none of these is in the man himself, but are outside him. Praise in him that which is neither able to be given nor taken away, that which is proper to man. . . . Mind and reason in a perfected consciousness.

> [Familiam formosam habet et domum pulchram, multum serit, multum funerat; nihil horum in ipso est, sed circum ipsum. Lauda in illo, quod nec eripi potest nec dari, quod proprium hominis est. . . . Animus et ratio in animo perfecta. (1925, 41. 7–8)]

Seneca's constant theme is the return to the self and its resources. F. H. Sandbach argues that from the earliest of the Stoics virtue (*areté*) was seen as coextensive with happiness and that neither was dependent on the external world (1975, 29–39 and passim), but this at least undergoes an intensification in Seneca. Seneca recommends that Lucilius avoid association with the public and attendance at the gladiatorial games, alleging an inevitable harmful effect on his behavior: "What do you think will happen to one's moral habits when the world assaults them?" ("Quid tu accidere his moribus credis, in quos publice factus est impetus?" [1925, 7.7]). Instead, "Recede in te ipsum" (7.8) or return to one's self. Elsewhere: "in se recedendum est" ("one must return to oneself" [1994a, 17]); "Utique *animus* ab omnibus externis in se revocandus est" ("the mind must be recalled completely into itself from all external things" [14; see also 1925, 25.6, 94.72]).

For Seneca the goal is the stable and sufficient self. The highest good is, in one instance, "the mind disdaining chance occurrence" ("animus fortuita despiciens" [1994b, 3])—that is, the mind able to stand apart from and unaffected by the events of an unstable world. Hence the wise man will be self-sufficient and self-contained (1925, 9.3). "What need of anything external to one who has all within himself?" [1994b, 16]). The stability and integrity of the self depend on breaking the link between it and the external world, or at least limiting it severely. Seneca delineates aspects of this world regularly in myriad examples, but his primary purpose is to characterize this world as a potential threat to the well-being of the self.

On the other side, he is never very precise about the constitution of the self. Instead, it is usually defined by the very self-world opposition: the self is interior to itself, what is within the boundary which demarcates individual and environment. Beyond that, one must fall back on a tradition of Stoic thought, perhaps dominated by Chrysippus: the *psyche* or mind as reason and assent (*iudicium* or *adsensio* [1925, 113.18]), what Pierre Hadot notes in Seneca as "the best part of the self" (1992, 226); passion arises from a distorted judgment about an "indifferent" object (neither good nor harmful in itself) and this leads to excessive, distorted desire (*adfectus*) or passion (Sandbach 1975, 60ff.; 1925, 16.9, 71.32ff., 85.6ff., 89.14–15). Seneca at times supposes an irrational element in humans (1925, 71.27ff., 92.2); but the general failure by the Stoics to recognize an irrational part of the soul is usually treated as a problem by commentators (e.g., Lloyd 1978, 235ff.; see Rorty 1979, 38ff.).

According to Seneca, the happy life entails a "liberum animum et erectum et interritum ac stabilem, extra metum, extra cupiditatem positum" ("a free, upright, fearless and stable mind, placed beyond fear and desire" [1994b, 4; see also, e.g., 1925, 124.12, 23]). But, turned around, the quotation indicates the threat the world poses to the self through the inevitable connection of world and mind. Foucault accurately notes that the philosophers of the post-Augustan period appear to have seen the self as much more surrounded by threats to health and morals than did the Greeks of the fourth century B.C.E. (1986, 56ff., 103). Pleasure is a specific threat: desire potentially links the self to the world—the place where desire can be realized. Aside from the fact that it arises from a lower, corporal function, the link that pleasure opens to the world can overmaster the self or make it vulnerable. If desire can't be totally extinguished (see above, *extra cupiditatem*) or moderated, then the self is threatened by loss of control: "pleasure controls those [too much devoted to it]; they are either tormented by its absence or strangled by its excess" (1994b, 14; see also 5, 11).

Yet the threat exists not in the world but in the self's vulnerability to it (1925, 50.4ff.). Desire is natural, but its excess and the failure of self-control or self-limitation places the freedom of the self "sub iugum," under the yoke (19.6 and passim). When this happens, "there begins to be a need for fortune [or what it provides], which is the greatest slavery of all; there follows a life which is anxious, suspicious, disturbed, fearful of accidents and uncertain in every moment" (1994b, 15). Hence the theme of Seneca's exhortations: "if we do not yield ourselves to servitude, not allow what is alien to possess us" (8); "Incorruptus vir sit externis et insuperabilis" ("Let man be uncorrupted and unconquered by the external world" [ibid.; see also 1925, 66.6].

Vulnerability is the condition of the self that has lost the capacity for self-control and is dependent on the world: committed to the satisfaction of desires that only the world can provide, or positioned to fear and to suffer loss because of changes in an inevitably unstable world. Seneca refers on occasion to Stilbo's (or Stilpo's) statement that nothing is good that can be taken away ("nihil bonum putare, quod eripi possit" [9.19]), that is, distinguishing what is proper to the self as opposed to the so-called goods of the world, which include the means of satisfying extravagant desires. The happy man is one "qui suis gaudeat nec maiora domesticiis cupiat" (who will experience inner joy at what is his own and desire no more than what belongs to the self" [1994b, 4]).

The traditional Stoic terms are *oikeion/oikeiosis,* what "belongs" to the self. The notion covers everything from the self-affinity or care of the self manifest in the impulse toward self-preservation in animals to the recognition by the human individual of "a natural *oikeiosis* to all mankind" in certain Stoics (Sandbach 1975, 34; cf. Rist 1978, 259–66). But Seneca doesn't emphasize the latter. In a parallel argument concerning health and riches—whether they are goods or merely "indifferent" things that are "preferable" (i.e., *adiaphora* and *potiora* [1994b, 22; 1925, 82.14, 87.36; see Sandbach 1975, 38–41])—Seneca says the following of the wise man: "non abigit illa a se, se abeuntia securus prosequitur" ("He doesn't reject these [that is, health and riches], but if they withdraw from him he remains undisturbed" [1994b, 21]).

The argument that wealth is preferable to poverty so long as the wise man does not become attached to it (see the second half of 1994b; see also 1994a) would again suggest Seneca's emphasis on the integrity of the self and of its self-relation as totally constitutive of its good. The doctrine of wealth as an indifferent also suggests a connection with the world, as long as it is kept under control. What Seneca does not emphasize, although he does occasionally acknowledge it, is the self's inevitable if minimal dependence on the world (1925, 116.3).

The extent of that dependence tends to vary in the various texts: an earlier dialogue (although dating is generally uncertain), *De tranquillitate animi,* maintains that "Multum et in se recedendum est" (17; quoted above), but argues as well: "Miscenda tamen ista et alternanda sunt, solitudo et frequentia" (ibid.). Solitude and self-withdrawal from the world must be alternated with public participation. On the other hand, in one of the late *Letters* Seneca argues that even the minimal means of subsistence should be refused (1925, 110.18–20; see also 18.10). It is a question of vulnerability, no matter how slight: "haec ipsa acqua et polenta in alienum arbitrium cadit." Even barley and water may be within the power of fortune or the external world; the freedom of the self is necessarily absolute if it is to be freedom at all.

Yet short of death, dependence is unavoidable for subsistence; this dependence, it should be noted, is part of an initial general dependence of the individual on its environment: *animus* and *ratio* are potentials that are activated only by empirical experience (1994b, 8); and assent is usually spoken of as occurring only after a sense presentation has taken place (*SVF* 1903, 2.974; see Stough 1978, 215ff.). This in part explains the logic of the "return" to the self. But the notion of the "world" involves Seneca's conception of nature. He refers at times to the traditional Stoic idea of a universal, living, rational world order, in which individual human reason participates as part of the living whole (for example, Diogenes Laertius 1925, 7.143): "I assent to [the Stoic notion of] the nature of things; wisdom rests in not departing from nature and in forming ourselves according to its law and pattern" (1994b, 3; see also ibid., 15; 1925, 74.20, 76.23, 107.7, 120.14; cf. Sandbach 1975, 35–36, 54, 59; and Diogenes Laertius 1925, 7.87–88 on Zeno).

But this is not a developed notion in Seneca: when he mentions it he usually returns to the individual self rather quickly. If the external world is determined by universal reason, Seneca still retains the perspective of the individual: the external world is "fortuna," "fortuita," an unstable process not predictable by and threatening to the self. The relation between universal order and individual choice was always problematic for the Stoics and their critics (Stough 1978, 203–31), but when Seneca speaks of *libertas* he means the freedom of the self from external constraint—unproblematically (e.g., 1925, 51.9). Seneca typically uses the above reference to universal nature merely to give context to his own focus: "Beata est ergo vita conveniens naturae suae" (1994b, 3; see also 1925, 41.9, 44.8, 122.19)—that is, the self in conformity with *its own nature.*

Pleasure, the link with the world, is of two kinds: one must differentiate these carefully, between those which "remain within natural desire" ("quae . . . intra naturale desiderium resistant") and those "which expand precipitously, are unlimited and which the more they are experienced the more they make one insatiable" (1994b, 13). The natural desires are for food, drink, and shelter as the means of subsistence. "My intention in eating and drinking is to assuage natural desires, not to fill and empty my stomach" ("desideria naturae restinguere" [ibid., 20]; see also 1994a, 9, 1925, 17.9, 25.2, 90.15, and 18ff.). Here the intention, in keeping with the principle of "conveniens naturae suae," is to limit the necessary link with the world to the minimum necessary to continue life (1925, 110.11, 119.2 and 10)—as long as one chooses to live.

If excess pleasure is unnatural (34.5, 48.9, 108.15), it becomes so by exceeding natural limits (what is necessary to the individual), or by an inner assent that results in the distortion of nature: elaborate and excessive meals, for example, that require regurgitation as the prelude to the next ostentatious course (think of the *Cena Trimalcionis*). There are numerous references to such meals and other forms of luxury in Seneca (e.g., 1994b, 11; 1925, 60.3, 90.18ff., 108.15, 110.12ff., 114.9). Limiting pleasure to that necessary to satisfy natural desires limits dependence on the world and therefore allows for the turn toward the self, the *sui cura*, self-control and self-management, in inverse proportion. The world offers not only sustenance but wealth, political power—all of those things which, when they threaten to withdraw or actually do, create inner turmoil. Seneca's goal is the invulnerable self.

The limitation of the relation of self and world is a form of the Greek Stoic ideal of *autarkeia* (1994a, 195); unlike for the Greeks, it can be achieved in Seneca if we do not become slaves to distorted natural needs vis-à-vis the external world. Minimizing and managing the link with the world by the self ends dependence and vulnerability, allowing the self to return to itself and become its own "artifex vitae" (1994b, 8; 1925, 18.6ff., 25.6, 50.6, 62.1, 80.3ff.), to belong to itself (71.36), to control itself (75.18, 85.10–12, 90.34, 93.2–3, 113.31), and to stand outside its own pain (85.29). In all such instances the self is conceived as the external agent able to turn toward its own interior self, to mind or thought.

The following quotations capture the necessary link between independence of the world and the *sui cura*:

> The mind must be recalled into itself from the external world completely: it must trust itself, rejoice at itself, look up to what is its own, withdraw as much as possible from what is foreign to it and turn its attention to itself.

> [Utique animus ab omnibus externis in se revocandus est: sibi confidat, se

gaudeat, sua suspiciat, recedet quantum potest ab alienis et se sibi adplicet. (1994a, 14; see also 1925, 31.3ff., 35.4, 42.10, 51.5, 66.39, and passim)]

The mind grows from within itself, it nourishes itself and administers to itself.

[animus ex se crescit, se ipse alit, se exercet. (1925, 80.3)]

Breaking the affective link to the world opens the self to its own resources, that is, to its own inner nature. Reason and judgment are the faculties that both are and also govern the self's resources and lead to a measured, ordered self-management and control. "[Ratio] omnia faciet ex imperio suo nihilque inopinatum accidet" ("[Reason] will do everything by its own power, and nothing unanticipated will occur" [1994b, 8]), with an understood causal relation between the two clauses: in a word, self-rule. This is the form interiority takes in Seneca; the difference of his conception bears the mark of prior Stoic thought: return to one's own interiority (that is, mind and reason); understand its difference from the world and minimize the contact between them.

According to Foucault, the fourth-century B.C.E. Greeks identified self-rule as an activity parallel in form to the activity of magistracy and management of the *oikos*; for the post-Augustan Seneca the ideal of self-rule takes the form of a nearly complete withdrawal from all external activities, entailing instead a turning of the self inward toward the self as mind and its potential for absolute self-control and invulnerability to an extremely erratic and dangerous world.

Self-relation in Seneca clearly takes the form of the return to the self, or as Foucault labels it, the care of the self (see, e.g., 1925, 49.12). The former is preferable since it points more directly to the self-world opposition that is fundamental to Seneca and from which the return arises. Breaking the affective link between the two is often made to seem relatively easy, a matter of limiting desire, which in turn will eliminate the fear of loss of the acquired means (such as wealth) of satisfying distorted desires in an unstable world.

It is worth noting that in the *Letters to Lucilius*—presumably among Seneca's last work, written during the three years before his death when he had left Nero's Rome and an envious Senate—the references to fortune and the instability of the external world become much more pronounced (e.g., 37.5, 45.9, 51.8, 70.7, 91.4ff., 101.5, 115.16, and passim). Seneca undoubtedly had some direct experience that fortified his sense of the world's instability. Often the world forces itself in on the self. Seneca can here admit that "All life is a form of slavery. One must thus get used to one's own circumstances. . . . there is nothing so harsh that the undisturbed mind does not find some solace in it" (1994a, 10). It is again a matter of self-control, of management of the link with the world.

The withdrawal into the self has a particular form in Seneca. If the wise man "in se reconditur, secum est" ("is concealed within himself and lives within himself" [1925, 9.16]), then his connection to the world diminishes; his activity or outward conduct is curtailed simultaneously with the return to the self. This represents a shift away from the focus on action toward a focus on interiority of self that characterizes the early Hellenistic period but not the age of Cicero. What is central to the self and is the locus of the return is the animus, roughly the mind or consciousness: "Nullum [bonum] est, nisi quod animus ex se sibi invenit" (27.3). It is not so much that the self stands outside its own mind; rather the mind contains its own agential function, and is able to turn toward itself. Letter 56 in *Ad Lucilium Epistulae Morales*, demonstrates Seneca's focus on animus as interiority quite clearly; in addition: "Summum bonum in animo contineamus" in the sense of a limitation to the mind (74.16).

For Seneca *honestum*, as noted earlier, and *virtus* relate to consciousness or thought, not action: "virtus . . . recta ratio est" (66.32). F. H. Sandbach points out that state of mind had being, since for the Stoics the psyche or animus was material (1975, 92; 1925, 106.4–5; cf. Diogenes Laertius 1925, 7.89). The animus as motive force is the center and essence of the individual self and the origin of impulse (impetus) (1925, 113.10, 17, and passim). The animus is also "Iustitiae . . . corpus" (113.13) or a material that takes on the form (habitus) of justice and other virtues. In this letter Seneca traces the process from the incitement by external stimuli to the action that eventuates: the animus is the focus of the process.

Seneca distinguishes between mind and body (1994b, 3, 5; 1925, 65.16ff.), although the animus, the seat of reason and judgment, regulates desires and the impulse toward action and thus the relation to the world. Reason and mind constitute the form of human nature, and self-reflexivity as well, as the ability of consciousness to see itself in relation to the world or turned toward its own resources (41.8–9, 76.9ff., and passim). The self is placed between itself and world.

Seneca defines reason primarily in individual terms, as human nature, and not as a part of the rational cosmos; this is what is referred to as identity today: "Animum intuere, qualis quantusque sit" (76.32). The self in its rational scrutiny of itself ("se sibi adplicere" [1994a, 14]), in its use of its own rational resources to manage its relation to the world in fulfillment of its own nature, comes to its own gaudium: a stable state of rational contentment that is opposed to the motion of desire, an inner joy as opposed to the outward expression of it, which is laetitia (but cf. 1925, 23.3 and below):

> We therefore ask how the mind moves along a steady, uniform course, how it is favorable to itself and observes its own joy and how this joy can be uninterrupted; [the mind] remains in a quiet and peaceful state, neither exalting nor depressing itself: that will be tranquility.

> [Ergo quaerimus quomodo animus semper aequali secundoque cursu eat propitiusque sibi sit et sua laetus aspiciat et hoc gaudium non interrumpat, sed placido statu maneat nec attollens se umquam nec deprimens: id tranquillitas erit. (1994a, 2)]

In Seneca tranquility (or, *aequanimitas* in, e.g., 1925, 91.18) often denotes, as above, precisely the same state as *gaudium:* "Hanc stabilem animi sedem . . . ego tranquillitatem voco" ("I call this stable place of the mind tranquility" [ibid.]). But there is a danger that this tranquility could be taken as Epicurean *ataraxia,* the stable state of mental pleasure promoted by the absence of fear and pain. This becomes an issue in the *De vita beata* when Seneca considers the claims of pleasure and its relation to virtue. This involves a response to Epicurean thought, but without any initial reference to Epicurus himself. When it comes to the latter, Seneca says that Epicurus's law of pleasure, sober and restrained as that pleasure is, bears a relation to Seneca's own law of virtue (1994b, 12). Pleasure remains a matter of limits.

Then Seneca redefines *gaudium* and *tranquillitas* in terms of virtue and the *summum bonum:* "these are in fact good; yet they do not complete the highest good [of virtue] but follow in its wake" ("sunt enim ista bona, sed consequentia summum bonum, non consummantia" [15]). This is not a denial that interiority of self is central but an attempt to substitute for the Epicurean state of undisturbed pleasure a rational but still inner state. It is the interiority or the state of rational consciousness that is central to Seneca's thought—what is "intra te ipsum" (1925, 23.3).

The question raised was whether a historical philosophic focus on interiority determined the form of self-relation that emerged. This seems true, since the self-relation in Epicurus is, in terms of its interiority, vastly similar to self-relation in Seneca: the inner state of being has simply been shifted from one of feeling to one of rationality. In both cases the focus on interiority allows for the form of self-relation as relation to one's interiority. Both Epicurus and Seneca see the potential harm arising for the individual from the world outside. Epicurus, however, begins with the continuum of self and context; everything is constituted of atoms within the void; everything "touches"; and the mind receives *eidola* or images from its environment incessantly. The danger lies in this continuity because *eidola* may be received that are detrimental to the desired peace of mind. It is the function of knowledge in the form of *doxai* to deflect that constant possibility. In Seneca the same inevitable continuity exists, but there is, as noted, a much stronger sense of the separate individual self, as a rational entity, which must stand against and limit the effect of the world.

Epicurus, as noted above, saw the individual as placed within a material world, and his doctrine allows only implicitly for self-reflexivity on the part of the individual. Maintaining a state of *ataraxia* is in fact self-management, but Epicurus's focus on the *doxai* as in promptu entities of consciousness ready to deflect the potential harmful effects of incoming stimuli tends to emphasize the technical structure of conscious process without giving rise to the notion of the self's reflexive concern for the self. Further, *doxai* such as those in *Pythocles* are developed by the master, Epicurus, for the use of not entirely proficient followers: Seneca substitutes self-relation for this Epicurean arrangement (although of course he also gives advice to Lucilius).

The Care of the Self makes the case that the *sui cura* characterizes western thought from 300 B.C.E. until the end of the first two centuries of the common era. Foucault says that earlier Greek thought is not directly concerned with self-reflexivity. But neither, as I have argued, are Epicurus and the early Hellenistic thinkers. Concern for the self characterizes Cicero, Lucretius, and others of the first century B.C.E. even less. It seems, then, that Foucault has taken a post-Augustan notion, that is, a heightened notion of the isolatability of the self and of self-insight—what is evident in Seneca—and made it the central context of thought since the death of Alexander.

F. H. Sandbach would offer support to Foucault: he assumes that an explicit relation to self characterizes the Stoic tradition from its inception (that is, Zeno), and that this is in part derived from Cynic and Megarian influence (1975, 22, 29–30). It is true that Stoicism is characterized by the scientific form of self-relation—that is, humans studying human nature—but there is no passage from the earlier Stoics that is as explicit about self-relation as the following from Seneca about his customary practice at the end of the day:

> I scrutinize my whole day and go over my words and deeds again; I don't hide anything from myself and don't neglect anything.

[totum diem meum scrutor factaque ac dicta mea remetior; nihil mihi ipse abscondo, nihil transeo. (1928, 3.36.3; see also 1925, 83.2)]

What distinguishes Seneca is his taking the position of the self under duress in arguing for a return to the self. His tendency is less to take an objective or scientific perspective on the process of the return of the self to the self than to render the experience of the self in the process: in a word, he stages the self seeking self-mastery in the context of the world. This is only in part due to the oft-noted connection between Seneca's life and his work. On the other hand, he is never completely detached from the traditional scientific study of human nature always current among Stoics—as in Letter 121 on the (self-reflexive) awareness of the animal and human of their own *constitutio* or nature, and the priority of the "mei cura" (121.17). Sandbach also discusses the self-reflexivity of the later Hierocles (1975, 170ff.), and notes "a new emphasis" on the opposition between the external and the individual's interiority in Epictetus (166; cf. Rist 1978, 265). But these are already well established in Seneca.

It should also be noted that the care of the self in Seneca, unlike the same inclination in Christianity, is not a process of self-knowledge or self-decipherment. The self knows itself already, the burden caused by its desires and the natural and necessary centrality of rationality, virtue, and *honestum*. Self-awareness is the given, as noted in the paragraph just above. Self-realization, however, must be achieved by a careful and nearly complete detachment from the world, and the defeat of the desires which made for the attachment in the first place; this gives natural primacy to reason and virtue, and strengthens their possession. But again, this is not a self-hermeneutic, as James Bernauer has noted (1987, 62).

All of this having been said, it seems most likely that modernity, based on the self-reflexive notion that the self is capable of an external, objective view of itself as related to/detached from the world or the "other," has some of its roots in Seneca and the post-Augustan age. Remember that the external world is at first a threat to Descartes's attempt to reach the truth of things. Another factor is the focus on interiority, which is an aspect of modernity as well, at least until it began to unravel well into the twentieth century. In Seneca the notion of self-relation derives from a focus on interiority coupled with the Stoic notion of *autarkeia*. Whether interiority functions in the same way for Descartes and the ensuing age of modernity remains to be seen. But clearly the post-Augustan age marks the beginning of an explicit self-relation and is thus in some degree the origin of modern self-consciousness.

Foucault says that the era of the Christian flesh was one in which self-decipherment and a hermeneutics of desire were the mode of self-relation, a turning inward of the self. Self-decipherment is present in the Hellenistic and Roman periods, becoming one of the elements of self-relation in Seneca (cf. Bernauer 1987, 62). Self-decipherment in its relation to the constitution of oneself as a subject of knowledge appears in the seventeenth century in Descartes as well; whether his focus is the same as that of the foregoing is a question which is situated by the analysis, and it is an important question for understanding the modern subject. Foucault's obscurity concerning the long Christian era in Europe is a hindrance to the understanding of the genealogy of this subject, but certain questions must be asked. Is the sixteenth century a period of self-decipherment (Foucault also promised a book on this century, and his interest in that period has been discussed by James Bernauer 1987, 50) and is it therefore closely related to Descartes's enterprise? Are the turns toward interiority in philosophy cyclic so that a genealogy of self-relation would produce different forms of interiority in different eras? Does Descartes in fact institute a new form of interiority within this genealogy?

‹◌ 6 ◌›

Renaissance Humanism, Interiority, and Self-Relation

I n *The Use of Pleasure* and *The Care of the Self* and in scattered references, Foucault generally speaks of self-relation in Christian Europe as taking the form of self-decipherment and self-purification. This means that the individual was obligated to examine its own desires, inclinations, and impulses or to apply a hermeneutics to consciousness and its hidden recesses. The results of these discovery procedures were then to be matched with a licit/illicit index of thoughts and behaviors. This suggests a measure of self-relation as well as conformation to an explicit code. In the previous chapter I discuss Foucault's turn toward self-relation, the provenance of this new genealogical impulse and the conflicts that arise with his earlier work, particularly *The History of Sexuality*, volume 1. And ultimately my inquiry is directed at a more explicit understanding of Descartes, modern philosophy, and modernity in general as constituting a particular historical ontology of human nature.

Foucault's ontology arises from the present. What characterizes human nature during the Enlightenment is the self-reflexive positioning of the individual, which, like Descartes, looks to its own interiority as constituting its identity: the subject of knowledge committed to knowing in particular, and through itself, the intricacies of its own inner nature and then the world external to that nature. In *The History of Sexuality* volume 1, Foucault suggests that the Christian tradition of self-decipherment and the practice of confession in particular stand behind this epistemological imperative as it was secularized from the seventeenth century onward. But questions are inevitable: was self-decipherment a constant and primary imperative over the intervening fourteen hundred years?

For example, James Bernauer assumes this constancy when he argues that "[w]ithin Christianity, there has taken place an interiorization or subjectivization of the human being" (1987, 52); and "[d]espite the intensification of self-examination, however, Roman culture did not issue in a need for a hermeneutics of the self, because it did not fashion the self as an obscure text which required decipherment" (62). Or was it merely one practice that arose in the rather peripheral monastic setting but was gradually universalized (as Foucault's text seems to suggest), one technique that was in place, ready to be adapted by the new secularizing forces of knowledge for the pursuit Foucault identifies as "the invention of man"? This invention of man is in fact the prime example of the scientific self-reflection that characterizes the modern age.

There are clearly other factors involved in this genealogy of self-relation. As the previous chapter indicates, one important issue is the periodic tendency of philosophic argument and moral advice to center on "interiority" instead of taking up a focus on exterior act and statement. The argument is, again, that this is not a historical constant and that an overall concern for interiority in any period profoundly affects the conception of self-relation during that time. The argument in this chapter is that among humanists in the fourteenth and the sixteenth century there is a distinguishable difference that circulates around this notion of interiority. This humanist tradition is only one of many intellectual traditions in the European Renaissance, but it may be indicative of overall tendencies. In the fourteenth century the locus of inquiry and thought is interiority or consciousness, but by the sixteenth century a tendency toward the textual or the externalized is firmly in place. Then interiority becomes a secondary term, in that thought, feeling, will, and intention are considered to be accessible only through the verbal text or the act considered as a sign or representation. This focus appears as once again transformed during the age of Descartes.

The notion of self-relation leads to a questioning of Foucault's earlier conception of the method of genealogy as contingent, subjectless history, and he clearly questions it with the notion that each culture conceives of the precultural or acultural individual that subjectivates itself or is subjectivated—that is, becomes a cultural subject by some means or other. Self-relation is one possible form of subjectivation. In other words, there can be a genealogy of the subject itself in terms of the various cultural means by which the individual undergoes subjectivation. The argument in this and the prior chapter attempts to rearticulate and to further this genealogy of self-relation during part of the Christian period that Foucault's arguments did not cover. This revision and extension takes the particular form of an argument that during the early Hellenistic period, in the post-Augustan era, during the fourteenth and then the seventeenth centuries, philosophic questioning is governed by a focus on interiority—and that this determines a particular form of self-relation. Further, while these eras of interiority produce a more intense form of self-relation, in the textual era of the sixteenth century self-relation seems to disappear as an important concern—only to return with Descartes in the following century.

There is no attempt here to complete the genealogy or to survey its permutations over the twelve hundred years of Christianity prior to the modern period. That is beyond my scope. What I attempt is to examine self-relation and interiority in the Renaissance or late premodern period in Europe, in the fourteenth and sixteenth centuries, as it manifests itself in the limited venue of humanist thought. This may provide some insight into how these concerns come to be constructed by Descartes and the seventeenth century; this latter provides the material for chapter 7.

There are some examples of work done on the Middle Ages from a Foucauldian perspective. Philip Barker in *Michel Foucault: Subversions of the Subject* attempts to construct the shifts in the "power/knowledge network" that occur from the tenth to the twelfth century in northwest Europe. His concerns are: the emergence of primogeniture and the lineal family unit, as well as the appearance of the transparent, self-reflexive subject in philosophers, such as Abelard, who were concerned with confession.

《◎》

The shift from interiority to textuality is particularly clear among the humanists of the Renaissance, whose prolific writings, while not philosophic, display strong theoretical tendencies. Petrarch is the best example of the tendency toward interiority and intensified self-relation in the fourteenth century, while the institution of imitation as it comes to fruition in the sixteenth century indicates a shift toward a focus on externalized activity such as verbal representation and visible or material action.

Petrarch is by some accounts the first and by all accounts one of the greatest humanists. The tendency among Petrarch scholars has been both to recognize his focus on interiority and to ignore it (see, e.g., Trinkaus 1970, passim). A great deal of Petrarchan poetry, both by Petrarch and his later imitators throughout Europe, is usually read as self-reflexive. It has always been said that these poems are about the men who love, the feminine object serving merely as a stimulus. And they are indeed analyses of love-devotion by the very ones caught in that obsessive web. What I seek here, however, is Petrarch's more direct articulation of self-reflexive positioning, which is more evident in some of the treatises on the religious life and on the relation of nature to art.

But even in these treatises Petrarch is often so vague in developing his position that his reference to interiority is obscure. In the *Secretum* Franciscus explains that victimization by Fortune leads to his *accidie:* in the words of Augustinus (that is, a representation of St. Augustine), Franciscus's spiritual adviser in the text,

> Tu ne igitur in tanto rerum humanarum turbine, tanta varietate successum, tantaque caligine futurorum et, ut breviter dicam, sub imperio positus Fortune.

> [In such a whirlwind of human concerns, in such a variety of successiveness, and with such obscurity concerning the future, lest you, to speak briefly, be placed beneath the dominion of Fortune. (Petrarca 1955b, 116)]

As in Seneca, the individual stands over against the onslaught of the world. It is easy to think of the *Secretum* as a Christian-Senecan inner dialogue (with a spiritual adviser) concerning the individual's attempt to reach salvation. And as we have seen, a focus on interiority lends itself to that kind of opposition between self and world just noted in the quotation. In the sixteenth century, human nature is coextensive with textuality.

Petrarch's description of the solitary man in the *Vita solitaria* (another text about self, world, and salvation) is similarly general, although here and in the previous passage the model of the individual under pressure—or free—from external forces is evident:

> Nulli penitus invidet, nullum odit; sorte contentus sua et fortune inuriis inaccessus, nichil metuit, nichil cupit . . . scit vite hominum pauca sufficere, et summas verasque divitias nil optare, summum imperium nil timere.

> [He envies none inwardly, he hates no man; content with his own lot and inaccessible to the injuries of fortune, he fears nothing, he desires nothing . . . he knows that very little is sufficient to maintain life; he does not desire great riches, nor does he fear the highest authority. (308)]

In these statements Petrarch resembles Seneca, although the self-reflexive turning of the self toward the self is so far only implied by the turning away from the external world and its threats (see Tripet 1967, 41ff.).

Petrarch elsewhere renders this same situation of the individual in a more specific manner, one that makes his orientation toward interiority evident. Augustinus concludes the first book of the *Secretum* with a specific description of the consciousness responding to the pressure of its surrounding environment:

> Conglobantur siquidem species innumere et imagines rerum visibilium, que corporeis introgresse sensibus, postquam singulariter admisse sunt, catervatim in anime penetralibus densantur; eamque, nec ad id genitam nec tam multorum difformiumque capacem, pergravant atque confundunt. Hinc pestis illa fantasmatum vestros discerpens laceransque cogitatus, meditationibus clarificis.

> [Numberless presentations and images of visible things crowd in through the corporal senses; although they gain entrance one by one, they thicken like collecting armies in the inner parts of the soul; and they oppress and confuse the soul, which is not born for this nor is capable of handling so many and such deformed images. Hence this curse of appearances tearing apart and lacerating our thought, [obstructing] clear meditation. (64; see also 45, 64; and Erasmus 1971, 1:54)]

The body-soul dialectic is focused within interiority: the chaotic external world is transformed into the turbulence of images and impressions within the mind; the effect of this is to beat down upon and disable by distraction its divine part. It is a failure of self-focus. In this passage the individual under attack by Fortune becomes the individual consciousness or mind, partly divine, but overwhelmed by means of its connection to the body and, through that, to the external material world. The goal is to exclude the external from its interference with interiority, or the turning of the mind inward toward itself.

Augustinus summarizes the state of the individual consciousness under the pressure of stimuli a little later, comparing it to an oversown field in which the competing plants choke and impede each others' growth:

> ut in animo nimis occupato nil utile radices agat, nichilque fructiferum coalescat; tuque inops consilii modo huc modo illuc mira fluctuatione volvaris; nusquam integer, nusquam totus.

> [so that in the mind too much occupied, nothing useful is fixed in its foundations; and nothing fruitful comes together; and you, lacking counsel, whirl around with extraordinary convolutions—never one, never whole. (1955a, 68; see also the "intestina discordia" of mind, 1965, 1:189–90)]

The mind is never whole until it turns inward to itself, separating itself from the world.

The *Secretum* and other similar writings lack the density that would be called philosophic, yet Petrarch is specific enough in developing the various elements of his model of individual interiority under the stimulus of the external environment. At one point in the *Secretum* Augustinus repeats the Platonic doctrine of the soul descendent into flesh and corrupted by it: "Nempe passiones ex corpora commistione subortas oblivionemque nature melioris" (Passions springing up from the connection with the body, and the forgetting of our better nature); and Franciscus draws from Augustinus's citation of Virgil the four passions that threaten the consciousness: pleasure, pain (doleo), fear, and desire: "ita quattuor velut flatibus aversis humanarum mentium tranquillitas perit" (the tranquillity of the human mind is destroyed by the four, as it were, averse winds [1955a, 64]). The passions are interior phenomena that arise from one's material nature spontaneously or as a consequence of the material connection to externality; all these potentially disturb stability of mind.

Petrarch, then, locates the scene of turbulence as within interiority. Whatever their origin, the elements of disturbance of mind are located as interior entities: imagines, fantasmata, passiones. Petrarch's treatment of Avignon in the *Secretum* as a source of stimuli harmful to stability of mind is a case in point. He has Franciscus (Petrarch's self-representation within the text) describe in vivid detail this *turbulentissima urbs:* it has smells ("graveolentes semitas" or noisome streets); sounds ("tantum confusis vocibus clamorem," "a great clamor of mingled voices," and the "stridorem" of grating cart wheels); and sights (the "spetacula" of extremely rich and extremely poor people intermingled). But the external causes are represented as within the interior of the self: "Que omnia et sensus melioribus assuetos conficiunt et generosis animis eripiunt quietem" (all of which overthrow the senses, accustomed to better things, and rip away the peace of noble minds [120]). Augustinus's reply invokes the same kind of model: "Quod si unquam intestinus tumultus tue mentis conquiesceret, fragor iste circumtonans, michi crede, sensus quidem pulsaret sed animum non moveret" (I believe that if the internal tumult of your mind were to be quieted, this surrounding noise would agitate the senses, but not disturb the mind [ibid.]). The *animus* must turn inward toward its own potential order as the only defense against an abusive exteriority.

This response is important because it makes another aspect of interiority clear: placed in an environment and connected as it is to a material body, the mind must necessarily undergo stimuli, often ones that are, as in the above case, potentially harmful. The problem is to control the incoming stimuli in such a way that they do not disturb the desired tranquil stability; Petrarch makes this evident in some of the previously cited passages.

One of Petrarch's remedies is to seek a less threatening environment, one set up as the diametrical other of the raucous and overwhelming city; this is in general what is known as "solitude" and is reminiscent, in the *Secretum* at least, of Petrarch's own Valchiusa, his home near Avignon. But in the *Vita solitaria* Petrarch claims to have discovered "qualis solitarie vite status interior sit" ("what the internal state of the solitary life is") and this has to do with the proper state of mind, not external circumstances:

> hec solitudo utique, non solitaria vita est, ea scilicet quam suspiro, quamvis exterius simillima videatur, eque hominum turbis educta, sed non eque passionibus expedita.

> [this solitude is not the solitary life that I long for, although it appears similar on the outside, equally apart from the crowds but not equally separated from the passions. (344)]

In the *Secretum* Augustinus reminds Franciscus of his retreats into positive and regenerating solitude:

> nunc in aprice vallis umbraculo dulci sapore correptus optato silentio fruebaris; nusquam otiosus, mente aliquid altum semper agitans, et, solis Musis comitantibus nusquam solus.

> [Now in the sunny bower of the sweet valley redolent with scents, you will enjoy yourself in desired silence; never otiose, always stirring your mind to higher things and, with the Muses as companions, never alone. (86)]

The passage suggests that the pleasing stimuli of a rural scene and its relative silence and harmony are beneficial to the mind, which may turn inward in undisturbed meditation in a way that is impossible under the assaultive impact of the city. This organized, stable, and self-referential consciousness, which is possible in solitude, is of course only the first step in the Petrarchan ascent toward the final end of salvation. This stage of "passionibus expedita" is the breaking of the affective link with the body and the world that allows the self to turn inward toward its own divine substance.

Yet solitude in the *Vita solitaria* is always something of an escape: it is necessary for Petrarch to develop a method to maintain mental tranquility in even the worst external circumstances:

sed ita ut, siqua me necessitas in urbem cogat, solitudinem in populo, atque
in medio tempestatis portum michi conflare didicerim, artificio non omnibus
noto sensibus imperitandi ut quod sentiunt non sentiant.

[thus if any necessity should drive me to the city, I would have learned solitude
among crowds and have reached the port amid storms, and by the little known
skill of commandeering all the senses so that what I sense I don't perceive.
(336)]

The method is based on Quintilian, 10:3, 27–30, who argues that if one
concentrates on the work at hand "tota mente . . . nichil eorum que oculis
vel auribus incursant ad animum pervenient" (with the whole mind . . .
then none of these things that enter the eyes and ears penetrate to the
mind [ibid.]).

Short of death, or the cessation of consciousness, sensation from
stimuli entering from the body or exteriority is inevitable. And since, as
Petrarch understands it, external solitude is a retreat more than a permanent
situation, there must be a method of diverting the potentially harmful effect
of these entering stimuli. Petrarch's ultimate statement of his method is as
follows:

Et profecto sic est. Nam et ego unum hoc in necessitate remedium inveni,
ut in ipsis urbium tumultibus imaginarium michi solitudinem secessu aliquo,
quantum sinor, et cogitatione conficiam, vincens ingenio fortunam.

[And it is certainly thus. For I found one remedy in this necessity: that
in the tumults of the city I would create for myself in thought a certain
solitude of imagination by a kind of withdrawal as much as I was able, thereby
overcoming fortune by innate ability. (338)]

Although Petrarch prefers a natural solitude, the city is the setting that
produces most clearly the sense of self-relation within interiority which
characterizes his texts. Self-relation becomes the return to the authentic self.

Petrarch's mediate end is a controlled state of consciousness, stable
and harmonious, achieved by the turning of the self as mind toward its
own substance. In the *Secretum* reason is called upon to curb cupiditates or
appetitus (41, 50). In the *Vita solitaria* Petrarch follows Quintilian's reasoned
act of will. In both cases interior operations work to control the content and
organization of mind. In the *Secretum* the process is given generally by
Augustinus:

Quid enim aliud celestis doctrina Platonis admonet, nisi animum a libidinibus corporeis arcendum et eradenda fantasmata, ut ad pervidenda divinitatis archana, cui proprie mortalitatis annexa cogitatio est, purus expeditusque consurgat?

[For what else does the doctrine of the divine Plato recommend, unless separating the mind from bodily desires and eradicating images so that it may rise up, pure and unencumbered, toward a vision of the divine arcana, to which thought of mortality is properly connected. (98)]

W. J. Bouwsma connects this process with Stoicism (1975, 19, 28–31, and passim). The Stoic doctrine of reason suggests reconciliation with divine reason and nature, but in the *Secretum* there is a fundamental opposition between external nature (or Fortuna) and individual interiority; and this is more nearly a Senecan Stoicism as described in chapter 5.

Once freed from the pressure of incoming stimuli and thus of the world, the animus, turning inward toward its own substance, will rise of its own nobility (1955a, 46). But the mediate end, and the secular level of the process—the level at which Petrarch agrees with and draws from the pagan philosophers, particularly Seneca—is the achievement of "that tranquility and serenity of mind" that is ultimately implied by the control by the mind of its link with the world.

In Petrarch the chaotic external world is a threat, but it is also an aid, and in Petrarch's writings there appear specific techniques based on experience which serve to break the affective dominance of the world over consciousness. Most prominent in the *Secretum* is the meditation on death, which is both a turning inward and a means to limit the effect of incoming sensible impressions. Franciscus's experience at night in bed is a "natural" example, although the result is "cogitationes immergor precipueque noctibus, cum diurnis curis relaxatus animus se in se ipsum recolligit" (I plunge into these thoughts every single day and especially at night, when the mind, relieved of daily cares, recalls itself into itself [58]). Once again, the absence of external interference leads to an intensified self-relation.

But Augustinus recommends a willed contemplation of death that limits the effect of currently incoming stimuli and at the same time, at least in a historical sense, makes use of a selection of these stimuli through recollection. For memory is based on experience of the world. To know death generally, Augustine argues, is not enough: "immorari diutius oportet atque acerrima meditatione singula morientium membra percurrere" (one must die for a long time and count over every aspect of dying with wise meditation). He proceeds to do just this for Franciscus—give the details of death in its most horrifying and disgusting forms—and then concludes:

> Que omnia [the details of death] facilius ac velut in promptu et ad manum collocata succurrent, si cui familiariter obversari ceperit memorandum aliquod conspecte mortis exemplum; tenacior enim esse solet visorum quam auditorum recordatio.

> [All of these come to mind more easily and, as it were, ready to hand if a particularly memorable visual image of death begins to appear intimately; for a visual memory is usually more lasting than an auditory one. (54; see Trinkaus 1979, 62ff.)]

The interesting aspect of this process is its interiority. Meditation is, of course, an interior function; but Augustine also locates the materials of this meditation as interior phenomena. The details of the *recordatio* are seated in the memory; they represent a selection from past impressions to which the individual has been subject, in effect a choice or limitation of what enters the mind to what is useful toward the important end of this meditation. These impressions are sifted out of memory and held *in promptu* so that may be called upon at a moment's notice. The successful meditation on death further prepares the now enlightened consciousness to control or to avoid the possible disorienting impact of the world or Fortune—that which promises only death in the end. The important part is that the entire process is located within interiority, that it represents the mind as focused inwardly upon itself and calling upon its own resources. Self-relation, as determined by this interior focus, becomes a return to the self by cutting off the world and by intensified self-focus on one's interiority.

How does Petrarch's interiority fit with Foucault's general notion of Christian decipherment? Petrarch's purging of the soul of passions is more Platonic, but it also entails a recognition of what has to be purged. And if there is no explicit code in Petrarch, that is the result of putting a humanist and more individualized text against texts from a more strictly religious and theological tradition. The code is implicit in Petrarch.

There are more similarities between Petrarch's method and Seneca's and Epicurus's, but primarily because they all represent a certain philosophic turn toward interiority. In the *Secretum* what replaces the Epicurean *doxai* are the details of death drawn from memory and focused on in meditation. In Epicurus *doxai* are the forms of knowledge derived from the Master to be absorbed and maintained in the minds of novice Epicureans, and usually collected into an *epitomé*—a collection of the most important *doxai*, ones that will ensure peace of mind. In contrast, the materials of the Petrarchan meditation derive more directly from individual experience. But the dissimilarity dissipates to some degree when it becomes clear that part of the logic of the *Secretum* is implicit in its form: it is a dialogue in which Augustinus serves Franciscus as a spiritual Master. And, because the *Secretum* involves a complex interaction between two interlocutors, Augustinus can also be said to represent part of the split Petrarchan self recommending a course of action to itself. Augustinus in fact mediates between self-relation and a relation that is theoretically between two distinct persons, emphasizing the former. But the latter draws a parallel between the framework of the *Secretum* and Petrarch's more general conception of the fruitful contact with the writings of the ancients, often referred to as Petrarch's doctrine of imitation. It might also be called a theory of reading, but the issue ultimately turns on the relation between the introjected other and the self.

In the *Vita solitaria* the contact with the greatest ancient minds is part of the overall process of interiority leading toward salvation. We are, according to Petrarch, in the position of "beneficii literarum a maioribus accepti" (receiving the gift of letters from the great); the prior reading of ancient texts becomes through recollection part of the process of the turning inward of the mind:

> Mittere retro memoriam, perque omnia secula et per omnes terras animo vagari; versari passim et colloqui cum omnibus, qui fuerunt gloriosi viri; atque ita presentes malorum omnium opifices oblivisci, nonnumquam et teipsum, et supra se elevatum animum inferre rebus ethereis, meditari quid illic agitur.

> [Send the memory back and let the mind wander through every century and all countries; dwell everywhere in conversation with all those who were glorious men; and thus forget current artificers of evil deeds, sometimes ourselves, and lead the mind, already raised above itself, into the realm of ethereal things, to meditate what occurs there. (1955a, 356)]

This is generally referred to as "il colloquio coi grande, sopratutto dell'antichità" (ibid., fn. 2; see Wilkins 1961, 21, and Bec 1976, 3–17). But what is interesting is that the process is an entirely interior one, the external contact with ancient writings thought of as a solitary conversation, that is, in the mind, and as being transformed into materials of memory; that, memory, is the actual locus of the mind's wanderings in the above passage.

Petrarch is more specific about the function of reading in the *Secretum* and in some of the letters of the *Familiari*. In the *Secretum* reading takes on the form of interiorization very clearly, the *sententiae* or thoughts derived from reading representing a limited selection from experience of a rather large scope, again controlled by the perceiving consciousness. The selection or limitation is clearly put when Augustinus speaks of the method for retaining what is chosen: "quod cum intenta tibi ex lectione contigerit, imprime sententiis utilibus (ut incipiens dixeram) certas notas, quibus velut uncis memoria volentes abire contineas" (When you arrive at your purpose from reading, mark the useful thoughts [as I said starting out] with fixed signs with which you will hold onto what you wish in memory, as if with hooks [126]).

> Quotiens legenti salutares se se offerunt sententie, quibus vel excitari sentis animum vel frenari, noli viribus ingenii fidere, sed illas in memorie penetralibus absconde multoque studio tibi familiares effice; ut, quod experti solent medici, quocunque loco vel tempore dilationis impatiens morbus invaserit, habeas velut in animo conscripta remedia.

> [When beneficial thoughts offer themselves from reading, which you observe either to excite the mind or restrain it, be unwilling to trust to the strength of natural ability, but conceal these things in the deeper parts of memory and with much effort make them your intimates; so that, as with experienced physicians, in whatever time or place the disease, impatient to spread, were to attack, you will have the remedy already well inscribed, so to speak, in the mind. (122)]

Petrarch is quite explicit about the disease: "Sunt enim quedam sicut in corporibus humanis sic in animis passiones" (Just as there are passions and affections of the body in humans, so also in the mind). Like the *doxai*, the *sententiae* are retained in memory to combat and neutralize the effect of potentially harmful incoming stimuli, if not to exclude exteriority altogether from the mind so that it may turn inward upon itself. The text continues:

> Quis enim ignorat, exempli gratia, esse quosdam motus tam precipites ut, nisi eos in ipsis exordiis ratio frenaverit, animum corpusque et totum hominem perdant.

> [For who could ignore, for example, certain motions so immediate that they destroy mind and body and the whole human being unless reason restrains them at their inception. (ibid.; see also 122, fn. 2)]

In book 3 of the *Secretum* Petrarch repeats the notion of the *sententiae* stored in memory and their use, although it is a response to Augustinus's jibe about the triviality of such a procedure:

Est autem, nisi fallor, grande solatium tam claris septum esse comitibus; itaque fateor talium exemplorum, velut quotidiane supellectilis, usum non reicio. Iuvat enim non modo in his incommodis, que michi vel natura tribuit vel casus; sed in his etiam, que tribuere possent, habere aliquid in promptu quo me soler.

[Unless I am mistaken, there is great comfort in being surrounded by such an outstanding group; and thus I confess I don't reject the daily use of my own supply of such examples. For it is an aid not only in these misfortunes that nature or chance have brought upon me; but even in these things which may occur—to have something in promptu with which to accustom or solace myself. (178; see also 126)]

These examples stand ready to ameliorate all possible interruptions of the individual's stable interior harmony. Even Augustinus agrees finally that such a process is useful—this interiorizing of the thoughts of others and the mode of recourse of the self toward the self of memory as a means of interior tranquility.

⟪◦◦⟫

Petrarch's theory of reading in the *Secretum* becomes, in the four important letters of the *Familiari* (or letters to friends), a theory of imitation. The two are very similar except that in imitation the recipients of the classical tradition seek to make these texts useful to their own speaking and writing. But the reader in the *Secretum* and the imitator in the *Familiari* are in similar positions, and the methods that govern the appropriate activity of each are theoretically parallel. Both raise the question of the individual in relation to the classical tradition and the method by which the individual will grow or change under the influence of the tradition. It is not so much that in imitation the focus is on the subsequent verbal production of the individual who imitates; the focus in Petrarch is actually on the transformation which occurs in the material received, that is, on the internalization of the material as the preparation that will ultimately result in enhanced speaking and writing by the imitator. In this sense imitation is almost identical to the theory of reading in the *Secretum,* in which *sententiae* selected from the tradition guard the tranquility of mind.

Imitation is also a question that continues to be discussed down through the sixteenth century; the changing attitudes lend themselves to the demonstration that there is a shift in theoretical focus in humanist intellectual activity from Petrarch's time to the later period: in brief, for

CHAPTER 6

Petrarch imitation is a matter that concerns the *animus* of both the classical author and the imitator; interiority is the locus about which questions of imitation circulate. In the sixteenth century imitation has to do with words or deeds of the model and the consequent statements and actions of the imitator—a focus on the externalized forms or representations of thoughts or things. Some critics mistakenly see the shift as a deterioration in creativity; it is rather a sign of an intellectual shift (cf. Greene 1976, 201–24).

There are several aspects of all proposed methods of imitation throughout the Renaissance that are similar. One of these is the conception of the model, the writer or the text to be imitated. In systems of imitation that are Sophist in conception, the model embodies the principle of the system and is the fountainhead or the origin of the tradition of discourse. This Master is the prior Subject discussed in chapter 1 and throughout this work. In Petrarch, for example,

> Siquem sane tam benigno lumine astra respexerint, ut ipse sibi sine externe opis adminiculo satis sit et per se ipsum magnificos sensus possit exprimere, multum habet quod dono gratie celestis ascribat . . . suum apibus morem linquat. Nos autem, quibus non tam magna contigerunt, apes imitari non pudeat.

> [If the stars were to shine on anyone with such a benign light that he is sufficient to himself without the support of any external prop, and from himself alone is able to produce great thoughts, then he possesses what he attributes to the gift of divine grace. . . . and he will leave his own practice to the bees. For us, however, to whom such greatness does not apply, it will not be shameful to imitate the bees. (1933–52, 1:8, ll. 119–26)]

In Castiglione, in the sixteenth century,

> Vero é che, o sia per favor delle stelle, o di natura, nascono alcuni accompagnati da tante grazie, che par che non siano nati, ma che un qualche dio con le proprie mani formati gli abbia ed ornati de tutti i beni dell'animo e del corpo. . . . e posson quei che non son da natura così perfettamente dotati, con studio e fatica limare e correggere in gran parte i defetti naturali

> [It is true that either by the favor of the stars or from nature certain ones are born accompanied by so many graces that they seem not so much born as formed by the very hands of some god and dressed out with all the goods of body and mind . . . and those who are not given such perfection by nature are able, with careful attention and effort, to erase and correct their natural defects for the most part (104, 105)]

by imitation of these masters. The same construction of the Subject or model appears in Roger Ascham's *The Schoolmaster* later in the century: "Surely Caesar and Cicero . . . [possessed] a singular prerogative of natural eloquence given unto them by God" (1967, 156).

These are theoretically similar statements of principle, of the arché of the system. They are necessarily given as justifications for the systems of imitation proposed. Any method of imitation assumes a tradition or precedent writer or text to be followed, and this raises the question of who is to be imitated and the question of the qualification for serving as model. But the model cannot be qualified from within the system. It is in fact extrasystematic or is in effect the principle or origin of system that is external to system—that is, prior to it—but justifies the system or serves as its center. The model is superendowed by nature or God with *ingenium* or the perfect capacity to speak and act well. It is necessary in such a system that the model not be trained but be endowed as a given so that the system of training or imitation may ensue from the model as both origin and standard (see, e.g., Cicero 1949, 1:2ff. and Derrida 1972, passim).

Petrarch's and Castiglione's methods of imitation differ in many ways, but they are fundamentally different in terms of focus: Petrarch treats imitation in terms of interiority, and for Castiglione imitation is the repetition of externalized activity. In the statements concerning the model quoted above Petrarch's emphasis is on the "magnificos sensus" or the thoughts, understanding and in general the capacity of mind; in Castiglione the model exhibits "grazia"—the desired perceptible quality—in speaking and acting. The focus is clearly now on externalized performance:

> E per darvi un esempio, vedete il signor don Ippolito da Este, cardinal di Ferrara, il quale tanto di felicità ha portato dal nascere suo, che la persona, lo aspetto, le parole, e tutti i sui movimenti sono talmente di questa grazia composti ed accommodati.

> [And to give you an example, look at Signor Don Ippolito of Este, Cardinal of Ferrara, who has brought forward such felicity from his own birth that his person, his look, his words and all his movements are truly composed of and fitting to such graces. (105)]

In the *Familiari* letters on imitation, Petrarch is concerned with the artist and his relation to the tradition, not the individual in need of ancient wisdom to help him maintain stability of mind in a chaotic world. Letter I, 8, to Thomas of Messina is one of the important texts, entitled "De inventione et ingenio" (Concerning invention and natural ability). Petrarch's emphasis from the first is on the transformation that the imitator of the ancients produces, given in terms of the familiar analogy of the bees:

> Cuius summa est: apes in inventionibus imitandas, que flores, non quales acceperint, referunt, sed caras ac mella mirifica quadam permixtione conficiunt.

> [Of which the best [advice from Seneca] is: you must imitate the bees for invention or finding because they bring back flowers: not what they originally encountered, but they produce wax and honey by a certain extraordinary mixing. (1933, 1:8, ll. 17–20; cf. Greene 1976, 208 and passim)]

The transformation is interior. What follows the above passage, however, is a consideration of whether it is appropriate to repeat the words of the model. Petrarch's answer is again to emphasize the transformation of the material within the imitator:

> Sed illud affirmo: elegantioris esse solertie, ut, apium imitatores, nostris verbis quamvis aliorum hominum sententias proferamus. Rursus nec huius stilum aut illius, sed unum nostrum conflatum ex pluribus habeamus.

> [But I affirm this: it is a more elegant skill if we, as imitators of the bees, produce in our own words any thoughts of other men. Again, we should have the style neither of this writer or another, but one constructed out of many. (ll. 32–35)]

Sententia means "thought" and/or "statement." If the meaning is the latter, then Petrarch seems very little different from sixteenth-century conceptions of imitation: style to style, given a variety of models.

But Petrarch moves immediately to the analogy of the silkworm, again focusing on the interior process of the imitator:

> felicius quidem, non apium more passim sparsa colligere, sed quorundam haud multo maiorum vermium exemplo, quorum ex visceribus sericum prodit, ex se ipso sapere potius et loqui, dummodo et sensus gravis ac verus et sermo esset ornatus.

> [It is even more favorable not [simply] to collect, according to the habit of the bees, what is scattered everywhere, but by the example of certain not much larger worms, which produce silk from their viscera, to understand and to speak more capably out of oneself and from oneself—with the proviso that the meaning is serious and true and the speech ornate. (ll. 36–40)]

Seneca's letter on imitation (1925, 84), which Macrobius repeats in his preface to the *Saturnalia,* and from which Petrarch draws here, is a good example of Seneca's own focus. In the letter he uses the analogy of the bees and others—the digestion of food, the chorus of many voices—to insist that the imitator transform his sources. The most frequent terms in the letter are *animus* and *ingenium,* the site of transformation:

> nos quoque has apes debemus imitari et quaecumque ex diversa lectione congessimus, separare, melius enim distincta servantur, deinde adhibita ingenii nostri cura et facultate in unum saporem, varia illa libamenta confundere.

> [we also ought to imitate the bees and to separate whatever we bring together out of varied reading, for the distinct can be preserved better; afterwards, aided by the care and faculty of our natural ability, to bring together the varied tastings into one flavor. [1925, 84, 5; see Pigman 1980, 1–32]]

In another part of the letter, the mind "formam suam impressit." Imitation is in both cases a matter of the transformation, within interiority, of material received from reading or from the exterior world. In Petrarch the process is specifically self-reflexive: the turn toward the self as the origin of a new production of thought.

Petrarch next moves to challenge Cicero on the question of what distinguishes humans from animals. This is a traditional question, and one that usually indicates the focus on either mind or text. Cicero privileges the human fact of speaking, as will the sixteenth century in its turn. But Petrarch distinguishes humans by their faculties of mind:

> Licet enim Cicero scribat videri sibi homines, cum multis rebus humiliores et infirmiores sint, hac re maxime bestiis prestare quod loqui possunt, tamen id vel oratori, ad commendationem artis quam tradebat, indulgendum fuit, vel sic accipiendum, ut ipsum loqui posse sine previo intellectu esse non possit. Alioquin multo michi potius videntur in eo precellere, quod intelligere, quod discernere, quod multa scire ac meminisse possunt, quod belvis natura non tribuit, tametsi aliquam intellectus discretionis et memorie similitudinem habere videantur.

> [Cicero wrote that it seemed to him that men, even if in many things weaker and lesser, stand before animals in this one thing, that they are able to speak; but the orator must be allowed to praise the art he practiced or it is to be accepted that for him to be able to speak without previous understanding is not possible. Otherwise it seems to me much more that men are able to excel

because they are able to understand, to distinguish, to know many things and to remember them; nature did not allow this to animals, although they seem to have certain qualities similar to understanding, discernment and memory. (1933, 1:8, ll. 47–56; see also 1955a, 52)]

Even animals are identified by the status of their faculties. Petrarch's disagreement with Cicero on this issue marks the difference of his focus.

《◎》

In the sixteenth century the expressive capacity is again the distinguishing mark of humanity. In the early part of this era Pietro Bembo has one of the speakers of the *Della Volgar Lingua* make the following statement:

> Et percio che gli huomini in questa parte massiamamente sono dagli altri animali differenti, che essi parlano, quale piu bella cosa puo alcuno huomo havere, che in quella parte, per laquale gli huomini aglialtri animali grandemente soprastano, esso aglialtri huomini essere soprastante.

> [And since in this particular men are completely different from the other animals in that they speak, what thing more beautiful is any man able to possess than, in this particular by which men stand totally above the other animals, to stand above other men. (3)]

The first oration of Bartolomeo della Fonte makes the same point (Trinkaus 1960, 97).

This is the capacity to give verbal form, generally referred to as eloquence, speaking, or discourse. When Philip Melanchthon responds to one of the Pico della Mirandola letters written to Ermolao Barbaro on the question of wisdom and eloquence, it is to reverse Petrarch's focus and therefore his emphasis. Melanchthon perceives Pico's claims as two: the attribution of absolute knowledge of things to the Barbari or philosophers; and their rightful disdain of eloquence. Melanchthon's point of attack is this latter separation of wisdom and eloquence:

> Nam cum hae duae virtutes hominis propriae sint ac summae, mente res bonas perspicere ac videre, easque dicendo explicare et ostendere aliis posse, paradoxum affers initio orationis tuae, quod cum ipsa natura pugnat, nefas esse Sapientiae Eloquentiam addere. Nam usus sapientiae plane nullus fuerit, nisi sapienter deliberata atque cogitata communicare aliis possimus, quod cum sine magna quadam copia et varietate orationis fieri non queat.

[For since these two virtues are the most proper to men and the best, to be able to perceive good things with the mind and by speaking to unfold and to show these things to others, you produce a paradox at the beginning of your oration: nature is made to fight with itself because it is unlawful to add eloquence to wisdom. For wisdom would be totally useless unless we were able to communicate wisely to others what we have thought and deliberated, and this can't be done without great copiousness and variety of expression. (9, col. 689)]

Melanchthon redirects Pico's position toward what is central for him, verbal representation. Only when things thought and deliberated are objectified in discourse as its content do they attain functional existence or become effective in communication. There is clearly another turn of the wheel: the sixteenth century privileges speaking as what distinguishes human nature, and they turn the previous admiration of Cicero into idolatry (almost). Self-relation as the (re-)production of the true self thus tends to disappear; its place is taken by the active production of speech or text—and if not true, then effective speech.

Petrarch would have difficulty conceiving of the issue in the way Melanchthon does. The focus on interiority allows for immediate access to the consciousness; it is not closed off or removed—although this is entirely self-referential, or access to one's own consciousness. Petrarch does, however, speak of interiority abstractly—that is, of all humans. And since Petrarch is specifically concerned with the process of change that can be made to occur within the mind to raise it toward God, he is not specifically concerned with the outward manifestations of those changes or the communication of them to others: they are beyond the focus. In the case of eloquence and thought, the imitation of great thinkers of the past would lead to an interior change in the imitator—from whom a certain eloquence would then naturally flow.

Consequently Petrarch's interest in the question of eloquence and wisdom takes on a different form: in the *Vita solitaria*, for example, the opposition between the active and the passive or solitary life becomes a question of the value of the eloquent public man or the orator. Petrarch concedes much:

Multa quidem, inquies, loquuntur utilter; audivi. Et sepe aliis prosunt; credo. Sed non statim sanus est medicus, qui consilio egrum iuvat. . . . Verba studio elaborata atque arte composita pro multorum salute non respuo et, quicunque sit opifex, utile opus amplector; verum hec nobis non rethorice scola sed vite est, nec inanem lingue gloriam, sed solidam quietem mentisintendimus.

[Many things, you say, are usefully spoken; I have heard them. And often they are helpful to others; I believe it. But the doctor who aids the sick with counsel is not necessarily healthy. . . . I don't reject words elaborated by studious effort on behalf of the health of many and, whoever the artisan, I embrace the useful work; but truly this is not for us a school of rhetoric but one of life; nor do we aim at some empty glory of the tongue but the substantive quietude of mind. (1955a, 324; see also 402])]

The analogy to the physician, a classical and Renaissance cliché similar to the one about the astronomer who falls in a ditch because he is always looking at the stars, is a case in point: the concern is for the rectified consciousness; whatever the useful eloquence produced or received, the individual self is ultimately responsible for its own self-rectification. Communication and self-focus don't seem to mix.

In *Familiari* 1:8 Petrarch returns later to the analogy of the bees: "perscrutemur doctorum libros, ex quibus sententias florentissimas ac suavissimas eligentes" [Let us examine the books of the learned, selecting the most delightful and flowery thoughts (ll. 151–52)]. He ends the letter shortly after by returning to his insistence on the transformation of the model within the interiority of the imitator:

Neve diutius apud te qualia decerpseris maneant, cave: nulla quidem esset apibus gloria, nisi in aliud et in melius inventa converterent. Tibi quoque, siqua legendi meditandique studio reppereris, in favum stilo redigenda suadeo; hinc enim illa profluent que tibi iure optimo et presens et ventura etas attribuet.

[Be careful that what you have selected not remain with you a long time: there would be no glory for the bees unless they converted what they had gathered into something other that is better. If you find any things by your effort of reading and reflection, I advise you also that they must be rendered through the honeycomb of your own writing; for from this will flow those things that by rights both present and future ages will attribute to you. (ll. 180–85)]

In *Familiari* 22:2, Petrarch summarizes the process and emphasizes his focus: "Vitam michi alienis dictis ac monitis ornare, fateor, est animus, non stilum" [I confess that when I seek to supply life with the words and advice of others, it is the mind that is important, not the style (ll. 97–98)]. In the same letter Petrarch makes the process more specific:

Legi apud Virgilium apud Flaccum apud Severinum apud Tullium; nec semel legi sed milies, nec cucurri sed incubui, et totis ingenii nisibus immoratus sum. . . . Hec se michi tam familiariter ingessere et non modo memorie sed medullis affixa sunt unumque cum ingenio facta sunt meo, ut . . . ipsa quidem hereant, actis in intima animi parte radicibus.

[I read in Virgil, Horace, Severinus and Cicero; I read not once but a thousand times; nor did I hurry but lingered over them, and I remained in them with the totality of my natural ability. . . . These things enter into me so familiarly and are fixed not only in memory but in my inmost recesses; they are made one with my natural talent so that . . . these things indeed remain, the roots driven into the deepest part of my mind. (ll. 72–80; cf. Pigman 1980, 12–13)]

He goes on to say that what is preserved in the memory of the imitator becomes his own, or, under the pressure of events, seems to come to mind as something new. Imitation in the sixteenth century becomes a matter of the repetition of words or actions, or in general a turn toward an externalized praxis. The interest in language and languages, which begins in the fifteenth century, comes to fruition in the sixteenth, in part because language is conceived as the exemplary external process.

And, as in Melanchthon, the emphasis on the value of communication becomes prominent, along with an emphasis on the production of the spoken or written text as its vehicle. This produces a pronounced shift in the notion of self-relation. Petrarch's notion of interiority is self-reflexive, but to a lesser degree than Seneca. The latter's pronounced return to the self does reappear to some extent in the exclusion of the external world by Petrarch in the turn toward the self as the first step of the spiritual journey toward God. In his notion of imitation, however, interiorized as it is, the relation to self is transformed into a self-other (*alienum*) relation, but one that ultimately results in the production of a new, more knowledgeable and wiser self—a self-augmentation. In the sixteenth century self-relation recedes, disappearing within the new dispensation of performance, the self-model relation and the relation to the world. The self-model relation is a discipline, but not a self-formation.

The most prominent among the second generation of English humanists in the sixteenth century is Roger Ascham. His major work, *The Schoolmaster*, provides, as he claims, the "plain and perfect way of teaching children, to understand, write, and speak the Latin tongue." Book 1 of the treatise begins in the same practical way, presenting an explicit method of imitation for training the young learner; but Ascham also gives thorough development to the question of imitation as a universal method, and so takes on some theoretical interest.

CHAPTER 6

Ascham's method of "double translation," his primary method, is as follows: the schoolmaster chooses an epistle of Cicero not inappropriate to the capacity of the young learner. Then:

> First let him teach the child, cheerfully and plainly, the cause, and matter of the letter: then, let him construe it into English, so oft, as the child may easily carry away the understanding of it. . . . After this, the child must take a paper book, and sitting in some place, where no man shall prompt him, by himself, let him translate into English his former lesson. Then showing it to his master, let the master take from him his Latin book, and pausing an hour, at the least, then let the child translate his own English into Latin again. . . . When the child bringeth it, turned into Latin, the master must compare it with Tully's book, and lay them both together: and where the child doeth well, either in choosing, or true placing of Tully's words, let the master praise him. (14–15)

Later in book 1 Ascham recommends, in a loosely parallel way, that young men at Court imitate the actions of good men in order to learn virtue (41).

Such methods are determined by the shift from interiority to text or exteriority that has occurred over the two centuries. Ascham, like others in the sixteenth century, focuses on the external. These external phenomena are assumed to be expressions or representations in the sense that they give form to or communicate what would otherwise be inaccessible. They are, in terms of the central Ciceronian metaphor, the *verba* that yield access to the *res ipsae,* either thoughts or things. As in Melanchthon, the mind as interiority is assumed to be inaccessible except through its verbal or actional representations; this in turn marks the *verba* as prior, the beginning and the focus of inquiry. The sixteenth century produces itself through a hermeneutic.

In double translation the initial work of the master in relation to the text is an attempt to get the learner to understand the "cause" and "matter" of the text, and this is done through the *verba* of the text itself. This and the child's translation of the text into English are tantamount to his absorbing the original situation and intention of Cicero. When he retranslates into Latin he takes on the problematic situation in which Cicero found himself and attempts to resolve that in exactly the same way as Cicero (successfully) did—with the same words, and in the same order. Cicero's word choice and order represent the best standard because Ascham and the tradition conceive of him as the most successful at dealing with situations by speaking and writing. The text or *verba* are the focus of the method.

Ascham claims that this double translation will: "work a true choice and placing of words, a right ordering of sentence, and easy understanding of the tongue, a readiness to speak, a facility to write, a true judgment, both of his own and other men's doings in what tongue soever he doth use," and that "right choice of words . . . is the foundation of eloquence" (14, 13). Ascham is arguing in effect that the repetition of style is the acquisition of wisdom: that to imitate the order and placing of the words is to express, and to acquire, the knowledge, intention, and skill that the particular text imitated gives form to. In repeating Cicero's words the learner becomes like Cicero. The focus is completely on the external verbal process or texture, which gives form to everything else. Interior changes are assumed to occur as a result of the learner's following Ascham's method, but interiority is not explicitly present in the theoretical matrix within which the method is developed. In the same way Petrarch assumes that the verbal performance of his imitator will improve, but generally excludes that aspect of the process from his analysis.

Ascham's notion of imitation is applied not only to young students. In a section entitled "Imitatio" he draws together commonplaces in Homer and Virgil and Demosthenes and Cicero, and others. In this section Ascham uses the method of verbal imitation to account for the existence of great epics, orations, and in fact every variety of verbal production. According to Ascham, to write in any of the various *genera dicendi* is to imitate the model text that stands at the fountainhead of that particular genre.

But with the learned speaker or writer as opposed to the young learner, imitation is not merely repetition, which now appears as merely training; imitation for the mature writer is adaptation. As Ascham explains in his treatment of the differences between Homer and Virgil and others: "This he altereth and changeth either in property of words, in form of sentence, in substance of the matter, or in one or other convenient circumstances of the author's [that is, the imitator's] present purpose" (1967, 118; see also 102–4). When the learned man seeks a model to imitate in order to resolve by verbal action his own problem-situation, he will most likely not find in the tradition of preserved literary expressions or in the works of Cicero one that is exactly appropriate; it will have been addressed to an at least slightly different situation. So the imitator will have to adapt or change the model text to make it fit the current situation. The adaptation is largely a matter of verbal changes. Yet to change the text is to change everything: it is the verbal form given to the *res*, thought, things, attitudes, inclinations, values, and a change in the text is a change in these. On the other side of the communication process, a change in the text is a change in the potential effect on the audience or reader. The text becomes the theoretical center of the discourse on imitation: the minds or interiority of the model, the imitator and the auditor are assumed to exist, to be affected and to change, but without specific reference; they are subsumed within the discussion of the text and its changes.

Erasmus's *Ciceronianus* offers an interesting parallel to Ascham in that it repeats the focus on the text. The dialogue is between Nosophonus, a strict Ciceronian, and the more liberal Bulephorus. Nosophonus takes the extraordinary position—although not for the sixteenth century—that Cicero is the arché of all speaking: there exists no word or form, no phrase, no figure or speech rhythm unless it has been invented by Cicero and validated for imitation by its specific occurrence in the texts of the Master (1971, I, cols. 980ff.). Bulephorus attacks this method, but merely to liberalize it and make it more workable. Both interlocutors, for example, agree that the primary method by which humans speak and act appropriately is imitation. Bulephorus raises many points, but one of these is that Cicero spoke in a limited number of situations, and even for those he did, the contemporary counterpart of these situations is different enough to obviate a word-for-word imitation of the Ciceronian text. Bulephorus suggests for such instances a form of verbal adaptation that is similar to Ascham's (cols. 996–97).

The first part of book 1 of *Il Cortegiano* centers on the question of courtiership and how it is acquired. A later part of the book focuses on the courtier's use of language, but the first section is concerned with the acquisition of the generally nonverbal activities necessary to the courtier. The method of acquisition is of course imitation, but in this instance the "text" is constituted by the physical acts that are the manifestations of the skill or "grazia" of the model; what are imitated are in fact model activities. As noted earlier, Castiglione—or Count Lodovico, the primary speaker of book 1—institutes as the principle of the system those who are born *formato* to perfect action without training. The Count's method applies to those born with natural potential that is not complete, and who therefore require training to actualize or give external form to it in more perfection.

Like Petrarch, Castiglione tends toward a variety of models; but his focus is different: the imitator observes the activities of the "ottimi maestri" and acquires the skill by repeating their actions; the imitator learns to perform acts. The Count explains the general method thus and specifies further by means of a description of a particular accomplished courtier:

> Chi adunque vorrà esser bon discipulo, oltre al far le cose bene, sempre ha da metter ogni diligenzia per assimigliarsi al maestro e, se possibil fosse,

transformarsi in lui. . . . considerate come bene ed aggraziatamente fa il signor Galleazzo Sanseverino . . . tutti gli esercizi del corpo; e questo perché, oltre alla natural disposizione ch'egli tiene della persona, ha posto ogni studio d'imparare da bon maestri ed aver sempre presso di sé omini eccellenti e da ognun pigliar it meglio di ciò che sapevano, ché sì come del lottare, volteggiare e maneggiar molte sorti d'armi ha tenuto per guida it nostro messer Pietro Monte, il qual, come sapete, é il vero e solo maestro d'ogni artificiosa forza e leggerezza, così del cavalcare, giostrare e qualsivoglia altra cosa ha sempre avuto inanzi agli occhi il più perfetti, che in quelle professioni siano stati conosciuti.

[Who desires to be a good pupil must, apart from doing things well, always put forth every effort to make himself like the master and, if it were possible, transform himself into him. . . . consider how well and how gracefully Signore Galleazzo Sanseverino performs . . . all the activities of the body; this because, apart from the natural ability that he possesses, he has made every effort to learn from the best masters and to have always excellent men nearby and from each to select the best of what they know; so for wrestling, horsemanship and the wielding of many kinds of weapons he has taken as a guide our own Pietro Monte who, as you know, is the true and only master of every artifice of nimble power; thus in riding, jousting and in whatever else, Sanseverino has always held before his eyes the most perfect that in such professions have been known. (1964, 123, 122)]

The focus of the method is clearly the activity, the expression of the skill. The imitator acquires the skill of the master by repeating the form in which the skill is manifest; he becomes like the master in performance, not thought or some abstract inner quality—although the former would be said to contain the latter. As mentioned, Castiglione is similar to Petrarch in the choice of a variety of models—not merely a different model for each distinct activity but for different aspects of a single activity. And the traditional bees reappear, but now used to direct attention toward the gathering and imitation of different parts of a variety of actional expressions (ibid.).

The methods of imitation proposed during the sixteenth century differ in many specifics. Ascham tends toward one model while Erasmus's Bulephorus and Castiglione's Lodovico recommend a variety—although often it's a matter of degree. Peter Ramus in his *Ciceronianus* recommends a different kind of imitation altogether—of the structure of the text. Yet in the sixteenth century all theories of imitation circulate about the text, the statements or activities of the model. What is interior is not referred to often, since it is assumed that the skill or knowledge of the model is contained or objectified in the model expression, and since the acquisition of the statement or act in performance implies acquisition of the content.

There is no space accorded for self-reflection in this method of producing actions and texts from a self-other relation. There is no self-relation except in the subject's attempt to recognize the particularities of its own speaking situation in order to adapt its words to that situation; and this is specifically not a turning inward toward the self but a turning outward to construct the circumstances that will determine the self's adaptation.

There are a number of other issues that reflect the distinct shift that occurs from Petrarch to the sixteenth century. In letter I, 9, of the *Familiari* Petrarch shows that he is aware of the opposition between interiority and text, and he ultimately assigns a priority to one. Petrarch begins the letter: "Animi cura philosophum querit, eruditio lingue oratoris est propria; neutra nobis negligenda" (The care of the mind requires philosophy; the erudition of the tongue is proper to the orator; we can neglect neither [ll. 3–4]). This is carefully structured opposition that Petrarch then easily dismantles: "But of the first [I write] elsewhere." Here the priority is correcting speech by means of the art of eloquence. Yet he returns immediately to the original opposition:

> Nec enim parvus aut index animi sermo est aut sermonis moderator est animus. Alter pendet ex altero; ceterum ille latet in pectore, hic exit in publicum.

> [For speech is no small indication of mind and the mind is no small manager of speaking. Each depends upon the other; but that lies hidden in the breast while this comes forth into public space. (ll. 11–14)]

There is then a suggestion that Petrarch inclines toward giving priority to mind:

> ille [mind] comit egressurum et qualem esse vult fingit, hic egrediens qualis ille sit nuntiat.

> [mind arranges what is about to come forth and gives form to what it wishes to be; this other [speech] when it emerges announces what the nature of the first one is. (ll. 14–15)]

The structure of the statement and the verb *nuntiare,* which reduces *sermo* to secondariness, change the balance in favor of *animus.*

Petrarch finally gives up any attempt at balance in the following, although the syntactic balance remains:

> quanquam ubi animo consultum fuerit, neglectus esse sermo non possit, sicut, ex diverso, adesse sermoni dignitas non potest, nisi animo sua maiestas affuerit.

> [although where there has been deliberation by the mind, it is not possible for speech to be neglected; so on the contrary there can be no dignity in speaking unless its grandeur is supported by the mind. (ll. 18–21; see Seigel 1968, 47ff., and Tateo 1960, 224–25)]

Interiority is prior: *animus* determines *sermo* in each clause. Petrarch continues by claiming that immersion in the Ciceronian fountain leads to dulcet and ornate speech, but to nothing of wisdom, deep seriousness, or coherence. Imitation of words, to him, excludes interior transformation. Coherence is the key term; it suggests the harmony of an undisturbed interiority that is the subject of the *Secretum*: "Quoniam nisi primum desideria invicem nostra conveniant, quod preter sapientem scito nemini posse contingere, illud necesse est ut, dissidentibus curis, et mores et verba dissideant" [Since unless our desires first come into some sort of order, desires that you know no one is able to limit except the wise man; this disorder of our own self-management makes our words and habits disordered (ll. 25–28]. The organized harmony of mind, achieved only by the control of what enters from the exterior world and the body, allowing thus for a return of the self toward its own interior self—all this is the center of Petrarch's concern; secondarily statements and acts ensue, their nature determined by the interior state, which is prior.

The final statement of the introductory part of the letter repeats, emphatically, the focus on mind as the prior reality:

> At bene disposita mens instar immote serenitatis placida semper ac tranquilla est: scit quid velit, et quod semel voluit, velle non desinit; itaque tametsi oratorie artis ornamenta non suppetant, ex se ipsa magnificentissimas voces atque gravissimas et certe sibi consonas elicit.

> [But the well disposed mind, the image of steadfast serenity, is always peaceful and tranquil: it knows what it wants, and what it has once wished it does not cease to desire; and thus, although the ornaments of the art of oratory may not be available, the mind produces out of itself serious and magnificent speech that is fitting to itself. (ll. 28–33)]

Oratory is simply the final act of the production of the self.

Petrarch does admit that the study of eloquence is useful at times when, even with the motions of the mind in harmony, appropriate speech does not emerge; but speaking and eloquence remain secondary to mind and interiority. He is even unwilling to admit the individual need for *sermo;* its usefulness is in communication to others:

> Que si nobis necessaria non foret et mens, suis viribus nisa bonaque sua in silentio explicans, verborum suffragiis non egeret, ad certerorum saltem utilitatem, quibuscum vivimus, laborandum erat; quorum animos nostris collocutionibus plurimum adiuvari posse non ambigitur.

> [Thus [eloquence] would not be necessary to us, and the mind, unfolding by its own strength its own strivings and its goods in silence, would have no need of words; but at least for the utility of the remaining ones with whom we live there is the necessity of labor, for their minds would undoubtedly be aided greatly by our conversation and speaking. (ll. 36–41; cf. Garin 1965, 19)]

Petrarch's focus on interiority, as the last quotation illustrates, is by its own form self-reflexive: the quotation suggests a natural inwardness that must often be broached of social necessity. Petrarch is always foregrounding his own turning toward the self and his own interiority, separate from the world. But this and other passages also reach a more general level: the issue of access to self or self-relation among humans generally, or the fundamental issue of the self's necessary presence to the self. Petrarch in this is similar to post-Augustan writers, particularly Seneca. And although he is not skeptical about the relation of external cause to interior effect, he does translate the former into entities of mind in order to introduce them into his analysis.

When Franciscus in the *Secretum* seeks fruitlessly for evidence of mental tranquility among men, he does not say he has observed all varieties of exterior life and activity; rather, as Truth "novit, quotiens humani more ingenii per omnes statuum gradus mente discurrerem" [knows, how many times I ran through in mind the qualities of human nature in all its degrees and circumstances (1955b, 114)]. The external world must be experienced and interiorized (or known intuitively), stored in memory, and then recalled during cogitation. In the case of Augustinus's warnings about the desire for temporal things, and especially love, it is the "visa rei species," the interior appearance derived from the external object, that creates the desire, not the external thing without interior mediation (154).

In the sixteenth century humanists take up a different theoretical position: they assume immediate access to the textual space between consciousnesses or to external process in general. Initial access to these phenomena leads to the question of how far they may be considered representations of the interior processes that preceded them, now assumed to be inaccessible except by the mediation of language or some comparable means of expression or form. The first issue is the movement from the *verba* to the unknown *res:* thought, intention, meaning, or the interiority of things in general. All questions circulate around the central issue of interpretation of the text or its production—but not a hermeneutics of the self.

The Pietro Bembo of book 4 of *Il Cortegiano* comes face-to-face with this question in his monologue on the Platonic "ladder of love":

> la bellezza estrinseca é vero segno della bontà intrinseca e nei corpi é impressa quella grazia più e meno quasi per un carattere dell'anima, per lo quale essa estrinsicamente é conosciuta . . . e questo medesimo interviene nei corpi, come si vede che i fisionomi al volto conoscono spesso i costumi e talora i pensieri degli omini; e, che é più, nelle bestie si comprende ancor allo aspetto la qualità dell'animo.

> [external beauty is truly a sign of internal goodness, and that grace is impressed in bodies more or less as a disposition of the soul, through which it is known externally . . . and this same thing intervenes in bodies, as one sees that physionomists often understand from the face the habits of men and sometimes their thoughts; and, what is more, in animals one understands the quality of mind from their outward demeanor. (Castiglione 1964, 522)]

What is available to perception, the external object, its surface texture, or its representation, becomes the starting point of the inquiry and ultimately its general locus. The mode of analysis suggested in the passage entails the assumption that the external object, its external qualities (the other person being in this case considered as an object external to the perceiver) and external process in general are the objectified forms of interiority: thought, inclination, desire, skill, and so on.

Michel de Montaigne may be considered among the most prominent of the antihumanists of the sixteenth century; his intention, especially in the "Apologie de Raimond Sebond" is to diminish human nature. Yet many of his theoretical choices are similar to those of the more benign humanists. There is a whole literature focusing on Montaigne and subjectivity, most of which is well articulated in Hassan Melehy's book, *Writing Cogito*. This literature is concerned with how the subject is constituted within the writing of the *Essays*. For Melehy, the Montaignian subject is "a fragmentary assemblage" (1997, 50), that is, controlled by the various phenomena of the world. This represents the institution of a modernity that stands in opposition to the cogito and Descartes's alternative institution, which privileges the subject as the unified substance in control of knowledge (and hence the world). The following discussion of Montaigne's attack on human nature's privileged Subjectivity may be taken as one instance of his general decentralization of the human subject.

The principle of Montaigne's argument against man in the "Apologie" is an inversion of the familiar Protagorean maxim. Montaigne argues against the humanist position that human capacities and activities, primarily the capacity for speech noted earlier, serve as a standard that places man above other creatures in the scale of being; this belief is simply an illustration to Montaigne that

> La presomption est nostre maladie naturelle et originelle. La plus calamiteuse et fraile de toutes les creatures, c'est l'homme, et quant la plus orgueilleuse.
>
> [This presumption is our original and natural malady. Man is the most disastrous and frail of all the creatures, and so much the more overbearing. (1969, 1:490)]

Montaigne goes further. He assumes, without specific mention, the standard argument of the century that speech and communication distinguish and privilege human nature, and then reinforces that by setting out to prove that animals communicate as well. He will show that, given this supposed distinguishing characteristic of humans, other supposedly lesser animals meet that standard. In one case:

> Et plus qu'il est ainsi, comme disent les cosmographes, qu'il y a des nations qui reçoyvent un chien pour leur Roy, il faut bien qu'ils donnent certaine interpretation à sa voix et mouvements.
>
> [And inasmuch as cosmographers say that there are some nations who have a dog for their king, it is necessary that they give a fixed interpretation to its voice and movements. (1:491)]

There is even communication among different species of animals: "En certain abbayer du chien le cheval cognoist qu'il y a de la colere" [the horse recognizes that there is anger in a certain kind of bark by a dog (1:492)], and even communication among animals without voice:

> Aux bestes mesmes qui n'ont pas de voix, par la societé d'offices que nous voyons entre elles, nous argumentons aisément quelque autre moyen de communication.

[Even with animals who have no speech, by the community of duties we see among them, we can easily argue some other means of communication. (ibid.)]

This passage turns Montaigne toward the recognition of the importance of gesture as a means of communication: "nos muets disputent, argumentent et content des histoires par signes" [our mutes dispute, argue and recount stories by signs]; lovers speak with their eyes; and hands speak "d'une variation et multiplication à l'envy de la langue" [with a variability and multiplicity that is the envy of language]. The return to human communication does not mean that Montaigne has forgotten other species: the emphasis here on natural communication by nonverbal signs does not privilege humans; animals are equally adept (1:499ff.). So much for the status of humans in the scale of being; yet clearly the point is made by Montaigne within the model that privileges signs and communication and text.

If we ask how Montaigne is able to know that animals communicate, we return to the theoretical position of the sixteenth century as presented by Castiglione's Bembo: from the observed behavior of animals without voice "nous argumentons aisément quelque autre moyen de communication." And more specifically:

Au reste, quelle sorte de nostre suffisance ne reconnoissons nous aux operations des animaux? Est-il police reglée avec plus d'ordre, diversifiée à plus de charges et d'offices, et plus constamment entretenue que celle des mouches à miel? Cette disposition d'actions de vacations si ordonnée, la pouvons nous imaginer se conduire sans discours et sans providence? . . . Pourquoy espessit l'araigné se toile en un endroit et relasche en un'autre? se sert à cette heure de cette sorte de neud, tantost de celle-là, si elle n'a et deliberation, et pensement, et conclusion?

[Moreover, what sort of our own adequacy don't we also recognize in the workings of animals? Is it a policy regulated by more order, diversified by more responsibilities and duties, and more constantly maintained than those of honeybees? This disposition of action and attendance so ordered (of the bees)—are we able to imagine them conducted without discourse and foresight? . . . Why does the spider open out its web in one place and loosen it in another? Why does it use one kind of knot at one point and another kind at another point, if it has no capacity for deliberation, thought and conclusion? (1:493)]

In these and other instances Montaigne assumes access to the external behavior and text(ure)s, such as webs, of insects and infers the faculties and capacities of mind, of which the objects and actions are representations or manifestations. From Montaigne's theoretical perspective, and that of the sixteenth century in general, the external processes of action or statement have priority in that they are the givens, the facts from which the interior and now hidden capacities or contents of mind must be inferred.

In Petrarch there is, characteristically, a general sense of the inadequacy of words that would be severely damaging to the sixteenth-century enterprise of interpretation of external manifestations. In the *Secretum,* for example, in the attack on the vanity of eloquence in book 2, these typical statements occur:

> Quotiens ego te querentem audivi, quotiens tacitum indignatemque conspexi, quod que clarissima cognituque facillima essent animo cogitanti, ea nec lingua nec calamus sufficienter exprimeret.

> [How often have I heard you complain, how often have I observed you silent and indignant because those things that were most clear and most easily known by the thinking mind could not be expressed by tongue or pen adequately. (1955a, 74; see also 734)]

Interiority, the region of thought, is clearly the privileged realm; speaking and writing are secondary and often inadequate.

This recalls the *Familiari* passage in which Petrarch claims that individual interiority has no need of words (1:8, ll. 36–41). The secondariness of verbal representation is a constant theme (see, e.g., 1955a, 342). Petrarch often bases his attack on the scholastic dialecticians on the distinction between knowing and speaking:

> Itaque si quem ex eo grege de diffinitione non tantum hominis sed rei alterius interroges, parata responsio est; si ultra progrediare, silentium fiet, aut si assiduitas disserendi verborum copiam audaciamque pepererit, mores tamen loquentis ostendent veram sibi rei diffinite notitiam non adesse. . . . Quid, obliti rerum, inter verba senescitis.

> [Hence if you question any one of that pack [of scholastics] concerning the definition not so much of man but of other things, the response is provided; if you go further there is silence, or if the perseverance of argument were to produce boldness and copiousness of words, this custom of speaking would show you that the true notion of the thing is not present. . . . Thus you waste away in words while forgetting things altogether. (52)]

The term *notitia* indicates Petrarch's priority: knowledge or the possession within the mind of the thing to be defined. This is reminiscent of *Familiari* I, 9, in which there can be no *dignitas* of speaking without the prior operation of thought; otherwise there is mere scholastic babble (see also 1955a, 736).

Finally, Petrarch's terminology indicates his focus on interiority. One of his key terms is *ingenium,* which he uses to indicate the natural or God-given capacity of mind; in the sixteenth century the same term indicates the capacity for verbal expression or act. Again, virtue in Petrarch is a state of consciousness. When he speaks in the *Vita solitaria* of the four levels of virtue, Petrarch places them in the mind. The "tertius gradus" consists of the "purgati animi virtutes" [the virtues of the cleansed mind]; and: "Quartus ac supremus exemplarium est locus, que supra hominem sunt et, ut aiunt, in mente solius Dei habitant" [Fourth and highest is the place of the exemplars or Ideas, which are above man and, so to speak, reside only in the mind of God (342)]. Virtue resides in the mind, human or divine. In the sixteenth century virtue becomes a question of externalized activity that is said to express virtue. In Ascham young men become virtuous or learn how to perform it by imitating the actions of virtuous men. In *An Apology for Poetry* Sir Philip Sidney compares moral philosophy, history, and poetry in terms of their capacity to give effective representation to virtue; in order to be effective, that verbal representation must best serve "the ending end of all earthly learning[,] being virtuous action" (1904, 1:160ff.; see also Garin 1965, 43ff.). On both verbal and actional levels, virtue must necessarily be expressed or performed.

I have quoted at length from texts in the original languages in order to demonstrate that thought positions itself in different ways and makes different assumptions during the fourteenth century and in the sixteenth century. Petrarch and his contemporaries in a sense reprise Seneca and post-Augustan thought by privileging interiority. In Petrarch this interiority is part of an overall emphasis on self-relation: the return to the self from the external world of disturbance in matters of religion and the recourse to one's interiority in imitation as a means to reproduce oneself and one's own style. The latter is less self-referential in that in imitation the self is juxtaposed to the model other, not itself. But in imitation the self does produce the learned self or augment it as a result of contact with the great minds of the past.

So the strong self-reflexive impulse in Seneca is both repeated and weakened in Petrarch. But in the sixteenth century self-relation is entirely transformed. In Ascham discourse and moral action are what is produced by imitation, that is, in relation to an other, and not in the relation of the self to the self. Self-reflection may perhaps be a theme of many religious texts of the century and in the meditative tradition.

The lyric tradition that is central to the late sixteenth-century literary efflorescence might also be held up in opposition to this textual thesis. Surely, even if the prose fiction of the era tends to present characters who have no interiority beyond brief preliminaries to action, the lyric poems of the era manifest interiority and self-reflection. Yet this may be the result of a modern attempt to read this poetry in our own terms. Shakespeare's Sonnet 73, for example ("That time of year thou mayst in me behold / When yellow leaves . . .") tends often to be read as the self-pitying lament of an aging lover, a meditation on loss; but it can as easily be read as a manipulation of the addressee—a representation by the speaker of his own impending death as a form of pressure on the person spoken to. In a certain way, then, Renaissance lyrics belong more to rhetoric than to our modern notion of the expression of feeling; they certainly fall more into the realm of representation than of self-reflection. In the humanist tradition self-reflection disappears. It will return in the next century with Descartes in the construction of the subject of knowledge.

Descartes, Interiority, and Identity

My subject in this chapter is the modern age taken in a broad sense, from the period in which Foucault says the deployment of sexuality began to displace and reorient the deployment of alliance down into the twentieth century. My concern is historical: another narrative of ourselves and our "historical ontology." Without attempting to construct a comprehensive new view of this era, I do intend to make some uncharacteristic connections among familiar notions of the modern as well as among familiar texts. A footnote to Foucault, one focusing on the historical nature of knowledge.

Foucault's histories of sexuality provide an immediate context: both the narrative of the emergence of the deployment of sexuality since the seventeenth century in volume 1 and his later concern with self-relation and the ascesis by which the self produces itself as a moral agent. The deployment of sexuality entails the production of human interiority and the tendency to construct that interiority as individual identity; this interiority is the locus of our sexuality or desire, or, more generically, "feeling," as Foucault sometimes puts it. Since Foucault only investigates self-relation from the fourth century B.C.E. through the first two centuries of the Roman imperium, more needs to be said about the historical form of self-relation in the modern period.

The immediate point of departure is a set of comments made by Foucault in an interview in 1983, that Descartes "succeeded in substituting a subject as founder of practices of knowledge . . . for a subject constituted through practices of the self" (1984a, 371; see also 1987, 14). Descartes broke the traditional link between a prior ethical ascesis and the access to truth. "After Descartes [Foucault says], we have a nonascetic subject of knowledge" (372). Simply put, "I can be immoral and know the truth." Thomas Flynn in "Foucault as Parrhesiast" treats in detail the modalities of "truth-telling" (102–18).

This characterization can be set over against Richard Rorty's more determinate characterization of the invention of the mind during the seventeenth century in Europe in *Philosophy and the Mirror of Nature*. For him Descartes is a primary actor in the "epistemological turn" of that century. Descartes is credited with the invention of mind as consciousness, that is, not merely rationality and intellect but "pains, dreams, memory-images, and veridical and hallucinatory perceptions" (1979, 54–55; see also Critchley 1996, 15); the mind as consciousness takes on a separate, nonspatial—that is, versus *res extensa*—existence; further, this construction of mind lends itself to the notion of self-relation: what separates the mind is its "ability to know itself incorrigibly," or, in more contemporary philosophical language, its "privileged access" to its own mental events (35).

Rorty also notes the skepticism that inevitably arises when immediate access is limited to the subject's own mental events (46, 94, 113, and passim). But it seems more likely that Descartes only reinvented the mind: James Bernauer presents Foucault's argument that the mind as the locus of images, feelings, memories, and so forth, had a long history in the west (1987, 52) and that Christian self-decipherment eventually formed the model for the modern "quest for self-knowledge" (62). Self-relation as self-hermeneutic may thus be said to have been utilized by Descartes in order to produce certainty about claims to knowledge—that is, he gave self-relation a new function. The self-hermeneutic leads to a hermeneutic of the world.

On the other hand, Descartes seems to have been one of the primary practitioners within a new episteme which privileged interiority, one which distinguishes the sixteenth from the seventeenth century in Europe. This is in part Rorty's point. Self-relation, as noted in the previous chapter, disappears in the major traditions of the sixteenth century, being replaced by the concern with the "exterior" processes of speech and action as central, and the commitment to a self-other ascesis in the production of accomplished orators and moral actors as subjects. Descartes is probably not the cause of the shift away from sixteenth-century concerns, and in fact could be read as an inheritor of the meditative tradition of the prior age; but he is also the exemplar of the "new" conditions of philosophizing that both reflect the fourteenth century and earlier eras and as well produce a new identity, the subject of knowledge.

Descartes, Interiority, and Identity

Since chapter 5, I have examined and exploited Foucault's last shift in thinking, which led him to begin a genealogy of human self-relation. In that chapter, I have sought to understand the implications of that shift, and then to augment his argument as it concerns the ancient world. In chapter 6 I attempt, by a excursion into the fourteenth and sixteenth centuries, to begin to break down the largely accidental assumption that for Foucault there existed a long and consistent "Christian" period of self-relation that endured for over many centuries. Here, in chapter 7, I make another attempt to expand on Foucault: to reread the modern era in terms of his final shift in thinking and the genealogy of self-relation. Some of his essays begin this revision, but the only comprehensive works he produced after the shift were the two last volumes on sexuality, and they were largely limited to the ancient world. My particular concern is the original compatibility of self-knowledge with objective knowledge or scientific discourses, and the split that emerges between them at the end of the nineteenth century.

Thus it would make more sense to consider Descartes as having adapted a historically prior model of ascesis in order to produce a new kind of subject, a subject determined in accordance with specific historical contingencies. The new, epistemological ascesis seems to Descartes to be incorporated with an ethical ascesis; in other words, one cannot be immoral and yet be a knower of truth, not without conscious choice; that is in itself an inversion: self-knowledge and objective knowledge are necessarily prior to one's construction of oneself as a moral agent. The twentieth century is another matter: Tom Lehrer's song about Werner von Braun and rocketry makes the point: I just send them up; where they come down is not my business. The new epistemological ascesis of Descartes is based on a renewed form of self-relation: the self's epistemological relation to its own interiority—an interiority which is in fact produced by the self-relation. Foucault says as much about the effect of the technique of confession by the beginning of the seventeenth century. And from Descartes on, that interiority is increasingly recognized as constituting human identity, universal at first and then increasingly individual.

The new ascesis allowed Descartes to produce two distinct but related forms of knowledge, experience and objective truth. The particular kind of experience noted here is self-experience and self-knowledge: the subject's relation to truth must detour through its own self-reflexive inquiry, that is, into itself as an object of knowledge; if I can know myself, my essence, then I come to the recognition of my identity as a subject of knowledge and as the foundation of knowledge. This ascesis also produces the new space of the secular, that is, once the self recognizes itself as an object of knowledge.

Knowledge of the material world, of ethics or manners, even theology, then becomes a set of separated forms of knowledge consequent to the constitution of the subject of knowledge. This "secular" ascesis becomes the incorporative principle subsequent to self-knowledge rather than arising in opposition to religious (and ethical) knowledge; moreover, it becomes knowledge.

This chapter has several sections: first, a more detailed analysis of Descartes's new form of epistemological self-relation and its necessary link to the production of knowledges; next, the representation of interiority in one typical eighteenth-century novel and one nineteenth-century one, with a particular focus on the status and relation of the two forms of knowledge—which is the ultimate focal point of the chapter; finally, the problematics of interiority and the relation of self-experience to knowledge in two turn-of-the-century works of fiction and in one prominent disagreement in the twentieth-century critical treatment of free indirect discourse.

The narrative here: after roughly two and a half centuries of compatibility the two forms of knowledge begin to undergo a discontinuous split. The crisis is often represented (as here) in literature in the twentieth century as the failure of objective knowledge, although the triumph of individual experience is often pyrrhic. There are complementary traditions as well: a continued assumption of the compatibility of the two knowledges in the sciences, attempts at reconciliation or distributions such as the separation of the domains of science and poetry, and so on. But one of the emerging issues was the discontinuity, the claim that self-knowledge was private and impenetrable to the institutional and public formation of knowledge—so to speak, "the invention of man." This may be read as an intensification of the notion that interiority constitutes particular identity.

⟨⟨◍⟩⟩

In part 1 of the *Discourse on the Method* . . . Descartes sets the stage for his self-inquiry by setting up a clear opposition between exterior and interior in relation to the subject: Descartes undertakes academic training and travel and then rejects both letters and his observation of behavior and belief in different cultures because they provide little more than a chaos of opinions, attitudes, and behaviors that obscures the singular path to truth (Bordo 1987, 52). In opposition to this influx of an irreconcilable set of notions, he resolves "to undertake studies within myself." In the *Meditations on First Philosophy*, a text similar in intention to the *Discourse*, Descartes focuses doubt more in the senses than in learning or general experience. The senses provide the basis for most of human belief, according to Descartes, so he concentrates his attack on them (1985b, 2:12ff.).

Foucault's notion of the increasing production of interiority as identity seems to have its origin here with Descartes's strategy of foundationalizing instrospection. This is a constant theme of the late Foucault; for example, in a lecture in 1978 on the conjunction of law and psychiatry he shows that in a contemporary legal case a typical demand was made of the defendant to confess, to offer a self-revelation "of what one is" (1988, 125–27, 137) that if not given would hinder the administration of punishment.

As noted in earlier chapters, this inwardness is not, however, unique in the history of thought: in the early Hellenistic period, a similar interiorizing takes place, notably in Epicurus, Aristippus, and the Cyrenaics, the Skeptics, and especially the Stoics. In Epicurus and the Stoics, for example, interiority takes a potentially "skeptical" form in that the relation between consciousness and exteriority is the first issue that must be addressed by philosophy. Descartes's more foundationalizing—that is, inventing the self—self-reflection is within this tradition, but his renewed notion of epistemological self-relation has in fact become a sign of modernity, particularly in terms of its emphasis on self-inquiry into interiority as the production of knowledge.

On the other hand, Descartes's notion of "our natural light" provided to humans by God through the functioning of the intelligible mind seems linked to Reformation texts of the prior century as well as to the determination by the Council of Trent that there is natural knowledge of God (although this natural light appears as a conclusion for Descartes, not an initial assumption); and from Foucault's occasional references to the Christian confession of the flesh, we can note profound similarities between Descartes' method and Christian self-decipherment: that is, the self seeks to know its own deepest desires and their provenance, with the goal of self-renunciation and purification under the aegis of divine law. But it is Descartes's adaptation of this ascetic process which is in focus here.

The work of Charles Taylor on modern "inwardness" and its historical construction in Descartes serves as a useful context here (1989, 109–207, esp. 143–58). Taylor sees Descartes as in part developing from the "radical reflexivity" of Augustine, that is, the construction of a self-relation that takes up a first-person perspective and is also experiential (but not necessarily empirical). Knowledge is constituted by interior representations for Descartes: "I am certain that I can have no knowledge of what is outside me except by means of the ideas I have within me" (1970, 123; quoted by Taylor 1989, 146). But Taylor's main point is that epistemological certainty is a function of reason or thought; this constitutes a historically new rationality that is "now an internal property of subjective thinking" that is not fundamentally dependent on a higher external reality (156). In other words, Descartes turns to his own interiority in order to construct the outer world.

To return to Descartes's interiorizing process: after his disappointment concerning the truth of the opinions fed into him or acquired in transit, Descartes finds himself detained by the weather in "a stove-heated room, where I was completely free to converse with myself about my own thoughts" (1985a, 1:116). This room, according to Baillet, was in a village near Ulm, and the sequestration occurred on 10 November 1619. This is not merely a localization but an important step in the process of interiorization. Isolation from the exterior world and tranquility are the keys: "finding no conversation to divert me and fortunately having no cares or passions to trouble me" (ibid.).

The same isolation takes place in the *Meditations* (2:12). "Conversation" refers to the outer world of opinion. In a letter to Elizabeth, the Princess Palatine, with whom he corresponded frequently in later life, Descartes describes the passions as thoughts or cerebral impressions aroused (that is, passive) by external sensations and internal ones—the latter deriving from the body. Descartes's contingent isolation and his good health are thus the primary step in self-interrogation: he is able to free himself of whole ranges of what might be roughly called "incoming stimuli"—an instance of partial self-neutralization or purification, so to speak. This first step, which is by Foucauldian standards a largely accidental pre-ascesis, opens up self-inquiry by allowing him to focus on the active part of his interiority: soul, reason, and will.

In the ensuing process of self-constitution, the relation to self is positioned as a continuing self-decipherment that produces a progressively limited and essentialized interiority as the object of knowledge. Oded Balaban argues that "the content of self-consciousness may be asserted to be the form of consciousness" and "that self-consciousness has not only a cognitive meaning but also constitutes the subject" (xi). It should be noted, as it has been deconstructively, that the constitution of the self as a subject of knowledge is *already* assumed in the self-reflexive splitting of the subject (that is, the existence of a self as potential knower of its own interior identity. Self-knowledge already implies a subject of knowledge.)

As noted, the *Meditations* focus on the senses as the basis of what Descartes has up till then accepted as true. And by centering on the deceiver and dreams in this text, Descartes also makes the interior/exterior or thought/external things opposition explicit, as in: "There are many . . .

beliefs about which doubt is quite impossible, even though they are derived from the senses—for example, that I am here, sitting by the fire" (2:12–13). He later decides that doubt is possible in this case because of the deceiver and dreams, but "beliefs" in the quotation means thoughts or images—that is, interiority—in relation to (or not) external objects, in this case material parts of himself (or so his senses tell him). In the Third Meditation Descartes argues that thoughts or ideas of (supposed) external objects certainly exist in his mind, but that he in the past mistakenly assumed "that there were things outside which were the sources of my ideas and which resembled them [i.e., his thoughts] in all respects" (2:25; see also 26). It is interesting that in this instance doubt indicates the failure of a certain kind of self-reflection—of the mind about the body—soon to be replaced by a more viable form—the mind turned toward itself.

The most familiar part of the *Discourse,* part 4, completes the process of self-inquiry and self-constitution: complete doubt, and then, in doubt, the self-reflexive discovery of the essential interior self: that it exists and that it is a certain kind of substance—thinking being—"by which I am what I am" (1:127) or which is his identity. A self-discernment. It is interesting that the basis of certainty for Descartes in the *Meditations* is proximity, that is, the closeness of the self as mind to itself. In Hassan Melehy's phrase, "The modern subject, following Descartes, is immediate presence to itself, pure autoaffection" (1997, 94). For example, Descartes says in the Third Meditation that "sense perception and imagination, insofar as they are simply modes of thinking, do exist within me—of that I am certain" (2:24)—that is, even if nothing exists external to mind. Certainty of their existence within the mind here depends on the immediate presence to the mind of the perceptions or imaginations and their being closely observed by the mind. Hence, "[w]hatever I perceive very clearly and distinctly is true" (ibid.).

The *cogito* might be paraphrased as follows: I, the subject of knowledge, external and objective, observe my more inner self or process of consciousness to be one of thinking (doubt is a kind of thought). Therefore I (exterior) conclude that I (interior to the prior "I") exist, since thinking cannot occur apart from being (see below). The fact that this conclusion is also a form of thought and that therefore an even more exterior "I" might be necessary in order to insure that this thinking is identical in form with "doubt-thinking" and also that an integral subject exists—ad infinitum—all this doesn't seem to bother Descartes. Proximity, as noted above, does seem to fit the two parts of the split subject back together again (cf. Bowie 1996, 123ff., and Frank 1996, 128–29).

What we see in this argument is that the subject of knowledge is produced simultaneously with self-reflection, that is, when becoming the object of self-inquiry and self-knowledge necessitates the existence of the self as objectifier or knower. The self-knower produces the self as knowledge, proving by a kind of circularity that its position as objective knower is justified. Stated more in Descartes's terms: self-knowledge is the first knowledge according to the logic of the ascesis: the interior self is the object of knowledge, from the analysis of which arises the subject of knowledge; this is the production, the instance, and the proof that the self can act validly as a subject of other knowledges, or produce knowledge of the external world.

The individual which constructs itself as a moral subject in Foucault's latest writings entails the assumption that the individual exists prior to its self-construction, as with Descartes. This should not be taken as a humanist assumption on the part of Foucault, that is, as a "return" of the subject. It is an assumption of the cultures he studies, a part of the "historical ontology" of human nature. Descartes produces the subject of knowledge by means of an epistemological, not ethical, process in which the subject is already entailed, but the point is that this subject of knowledge is fundamental to our own, modern "historical ontology" as well, not as a transcendent truth of human nature.

There are numerous further details of Descartes's self-inquiry: for example, having educed one true proposition, the *cogito* itself, he "see[s] clearly that in order to think it is necessary to exist" (ibid.), and this leads to a rule about the relation between clear conceptions and evident truth (it is necessary to remember that this is a transcendental inquiry, not an empirical one). At this point in the *Meditations* Descartes works from the interior of ideas to exteriority by means of rational inference in a much more detailed manner than in the *Discourse*—for example, in the Third Meditation. Descartes has of course been attacked by recent philosophers of mind for, in the words of Dieter Sturma, "the original theoretical sin," that is, producing the "reifications that accompany the concept of the res cogitans" (200–201).

But the important point is that self-inquiry, self-analysis, self-experience, and self-knowledge of one's constituent interiority is necessary to found the possibility of knowledge in the subject; it consequently serves as "the true method of attaining the knowledge of everything within my mental capabilities" (1:119). Thus, as he shortly after brings the self-inquiry to completion, Descartes moves on to knowledge of nature and the exterior world in general. This shift occurs in the Fourth Meditation:

"And from the mere fact that there is such an idea [of God] within me, or that I who possess this idea exist, I clearly infer that God also exists. . . . And now, from this contemplation of the true God . . . I think I can see a way forward to the knowledge of other things" (2:37). But the Fourth Meditation is actually preliminary to the certainty of knowledge of external objects (see, e.g., 2:44). Descartes gets around to this only in the Sixth Meditation: "It follows that corporeal things exist" (2:55). This reverses the Epicurean orientation, which uses knowledge to establish moral self-maintenance. But Descartes eventually goes on to talk about the relation of knowledge to moral agency.

There are two kinds of knowledge at issue here: first, the ascesis or self-relation that produces self-knowledge through a process of self-experience of one's interiority. This is perforce individual knowledge. In Descartes this individuality of self-knowledge is only a part of the process, the institution of the subject of objective knowledge, that is, knowledge of the second kind. In fact, Descartes poses himself as a singular individual who undergoes a private ascesis, one which should not serve as a model for others (1:112, 118, passim); at the same time Descartes positions himself within the "normal," as a subject of reason or the "good sense" that "is naturally equal in all" (1:111). The epistemological ascesis insures the coincidence of rationality with human identity, and hence universality.

The individual, by knowing itself and thereby producing itself as a subject of knowledge, opens the possibility of scientific or objective knowledge. This knowledge by definition transcends the individual subject: it is knowledge which is compatible with self-knowledge and arises from it, but it is different in kind. Andrew Bowie, for example, maintains that rationalism "sees the necessities of thought evident in mathematics and logic as imbued in the very nature of things, so that the task of thinking is to construct the whole pattern of reality on the basis of these indisputable a priori foundations (1996, 107). The two kinds redouble each other. Rationality is produced by an inquiry into the inner, essential self considered as an object of knowledge; hence it is objective knowledge. With "the invention of man" that begins in the seventeenth century and intensifies in the nineteenth, scientific knowledge becomes increasingly self-reflexive, producing the human sciences of medicine, psychoanalysis, and so on. Modern thought has been described as the attempt to think "the unthought" of its thinking and so to excavate or to produce the truth of human nature; this has been called "the invention of man," (that is, as a scientific object)—an object that still occupies the position of the subject of knowledge (Foucault 1970, 303–31; see also Hoy 1988, 18, 36–37). Foucault's image of this objective self-reflexive knowledge in *The Birth of the Clinic* is the autopsy: humans penetrating into deeper and deeper levels of human interiority—that is, into themselves.

What happens to the purely ethical ascesis in Descartes, the a priori necessity of constituting oneself as the moral subject of one's actions? I have argued that Descartes adapted that ascesis toward the end of producing a subject of knowledge; but it also remains an ethical ascesis. The turn that philosophy takes along with Descartes forces an epistemological problematic: do we know? if so, how and what do we know? what are the limits of knowledge? and primarily for Descartes, what is it that knows? In his "stove-heated room" Descartes intends to reject all opinions and replace them with truths produced by the application of "the standards of reason," beginning with the epistemological reduction or ascesis. Only then does the question of what is traditionally thought of as moral activity occur. As one critic puts it,"the privileged position of a morality was increasingly identified with rational knowledge and the subject who was in a position to know it" (Harootunian 1988, 119).

By means of the truths which replace opinions, Descartes argues, "I would succeed in conducting my life much better" (1985a, 1:117). Virtue thus becomes the resultant of rational knowledge: reason, which produces "a true knowledge of good," is the prior foundation of action (Letter to Elizabeth, 1 September 1645 [1970, 169–70]). Descartes, in other words, allows for the production of the self as a moral agent only after the production of the self in relation to knowledge.

Thus moral behavior becomes part of objective knowledge, in the sense that it necessarily follows from both the cartesian ascesis and consequent knowledge of the world; then the individual can calculate the potential good of any intended action. The autopsy, mentioned above as the medical form of objective yet self-reflexive knowledge is, like moral knowledge, distinct from the primary cartesian ascesis and posterior to it.

The prior ascesis, which produces interiority by representing it to the self, persists, but tends in the future to become detached from scientific inquiry and to constitute a different and even opposed kind of knowledge. In the many forms which it takes in our modern knowledge-society it most often comes to constitute unique individual experience and identity.

To pursue this eventual conflict of knowledges, we must jump far ahead, filling in only a few blank spaces. For example, Kant in his first Critique dispenses with the ascesis. The focus is human interiority or more precisely the already given subject of knowledge in terms of its faculties of cognition, their operation, and the limits on the human knowledge consequently produced. Kant's approach is transcendental—that is, the inquiry into human cognition is prior to empirical experience—and certainly individual self-inquiry and experience have no place here. David Hoy argues that Kant held that "Genuine self-knowledge is in a sense impossible, since the self that we make appear to ourselves as an object of knowledge will never be identical to the self that is constructing that object" (Hoy 1988, 16); hence the ascesis is irrelevant and is replaced only by transcendental apperception. In terms of "the invention of man," however, Kant's Critique is scientifically self-reflexive, an objective human perspective on human nature.

The Earl of Shaftesbury at the beginning of the eighteenth century seems poised between Descartes and Kant in terms of the necessity of the prior ascesis. Shaftesbury, whose thought apparently derives from that of the Cambridge Platonists (roughly contemporary with Descartes), continues the emphasis on interiority but also produces a form of that interior identity different from Descartes and the rationalists. This is an important shift as it applies to the novel, as will be clear shortly. This shift in interior identity also facilitates the split between objective knowledge and experience.

Shaftesbury considers the argument of Descartes's self-inquiry logically suspect, although he is willing to accept self-existence as evident. Thus it is peculiar that at times he seems to reproduce the cartesian ascesis, arguing that individuals must turn their eyes toward their own interiority or "take the inward way" as a first step, even to the point of doubting the existence of the external world. The self-reflexive process is necessary to found the self as a subject of knowledge, which is ultimately the result of an inquiry into the nature of the affections. Then humans are able "to trust [their] own eyes and take for real the whole creation" (Ashley 1964, 2:286–87).

Yet in the *Inquiry Concerning Virtue...* Shaftesbury takes up a position much like that which Kant will take up later: human identity is constructed as an unreflective natural inclination motivated by the affections (1:243), which are, incidentally, largely social. And this is the usual *métier* of Shaftesbury: the objective inquiry of the scientific knower into human identity, one which is also self-reflexive in the objective sense. But Shaftesbury is significant because of his fixing of human identity in the feelings instead of reason; however universalized his approach, he produces an ethical substance that will become central to individual identity in the following two centuries.

⟪◌⟫

Literary texts of the period reflect these essentially modern concerns with self-refexivity, interiority, and the relation of the two forms of knowledge.

This may be particularly true of the novel, which has been traditionally assumed to be coincident with modern or bourgeois society. Fictional texts are usually taken as exemplifications, but ultimately they are as productive of interiority as modern philosophical texts. They only differ in one respect: they call attention to narrative structure or, what is the same thing, the positionality of the subject of knowledge and the structure of knowing. This question is as relevant to philosophical texts—as has been made clear—because they are in one sense narrative fictions. Witness the effect of the splitting of the subject in Descartes's *Discourse,* in which the later subject, beyond the narrative, recounts the reconstructed autobiographical process of his own constitution of himself as a subject of knowledge—that is, from the perspective of the later subject of knowledge. But for the purposes here, so-called literary texts are the most interesting.

Shaftesbury leads us to Henry Fielding, who represents one of the traditions of the novel in the eighteenth century. In *Joseph Andrews,* for example, feeling—benevolence, good will, or, in opposition, self-love—constitutes the moral identity of the characters. The older form of identity, by means of alliance or relation, to class, family, nation, religion, gender, and so forth, but in Fielding predominately to the human community, is partially refounded on individual interiority, specifically feeling or the social affections. The primary characters in *Joseph Andrews* act unreflectingly on their feelings of benevolence; an interiority constituted by self-reflection and self-experience of one's feelings is generally absent from the text. Interiority or the affections are necessitated but not represented as self-discovered or produced, with the exception of Lady Booby, who is self-focused or -obsessed and therefore given to inner struggle with her better inclinations. This raises the question of narrative structure.

Joseph Andrews comes under the rubric of third-person narration, which foregrounds the position of the objective or scientific knower. The subject of knowledge is outside, detached, able to render an objective, rational judgment. This structure seems relatively uncomplicated in the novel, except that it at the same time elides our usual separation between author and narrator—in order to form a rhetoric of truth—and collapses the expected distance between author-narrator and reader, who is directly addressed at strategic points and is the recipient of one complete chapter. By this means the same affective relations are produced between reader and characters as are produced among the characters.

The author-narrator is also related by benevolent feeling to his characters. This is expressed in displaced fashion in Parson Adams's encomium of Homer's "pathetic" writing: "The images [of Andromache] are so extremely tender . . . that I am convinced that the poet had the worthiest and best heart imaginable" (1961, 167). Fielding, in an epic of his own devising, would expect to duplicate that affective relation, and that relation is clear in his treatment of Adams, Joseph, and Fanny throughout. On the return to the parish of Lady Booby, Adams is produced as one who "exprest a satisfaction in his face which nothing but benevolence made happy by its objects [that is, the parishioners] could infuse." Along with Joseph and Fanny, "no three persons could be more kindly received, as, indeed, none ever more deserved to be universally beloved" (236). The author-narrator's as well as the characters' self-experience of the natural feeling that arises from relation is marked here, though neither is directly represented except as outward manifestation.

Fielding has it both ways: the author-narrator is objective and affective as well: he is the outside subject of knowledge of the truth of the characters and the person joined by good will to these other "real" persons of the story. And he "knows" these characters by means of his affective relation to them: scientific knowledge is effected by and founded on the self-experience of affective bonds. The two forms of knowledge are inherently compatible—so much so that knowledge of human nature comprehends and encloses interiority without any necessity for representation of it. The characters individually manifest the institutional knowledge of human identity.

Thomas Pavel proposes in an essay a somewhat similar schema for understanding the shift in the meaning of interiority in the middle of the nineteenth century for writers of fiction; earlier: "the self was understood as the locus of strategic and moral debate closely related to action and held in a language shared by an entire community; [thus] inner thoughts were taken to be as clearly articulated as public ones, and accordingly, the difference between them and overt speech was a matter of contingency" (1992, 25).

The representation of Lady Booby's thoughts would answer to this schema nicely. Pavel in effect constructs an interiority that in its first stages is continuous with exteriority; after the mid-nineteenth century, he says, a distancing of action from thought occurred, and there appeared "representation of nondiscursive elements through inner discourse" (ibid.). By the latter he means "sensations, memories, and diffuse desires" (26). Why this distancing occurred is not made clear. Pavel is in fact arguing that thought is progressively deinstitutionalized, while the opposite is actually the case.

Thus in the nineteenth century the representation of interiority in fiction becomes an important and, following Pavel, a different issue. The development of free indirect discourse is a case in point, in Jane Austen, Flaubert, Emile Zola, and others. Charles Dickens's *Great Expectations* manifests a similar concern about the representation of interiority. Incidentally, Dickens's novel is in some senses a reprise of *Joseph Andrews,* so a few of the same questions may be addressed to it. The structure of the representation of interiority in *Great Expectations* is different from that in Flaubert and other examples of free indirect discourse: it is a first-person narration. This kind of narrative is structurally self-reflexive, entailing as it does a double narration. The older, mature Pip stands at the end of the narration, virtually outside it as an objective observer, and stages or frames the immediate self-relation and expression of inner experience of the younger Pip. The novel centers on a series of these moments of interiority—especially the moments of self-reflection and self-decipherment, often misguided, within the overall structural frame of self-reflection.

The lesson of *Great Expectations* is the same as that of *Joseph Andrews:* a matter of benevolence or love that binds humans (although in the former, interestingly enough, it is no longer the human community but a very restricted group of relatives and friends). Now, however, it is a lesson to be learned by experience—by event and a process of self-reflection that eventually produces self-knowledge. *Great Expectations* is a typical Bildungsroman, a narrative of inner growth and maturation. The events which propel Pip toward self-knowledge are devastating at first, but eventually he transforms himself by producing deeper and more hidden feelings—ones present in the first self-representation of the thought of the frightened young Pip in his encounter with the escaped convict. The process is thus one of self-recognition.

The end of the novel brings the narrative separation of the two Pips toward closure, allowing for the smooth emergence of individual experience into objective knowledge. As with Descartes, whose *Discourse* is also a first-person narrative, self-reflexivity in the form of self-examination and self-knowledge is the structure of the ascesis or method by which the individual constitutes itself as a moral subject at the same time it qualifies itself as a subject of knowledge. This subject of knowledge, that is, the objective observer of human nature set apart from daily human intercourse yet bound affectively to it, is produced by self-experience. In the original ending of the novel this is the position of the older Pip. The two kinds of knowledge are compatible and necessary to each other, one growing out of the other. That is guaranteed by the narrative structure: the two Pips are the same character.

The representation of interiority becomes important in the nineteenth century, but it is often tinged with irony and a certain embarrassment. In *Great Expectations* self-reflection is indistinguishable from self-absorption and self-love. This is one reason why self-reflexivity and the representation of interiority are not factors in Fielding's novel except for the characters motivated by self-love. In Dickens, a century later, it is necessary to represent interiority in order to constitute individual identity, but even as it occurs it must be transcended. As Pip matures in the final third of the novel he necessarily becomes a subject of action and much less a self-reflective subject of thought.

Something of the same occurs in other novels of the nineteenth century; in *Madame Bovary*, for example, the representation of interiority cannot be separated from irony that takes the form of the expression of the "innerness" of the character in language that is in itself inaccessible to the character (see Pavel 1992, 26). The objective narrator knows the character as she does not: self-reflection on the part of the character produces a flawed self-knowledge that is the result of self-absorption and that is what is incorporated into the narration's perspective. As Foucault might say, the discursive element has yet to undergo a positive inversion. In the twentieth-century modern, however, the self-absorbed constitution of one's identity is central and rarely completely ironic.

On the other hand, the nineteenth century was witness to an increased concern with the representation of interiority, self-experience and self-knowledge, and the individualizing effects of such a concern. The emergence of the production of inwardness within discursivity seems increasingly to unsettle the relation of knowledge and experience so that by the end of the century self-experience comes to contest and even oppose objective knowledge. This is doubtlessly connected to a contradiction that arose within the Enlightenment project. One function was to articulate reason's powers in knowledge and politics (and knowledge-politics). Foucault says there emerged a confused opposition between a rationalization-prone society and individual liberty (for example, in Mill) that it was the task of philosophy since Kant to adjudicate (1988, 58–59). The contradiction is in the fact that Enlightenment self-reflexive reason produced the individual subject as well as subjecting it to institutional knowledge.

Literature in its nineteenth-century form of concern with the interiority and particularity of individual characters in the novel seems to have entered the lists as well as philosophy—that is, with the claim that interiority is privileged. This was not a problem for Descartes, in whose time the "human sciences" were yet to take shape; the negativity attached to self-absorption mentioned earlier might also be read as the preliminary instability that led to a discursive shift in the splitting of the two knowledges and the more intensive identification of interiority as identity.

This split might be read as a "genealogical moment," for Foucault argues in *Power/Knowledge* that genealogy "entertains the claims to attention of local, discontinuous, disqualified, illegitimate knowledges against the claims of a unitary body of theory which would filter, hierarchise and order them in the name of some true knowledge and some arbitrary idea of what constitutes a science and its objects" (1980b, 83)—only to undergo a further stage of institutionalization through the representation of these illegitimate knowledges. Interiority has been subjected to knowledge throughout the nineteenth century, so the genealogical moment referred to here seems to be a closure or refusal that leads to intensification, since an alternative to incorporation into objective knowledge is not readily available. Hence the denial, in the two novels to be taken up, that interiority can emerge seamlessly into the appropriation by knowledge. This, in turn, can be said to found one of the traditions of the twentieth-century modern: the artist-hero, self-absorbed and self-constituted as elitist other, self-defined as different from the vulgar: T. S. Eliot: "The seventh day *they* motor." The subject becomes the other of discourse, the unrevealed.

The conflict of the two kinds of knowledge is apparent in *Heart of Darkness* (1899). The story is structured by two first-person narratives, one enclosing the other, the unnamed narrator telling the story of Marlow telling a story of his relation to Kurtz. The remarkable thing about *Heart of Darkness* is that in each instance the outside, objective observer—in contrast to the older, mature Pip—does not know and even cannot know. The subject of knowledge is in crisis. To put it another way: at the center of the inner narration is Kurtz and his self-experience—what Marlow the narrator characterizes as self-gratification or the gratification of "monstrous . . . passions." That Marlow incessantly attempts to "know" and characterize this interiority of Kurtz is an important issue, and we will return to it in a moment.

Marlow begins his journey up river as a rather cynical and detached observer of the greedy ineptitude of the "pilgrims" at the outer and central stations: he stands above and overhears the manager and his uncle at one point as they relish the thought of Kurtz's demise. As Marlow moves closer to Kurtz he becomes less detached; in other words, his own self-experience becomes a factor. The image of the binoculars, by which Marlow, standing safely on the boat at the inner station dock, is thrust immediately into the center of the compound and comes face-to-face with the inward-facing heads on stakes, serves as a sign of that. Marlow is affected by the wilderness and by Kurtz; while the latter goes completely over the edge, Marlow is somehow restrained; he merely looks over the edge at Kurtz, who lies at the bottom, immersed in the darkness. This is the "text"; but there is a subtext, one that centers on the discontinuity of institutional and self-knowledge.

Consider, however, the outer level of the narration. The unnamed narrator is part of a group of men formerly of the sea who listen to Marlow's story; this narrator reports not only the story but Marlow's frequent breaks from it in order to address the listeners directly. His statements to them are all of a piece: you are all enmeshed in civilization; you are urban and cossetted, made safe by a policeman on every corner. The listening group forms a community of knowers, the recipients of communicable cultural knowledge. Cultural knowledge is in fact structurally the same as scientific knowledge—depending on how specific the institution is which presides over the production of knowledge. Discursivity and communicability are the signs of objective knowledge. Marlow says again and again that they, his listeners, subjects of knowledge, can never understand his experience in the heart of darkness: "You can't understand. How could you . . ." (122). Yet he is at the same time attempting to make his and Kurtz's self-experience discursive: he constructs by the fact of his narration the possibility of objective knowledge detached but deriving from self-experience and moving into the cultural arena.

This latter claim focuses attention on the economy of knowledge and experience in the inner narrative: if Marlow's group, idling away time on a boat anchored in the estuary of the Thames within sight of the center of a great civilization, can know Marlow's experience half a world away, in "darkest Africa," then Marlow can know Kurtz's interiority: "The thing was to know what he belonged to, how many powers of darkness claimed him for their own" (121). This is of course to place Kurtz within the categories of knowledge-constitution. Yet everyone who has read *Heart of Darkness* knows what the central enigma is, what might be called the absent center: what is missing is Kurtz's interiority, his own first-person narration. And this puts Marlow's knowledge in doubt. The heart of darkness is not dark because it contains "unspeakable rites" (123) or "forgotten and brutal instincts, gratified and monstrous passions" (143) or "abominable satisfactions" (149), but because it cannot be known, except as self-experience. When Marlow characterizes Kurtz in terms of the "Hollow[ness] at [his] core" (133) or "the barren darkness of his heart" (146) he is admitting to the discontinuity between experience and knowledge. "His was an impenetrable darkness," says Marlow of Kurtz (147).

Kurtz is always an enigma to Marlow, despite the fact that the latter's narrative emphasizes the contagion that spreads from Kurtz to himself, and the similarity of their experiences. Marlow's binocular metaphor virtually claims that he enters Kurtz's consciousness. Marlow does indeed *know* about Kurtz: the reports of "the unspeakable rites . . . offered up to him" were "reluctantly gathered" from hearsay. He knows Kurtz through the form of a series of oppositions, that is, within language and discourse. Kurtz is fixed within a structure defined by: light/darkness, civilized/primitive, reason/passion (or restraint and its absence), the licit/illicit (for example, "this alone had beguiled his unlawful soul beyond the bounds of permitted aspirations" [143]), and so forth. At the moment of experience, however, language fails; witness the eloquence of Kurtz's Report.

Kurtz's impenetrable darkness can be characterized: simply put, detached from European civilization, Kurtz turns inward self-reflexively, and this takes the form of self-experience; "his soul . . . had looked within itself . . . had gone mad" (144)—Marlow labels it the monstrous self-gratification of every desire. But of course noncritical self-experience is by definition self-gratification, or, as earlier, self-absorption.

This characterization remains along the lines of Marlow's insights as an observer and a discourser precisely because self-experience is seen as discontinuous with discourse and knowledge. Descartes argues that self-reflexive knowledge of one's interiority is the foundation of knowledge, but for Conrad there is a fundamental differentiation. On board, going down the river, with Kurtz "as good as dead," Marlow has a kind of negative epiphany about a supposed epiphany of Kurtz: "And for a moment it seemed to me as if I also were buried in a vast grave full of unspeakable secrets. I felt an intolerable weight oppressing my breast . . . [in] the darkness of an impenetrable night" (139). There is a claim to sympathy and connection here: "I also," Marlow says, experienced what Kurtz did. But "secrets"? hidden from whom, if not Marlow? Secrets, the impenetrable, that which cannot be known. "Unspeakable": that is, if known, never to be contained in discourse: but of course discourse is knowledge. Thus the site where Marlow wishes most strongly to claim intimacy with Kurtz is infiltrated by counter argument.

At other points Marlow makes a clear distinction between his own self-experience and Kurtz's. The moment of Kurtz's self-recognition—that is, his rational or civilized self-reflection on his self-experience once he is descending from the wilderness and is near death—all of this is put by

Marlow in the form of a question because he is only the observer, unable to penetrate Kurtz's interiority: was this "the supreme moment of complete knowledge?" (147). Here the discontinuity seems to be emphasized. The distinction is even clearer at another strategic point in the narrative where Marlow seems intent on marking the difference between his knowledge and Kurtz's experience: "he had made that last stride, he had stepped over the edge, while I had been permitted to draw back my hesitating foot. And perhaps in this is the whole difference; perhaps all the wisdom, and all the truth, and all sincerity are just compressed into that inappreciable moment of time in which we step over the threshold of the invisible" (149). Marlow admittedly speculates, because Kurtz's interiority is not accessible to him. It should be noted that this is the moment of total self-experience for Kurtz—this stepping over—and not his moment of self-recognition, which comes later. At the moment of stepping over, he clearly has no objective knowledge, even of his own interiority.

There are a number of other issues: even if Kurtz's experience becomes accessible as Marlow's self-experience, it is still unspeakable to anyone else; Marlow's first-person narration is also end-loaded: his immediate inner experience in the heart of darkness seems remote; seen through the wrong end of the telescope, it is attenuated and obscured at the moment of telling by the framing of philosophic and scientific language and by objectification; and finally the outer narrator: his description of the difficulty of Marlow's stories with their surrounding luminosity, that is, allowing for understanding only in terms of an intuition of the self-experience of the other, not its articulation; this narrator only learns from Marlow's story that "the heart of an immense darkness" is "out there," proving the incommensurability of knowledge and experience.

Marlow's first-person narrative promise of access to another's interiority is thoroughly ironic. The third-person-narrative structure of *The Awakening*, published in the same year as *Heart of Darkness*, would suggest a similar access by different means—that is, by use of free indirect discourse and other techniques available to it. Both novels are about self-experience or, what is the same thing, self-realization, the actualization of one's inner potential. The person *is* its inner experience, not its external motions. Since the interest in Chopin's novel is thus focused on the emotional changes Edna Pontellier undergoes throughout, it would seem natural to represent that interiority completely. Peculiarly enough, this is a promise not quite fulfilled, and this makes the two novels companion pieces.

In *The Awakening* objective knowledge takes the form of the cultural, although the scope is more curtailed and specific and gender oriented:

Edna Pontellier becomes part of a New Orleans Creole subculture, which is represented as different from, for example, Accadian or Cajun culture. The knowledge of this culture is embedded in a set of attitudes and social roles and duties. Edna Pontellier's interiority is posed against this social truth in the novel. But the same opposition appears in the relation of the narrative perspective to Edna's self-experience. This perspective mediates Edna's self-experience and strictly frames its representation. It is objective without quite being the voice of the culture. For example, when Edna finally learns to swim, she is likened by the narrative to a child first learning to walk, "boldly and with overconfidence"; further: "A feeling of exultation overtook her, as if some power of significant import had been given her to control the working of her body and soul. She grew daring and reckless, overestimating her strength. She wanted to swim far out" (1981, 36). This is clearly Edna's self-experience; but it appears by way of a thoroughly mediated access: the objective, cautious, even ironic narrative perspective. And it is not merely the irony: typically, the narrative only summarizes Edna's burgeoning self-experience instead of providing immediate access to her consciousness. The short chapter 28, after Edna sleeps with Arobin, provides another illustration.

Why limit access to the interiority of the only character who matters in this novel, and the only one who undergoes any sort of significant inner transformation? There is no doubt that Edna's self-experience is central here: she emerges from the cocoon of rather indifferent social propriety to undergo the experience of a succession of her emotions and her desires—and their gratification as often as not. It is the experience of her inner self, of all her emotional potential as an individual. This is staged in one instance, during her sleepy Sunday afternoon at Madame Antoine's, when she luxuriously examines and feels the round firm sensuousness of her body (48). Her new identity is the product of this intense self-focus or -experience; it in fact is that self-experience.

The objectifying, summarizing narrative that frames and distances Edna's interiority could be said at the same time to obscure it from prying eyes, to allow it to remain Edna's interiority. Edna herself tends to be private, self-circumscribed, and isolative. She moves to her own home to be alone; she realizes that males constitute, like signs, a chain of substitutions, and that eventually all of them will fade from memory.

Toward the end of the novel, when she has just undergone the devastating experience of witnessing childbirth, and when Dr Mandelet offers to allow her to pour out her confused feelings to him, she makes a signal refusal. She is her inner experience, however disturbed at the moment, and she deliberately chooses to cloister it: once communicated, it is no longer inner or individual; no longer her unique identity if shared. In a similar way the narrative perspective, by its very objectivity, seems to grant Edna the space of her own interiority; even the irony about Edna's transformation can be seen as a technique of nonpenetration, a way of remaining outside and detached. But not completely so: that comes at the end by Edna's own act.

This provides a new perspective on Edna's suicide. The confusion that comes from witnessing childbirth is based on her desire for freedom and her visceral knowledge of her connection to her children, which she defers but must eventually face: she says to Mandelet, "I want to be let alone. Nobody has any right—except children, perhaps—and even then, it seems to me . . ." and trails off. Then: "I shouldn't want to trample upon the little lives. Oh! I don't know what I'm saying" (147).

Edna's interiority, even in its severely mediated form, disappears shortly after and is not represented again until the next day when she stands poised on the beach at Grand Isle. Her thoughts—partly interior monologue—are reported by the narration as what has occurred the previous night. In these thoughts her children are still her "antagonists," the unbreakable link that binds her to the social world. "But she knew a way to elude them" (151). Then the narrator brackets Edna between the sea and the sensuous self-experience of her nakedness, her memory of her loosening attachments, that is, her interiority. Edna's final narrative act is to swim directly out into the Gulf; suicide, yes, but it is fundamentally an act of "eluding" the narrative perspective; she simply swims out of it, refusing in a final act to allow her interiority to be compromised.

There is an irony here. In order to preserve her interiority intact, Edna herself opens it up to the outside—the sea, the meadow, and the unlimited. This is precisely in the terms of the narrative perspective, for which these are the outward signs of Edna's innerness. In one sense, then, she remains contained by knowledge. Nonetheless, Edna does escape this control. She simultaneously moves in mind into memory, barricading her interiority, and moves outward, beyond the grasp of the narrative—with the apparent compliance of the narrative perspective.

As in *Heart of Darkness*, in *The Awakening* the narrative of interiority faces the problematic of its own production. The representation of interiority by whatever technique disrupts the interior/exterior opposition. Objective knowledge is always knowledge-power, the production of truth under the auspices and control of the institution. Objective knowledge, persuading itself of its own distance from power, ends by opening up avenues along which power penetrates—simultaneously (see Foucault 1988,

43, 106). The truth of interiority produced or represented, that is, as the object of knowledge, is no longer interior and protected. That is the dilemma that Edna faces, and problematically escapes. In *Heart of Darkness* the claims of knowledge to comprehend inner experience are always seen to fall short.

In both novels, in contrast to the earlier examples, the narratability of interiority is called into question, as well as language and discourse themselves, by which knowledge is produced. The fundamental disjunction of knowledge and self-experience is represented in the later novels by the testing of limits and attempts to broach the discontinuity. This suggests that these texts assume the disjunction from the outset, test it, make forays into understanding interiority and end by affirming the intractibility of the difference. Interiority is then confirmed by its absence from discourse, although it took a century of producing that interiority to make such a conclusion an arguable one. It is a strategic reversal of a discourse of compatibility.

Conrad and Chopin could thus be considered as a reaction against the instrumentality of reason or scientific and political rationality in the human sciences, the resistance to the penetration of knowledge-power. Richard Rorty, in his work on the seventeenth-century invention of the mind as interiority, mentions what he calls "the sentimental intellectual's conviction that there was a private inner realm into which publicity, 'scientific method,' and society could not penetrate" (122–23). From our own perspective this sentimentality seems inevitable, as well as its passing from the postmodern scene. Thomas Nagel in *The View from Nowhere* sees both an integration of the two perspectives (objective and subjective) and an impossibility of reconciliation.

But what is interesting at this point are Chopin's and Conrad's resources for this reaction: against the history of reason they have recourse only to its other, irrationality, madness, and egocentrism. And they throw up a barrier to penetration by setting off a separate and unknowable truth of the individual interior self; yet by doing this they, like Freud, set up another realm that holds out the promise of yielding its secrets to objective knowledge. They unwittingly do the work of knowledge.

These texts also seem to introduce the twentieth-century modern: the artist as alien, who produces him/herself by self-inquiry, self-experience, self-knowledge, and the consequent self-constitution as a unique interiority discontinuous from the social. There remains the paradox, just noted, that interiority exists only by being represented in discourse and thus becoming part of institutional knowledge. In the twentieth century there are prominent attempts to limit narrative control such as stream-of-consciousness narration, the intensified use of indirect discourse, dreams, surreality, which all propose the attenuation of objective knowledge. I. A. Richards and others approach the problem by distinguishing the two discourses of science and poetry, exterior and interior truth; but Richards also constructs interiority as a form of psychological intelligibility in his *Principles of Literary Criticism*.

Not all of the first half of the twentieth century is of a piece. Fiction often continues to integrate narrative knowledge with the self-experience of the characters, as in *Death in Venice*. And in the thirties and forties a shift occurs which alters the problematic of interiority. Interiority doesn't disappear, but becomes textualized. And self-relation takes on a different form in this new textual era: the individual stands outside itself and observes itself in relation to the world (see Nagel 1986, 4–5 and passim). This is the same capacity to stand "outside" that is a function of the Subject noted in previous chapters. This is the era of language and discourse, of the intentional fallacy and then of structuralism. Up until structuralism interiority was assumed to be expressed or manifested by the text. It was not a long step toward saying that only the text existed, that writing or discourse produced interiority and therefore the subject and its identity; this was said by the sixties.

◖◍◗

There is another example of the modern conflict of knowledge and experience on a slightly more theoretical level, the critical discourse of the seventies and early eighties concerning free indirect discourse. A particular difference within the more traditional part of this criticism demonstrates how the problematic of interiority persists in the textual era alongside post-structural notions of originary absence and the demise of the subject. Free indirect discourse was a response to the increased attention paid to interiority in the nineteenth century, and continued into the twentieth century along with techniques such as stream-of-consciousness. Roy Pascal's *The Dual Voice* is concerned primarily with the earlier century. The title is indicative: Pascal argues the traditional continuity of objective knowledge and inner experience within the structure of free indirect discourse. There is no representation without a representer: the narrative perspective or "voice" seamlessly transforms the characters' interiority into discourse; the narrative perspective is the embodiment of the formal and textualizing impulse. We must remember that Pascal operates under the aegis of fictional realism, that is, under the assumption that the origin of the representation of interiority is an actual if hypothetical consciousness, which is brought into discourse.

Against Pascal's traditional reading the linguist Ann Banfield poses a forceful alternative argument in *Unspeakable Sentences.* These are the sentences of narration and represented speech and thought, the latter her name for free indirect discourse. These sentences are in effect unspoken by the (previously supposed) narrator or agency of narration. Banfield in fact denies the existence of a narrative agency within the text, putting into doubt by elimination the textual era's normal distinction of author and narrator. Banfield thus produces what appears in most of her book as a direct, unframed representation of interiority arising as the inner self-expression of the self-experience of a character. There is immediate access to this interiority, although the self-representation is linguistic. This would indeed be the triumph of interiority, its rupture of the external frame of objectivity, notwithstanding the continued irony of its exterior representation.

Yet Banfield makes ultimate reference to the author if not the narrator. In a literate society such as nineteenth-century Europe had become— that is, a society of writing—she argues that free indirect discourse found its development. Writing allows for a deferral of the speaker/author and the present or "now" of the act of writing; in other words these are left outside the text. Objective knowledge is now external to the text. The text self-circumscribes its own interiority. Within the text are representations of the interiority of the characters intersticed with constative (fictional) narrative sentences (for example, "The war ended."). According to Banfield the frame of objective knowledge has disappeared from the text insofar as it knows interiority; but of course it has only been displaced into authorial space.

Here is the classic argument about the relation or difference between objective, scientific knowledge—the external perspective—and the interiority of self-experience and self-knowledge. One, in a direct line from Descartes, but without benefit of an ascesis, asserts both the duality and the coincidence of the two forms of knowledge. The other asserts the priority of the self-production of interiority, but not without a certain sleight of hand. Both views are traditional from a nineties' perspective: Banfield's deferral is not poststructural; for her the author remains the origin of signification.

There is no attempt here to extend this analysis into the poststructural era, but the death of the subject is familiar, as well as the later claim that such news was greatly exaggerated. The former suggests at least the beginning of the end of the era in which interiority is identity. "The postmodern paradigm is not profundity but complexity" of the surface or text

(Hoy 1988, 28). Is it a coincidence, then, that a new impetus was given to the old relational identity based on gender, race, and ethnicity in the same decade that God died and Derrida and Foucault appeared on the scene? The question that needs to be asked is whether this new identity is discursive or whether it is founded on interiority—how it *feels* to be a woman or African-American.

⟪ 8 ⟫

Kant and Subjective Traditions

This chapter turns to Kant, that is, to another part of the tradition of the subject of knowledge taken up in the previous chapter. Chapter 7 establishes the necessary priority of interior self-knowledge to objective knowledge in Descartes and analyzes the subsequent itinerary of the relation between the two knowledges down into the twentieth century, along with emerging notions of human identity. Now it is important to return to these questions, not through literature, as in chapter 7, but through some philosophical texts, those of Descartes, but primarily of Kant. No chapter can cover the modern philosophical tradition, but it is possible to show how Kant's first two Critiques enter into the debate about subjective and scientific knowledge.

Descartes's return to an episteme of interiority encompasses a new form of self-relation as the production of the self as knower of the *res extensa*. Kant similarly grounds knowledge in the faculties of intuition and cognition given to human nature, but without the prior excursus into self-knowledge that Descartes thought necessary. In Kant the priorities are reversed, and with that come complications. First, the aesthetic and analytic lead to rational speculation about self-knowledge, since the notion of apperception or the "I think" arises there. This is true for Kant despite the fact that the aesthetic and analytic assume the position of the subject of knowledge already exists. The Dialectic in Kant is devoted in part to showing the inevitable effort to produce self-knowledge and the equally inevitable failure of this attempt.

The split and self-reflexive subject is actually a product of the second Critique: the subject here "recognizes" itself, but without an ascesis, as the subject of knowledge; or it assumes the self-produced knowledge of itself as a noumenon or origin in order to warrant the objective nature of moral knowledge. Kant's influence on the modern subject of knowledge thus seems to have come from this latter Critique; yet the first Critique is based on the a priori existence of the subject of knowledge. Together the two Critiques promote the notion that self-knowledge, if possible, is continuous with objective knowledge, although in different ways.

Descartes had introduced the notion of split subjectivity or self-reflexivity and self-consciousness into early modern notions of subjectivity as the necessary constitution of the subject of knowledge; this notion continues to function in the larger discourse of subjectivity within the modernist project. Descartes's task has been to establish a (new) point of certainty in the *cogito* (and later in the *sum*), that is, the constitution of the subject of knowledge by self-reflection on its own interiority; this is the issue on which most commentators agree (e.g., Caton 1973, 35–36 and passim; Judovitz 1988, 25, 47, 77–79; Bowie 1990, 15).

Descartes is not really at issue here, except as a predecessor of Kant and a convenient label for a clearly different epistemic way of thinking about subjectivity. The effect of Descartes, the rationalists in general, the empiricists of the eighteenth century, and Kant as well, with respect to the ancient discourse of subjectivity, is twofold: first, instead of Subject and subject, we now have one subject, variously identified but clearly normalized. At the same time Descartes and others initiate a split in that subject. The normality and universality of the subject is obvious in Kant's delineation of the finite rational being incorporated with sensible intuition; in one commentator's words, "a conception of man that . . . [is] essential and normative" (Van de Pitte 1971, 3).

For eighteenth-century taste critics from Addison to Burke it is a less critically specified but nonetheless universal human subject in terms of its primary and secondary levels of response; the marginal case often turns up in these writings in the form of the blind or deaf individual, but always as the limit case which establishes the normal human response (yet the tendency itself is not universal in the eighteenth century: Baumgarten and Hamann, for example, are concerned with "sensuous particularity" [Bowie 1990, 4–7 and passim]). If it weren't for Foucault we might be tempted to look for a parallel process of political democratization during this era—that is, with the rights of this newly invented and foundational subject.

Second, there is an interiorization of the subject. We might call this an epistemic shift from the concerns of the sixteenth century, as long as that means that inquiry is now focused on interior processes of reason, sensibility, and, ultimately, consciousness—either as constituting/constituted and/or altered by incoming stimuli or as independent of that. This is consonant with Rorty's claim that Descartes invented/produced the "mind." Kant's tendency to focus on appearances instead of things in themselves, as well as on the formation of the will in practical reason instead of on action, are illustrations of this priority.

The central question often becomes, during such an episteme, since we are "locked within," whether we know or how we know. Descartes begins with a similar kind of skepticism. Even the opposition rationalist-empiricist is incorporated within this focus. The subject is in fact structurally the center of this model. For this reason Kant's objective-subjective opposition, based on his universalization of human nature, is often ironic, since what is objective is based on the normal subject (see, e.g., Bowie 1990, 11ff.). Knowledge or the formation of the will produced by the a priori categories of the understanding or by a priori practical laws is in both cases clearly "subjective," since the nature of the finite rational subject—at the abstract or universal level at which Kant conceives it—is prior to both knowledge and the formation of the will.

The subject—the *human* subject, though Kant is aware of the possibility that other thinking subjects exist—is the necessary foundation of the system of philosophy; or, rather, its transcendental faculties serve to ground philosophy. Kant seems to have been in the process of determining this during the 1760s, if the following note is from that period:

> everything passes in a flow before us, and the variations in taste, and the different aspects of man make the whole play uncertain and delusive. Where shall I find fixed points of nature which man can never shift and which can give him indications as to the shore on which he must bring himself to rest. (*Schriften* 20:46 [a marginal note in Kant's copy of *Observations on the Feeling of the Beautiful and the Sublime*], quoted in Van de Pitte 1971, 43)

Even prior to the opposition transcendental/empirical, Kant here sets the stage for the focus on the interiority of the human subject as containing the potential foundation of philosophy.

The whole question may be put in a more direct and focused (if more general and less definitive) way, as Andrew Bowie does in a recent book: "Modern philosophy begins when the basis upon which the world is interpreted ceases to be a deity whose pattern has already been imprinted into existence and becomes instead our reflection upon our own thinking about the world" (1990, 1). That is succinct and to some degree accurate; but the shift to interiority pursued here is more methodological in character.

The question of the subject as the framework of Kant's system is often posed in Kant scholarship as a question of anthropology: is that "science," in terms of Kant's system, merely a peripheral set of empirical observations set down for popular reading late in the philosopher's life— as in the *Anthropology*—or is it in fact structural? Van de Pitte, who also summarizes and focuses this debate, indirectly argues that Kant's Critical Philosophy assumes the human subject as its structural basis (1971, 4– 5, 115, and passim). It can be argued that "the principles . . . in the first Critique, although resting on a certain analysis of subjective functions, take no concrete human nature for their foundation" (Williams, quoted in Van de Pitte 1971, 32), or that Kant is developing, in the first Critique, the a priori basis of the relation of human nature to reality (47). Van de Pitte's contention (the latter) is ultimately a weak one: he often conflates the practical or moral with the empirical; his claim about the systematic relation of a priori "subjective functions" and concrete anthropological knowledge is merely the coincidence of Kant's structural use of the subjective model—a question Van de Pitte does not address directly; and, certainly, Kant's philosophical texts never descend to the level of an interest in historical individuals (except for the names, such as that of David Hume, attached to philosophical positions), in the way history is traditionally understood. As Van de Pitte allows, Kant is only interested in "a truly normative anthropology" as opposed to psychological or empirical subjectivity (81); such an opposition is, however, an effective argument that Kant's anthropology, as it concerns the individual subject, is largely peripheral—if it at the same time reflects the structural function of the subject.

In the previous chapter Descartes is shown to have insisted that self-knowledge is prior to and constitutive of the subject of knowledge. From that perspective Kant may be seen to have understood Descartes's necessity and to have dismissed it, for he assumes from the outset that the human subject constitutes knowledge according to its interior faculties. Descartes would thus only appear in the Dialectic of Pure Reason. Kant's intention implies a recognition of self-relation, but not of the individual. The Critiques thus take the form of scientific self-reflection (the study of human nature by humans, as in the autopsy), which results in the "invention of man."

All this is by way of background or context for a discussion of Kant and the subject. It is not a history of constructions of subjectivity but rather an attempt to put in motion several of the discourses of subjectivity that can be brought to bear on Kant's own construction of the subject, of self-relation and knowledge, in the first two critiques, and which give focus to certain aspects of that construction.

One striking thing about Kant's notion of the subject is that one critique constructs a split and self-reflexive subject and that the other critique argues strongly against the knowability of such a structure; there are arguments to be made which further exacerbate this discontinuity or ameliorate it. The existence of two critiques of reason might be taken as an illustration of the split in the subject (of a different sort), or a reason to look for a continuity which subsumes one kind of reason under another. Other interesting notions arise as a consequence of the splitting of the subject in the *Critique of Practical Reason*. At the upper level of the split, the subject as noumenon, we have a subject endowed, like the Sophist Subject, with the capacity to act as an origin, specifically a practical origin (of intention and act). This same split between sensible and intelligible subject also gives rise to a proliferation of self-reflexivities; and one of the consequences of that is the constitution of an "external" perspective from which to view the whole—that is, the unified—split subject. It is this external, "scientific," objectifying perspective—that is, the position and its substantiality—which should be kept in mind during the following brief journey through the two critiques of reason, for it is the site of knowledge contained in the subject.

The *Critique of Pure Reason* is variously divided in terms of how it provides insight into subjectivity. On the one hand, human nature is the principle of knowledge; or, knowledge is a construction by the universal or abstract human subject. This is the structural assumption of the three main sections of the text, of the Transcendental Aesthetic, the Transcendental Analytic and even including the Dialectic, in which the ideas of pure reason transcend the possibility of human knowledge while yet conforming to human nature. On the other hand the Dialectic represents a distinctly different tack concerning the knowability of the subject. The best known statements in the *Critique* come in the second preface and mark Kant's strategy for a Copernican revolution in epistemology (which is actually a reversal of Copernicus in that Kant retains the human subject at the center): Kant says that "we suppose that objects must conform to our knowledge" (1929, Bxvi).

In place of a detailed discussion of the Aesthetics and Analytics, let the following summary by Kant suffice for those two initial sections of the *Critique:*

> Our knowledge springs from two fundamental sources of the mind; the first is the capacity of receiving representations (receptivity for impressions), the second is the power of knowing an object through these representations (spontaneity [in the production] of concepts). Through the first an object is *given* to us, through the second the object is *thought* in relation to that [given] representation (which is the mere determination of the mind). Intuition and concepts constitute, therefore, the elements of all our knowledge. (A50, B74)

The third part of the *Critique,* transcendental dialectic, marks a shift away from the two earlier sections. The dialectic contains the critique of pure reason, which of its own nature must refuse the limits of intuition and understanding, creating transcendental ideas which promise, although without certainty, the completion of human knowledge. The issues which most concern subjectivity in the dialectic are the paralogisms and the third antinomy of pure reason, the conflict of freedom and natural necessity. In the paralogisms, the unity, identity, and ultimately the priority of the subject are considered; in other words the para-logic by which reason develops, from the fact of consciousness or apperception, the mode of being of the subject, is brought under critique.

In the third antinomy Kant attempts to reconcile the two causalities, of freedom and necessity, touching naturally enough on the freedom of human behavior and introducing another faculty, practical reason. In the antinomy the question of a human subject as an origin of its own actions beyond natural causality is the issue. Freedom is parallel to the Sophist doctrine of the originating Subject, at least in practical reason. Kant argues both the necessity of thinking that the subject acts spontaneously and the impossibility of knowing that such freedom exists. The result is a new or modified discourse of subjectivity in which the subject is both an origin and is not, the subject external to discourse and the subject within discourse. Since Kant takes up practical reason in the Dialectic of the first critique, we have here the discontinuity between the two critiques mentioned earlier, which is actually a question about whether self-knowledge is at all possible. In a reversal of Descartes this question of self-knowledge is produced after the basis of objective knowledge is established.

But we also need to look at how the text itself produces subjectivity. In the aesthetic and analytic, we have a narrative structured as a result of the possibility of the positioning of the scientific/philosophic observer of the human subject, an external position from which the subject is seen as an essence constituted by a structure of faculties or capacities which, in turn, determines the nature of knowledge. Kant's perspective in the Dialectic shifts from the external, as in the first two parts, to the perspective of the subject-in-the-process-of-thought, and that should alert us to the possibility that an external positioning is not necessarily given, but is constructed. In the dialectic Kant says that the thinking subject knows other human subjects only by projection of its own faculties, and this proposes as well a self-reflexivity which is not elsewhere produced in the first critique.

What all this suggests is that the aesthetic and analytic are preliminary and that they represent instances of paralogical reasoning based on the assumption that the subject may take up a position external to itself. The possibility of the subject observed by or observing itself (or the subject-in-general) argues that it is a noumenon or that it can know itself as a thing in itself. Such notions are specifically discredited in the dialectic, so we have conflicting positions about the subject as split and as self-reflexive even before the introduction of practical reason.

Thus as Kant founds objective knowledge in the interior faculties of human nature, he—as the inquirer into human knowledge—takes up the position of the noumenal or external subject of knowledge. In Descartes this knowledge is necessarily preceded by a self-reflexive ascesis. The subject in Kant is *already* a subject of knowledge as well as its object. This is the theoretical path taken by emerging scientific discourses in the modern era, although these are in actuality much more empirical. But this same objective or noumenal position is precisely what is questioned in Kant; thus the aesthetic and analytic become parallel to practical reason in terms of this assumption—the one that is questioned.

Early in the chapter reference was made to Descartes and split- or self-referential subjectivity, a phenomenon which seems peculiarly rationalist or typical of early modern philosophic thought. Self-referentiality is not, for example, an important issue in Renaissance thought, although the notion can be detected in the meditative tradition and elsewhere. In Descartes and others, the issue of the subject necessarily thinking itself may arise from what I have called the interiorizing cast of such approaches to philosophy—that the subject as reception, thought, and consciousness initiates inquiry into the productive capacities of the faculties of the human subject, so that a turning back on itself first as instrument and then as object is the logical protocol of philosophic process. What is notable about Descartes specifically is that split subjectivity is an interiorized repetition of the two diachronic levels of subjectivity in Sophist thought, and that this interiorization and unification of subject(s) introduces self-reflexivity.

Unlike Descartes, Kant seems intent on closing up the interior space in which the subject tends to double itself and to get rid of self-relation as essential or even possible. This in the face of Descartes' claim that only self-reflection can produce the subject of knowledge necessary to Kant's positioning in the aesthetic and analytic. Such a claim can most clearly be made in relation to Kant's notion of transcendental apperception and in the paralogisms, in which apperception figures prominently. Apperception is precisely the locus of many attempts to show how the unity of the subject is claimed yet frustrated by the mode of analysis Kant employs, but it offers the clearest entry of Kant into the arena of self-relation. Apperception, simply put, refers to consciousness as thought or self-awareness. Pure apperception is, more precisely, the form of thought. At the same time, the categories and concepts of the understanding are the a priori forms by means of which we synthesize and think objects through appearances. But pure apperception is the a priori synthetic unity which supervenes on and makes possible those synthetic unities. Kant explains:

> the possibility, indeed the necessity, of these categories rests on the relation in which our entire sensibility, and with it all possible appearances, stand to original apperception. In original apperception everything must necessarily conform to the conditions of the thoroughgoing unity of self-consciousness, that is, to the universal functions of synthesis, namely, of that synthesis according to concepts in which alone apperception can demonstrate a priori its complete and necessary identity. (A111–12)

As Kant says in the analytic, the "supreme principle" of the possibility of understanding "is that all the manifold of intuition should be subject to conditions of the original synthetic unity of apperception." The manifold, in other words, responds to the possibility of "being combined in one consciousness": "for without such combination nothing can be thought or known, since the given representations would not have in common the act of apperception 'I think,' and so could not be apprehended together in one self-consciousness" (B136–37). Transcendental apperception is thus the a priori ground of the unity of consciousness in the synthesis of the manifold of intuition (see, by contrast, Georg Mohr on apperception in relation to consciousness of freedom, 1995, 35–36). Self-consciousness seems to be identical with consciousness, and, moreover, apperception is an automatic function of the mind undergoing possible experience.

Aside from apperception, we can only *know* ourselves, because knowledge entails both intuition and understanding, in a certain way: so far as inner intuition is concerned, we know our own subject only as appearance and not as it is in itself (Kant 1929, B156, 168). Hence the frustration of the subject's knowledge of itself through intuition.

In the light of these negative claims, it seems somewhat wrong-headed to claim, as Bowie does (quoting Dieter Henrich), that Kant's epistemology is structured "as the justification of 'forms of cognition from the form and nature of self-consciousness.' It is the status of this self-consciousness which is the central issue" (1990, 15). It is more likely that structures of mind are prior, in potential, to consciousness (and it is difficult to speak of *self-*consciousness in the first critique); and these structures are *spontaneous* but coterminous with apperception, *in act,* since transcendental apperception is also spontaneous. What concerns Bowie here (e.g., 19) is the need to demonstrate the possibility of the identity of the subject through apperception. But what Kant says precisely is that a formal identity is possible but not a substantial one. And we are always at the level of consciousness in the *Critique of Pure Reason;* self-consciousness implies a substantial identity in that it assumes a transcendental or intelligible positionality of the subject— that is, the subject as thing in itself.

Apperception—and this is the point to which my description of the consciousness or apperception has been leading—offers the same frustration: "The 'I think' expresses the act of determining my existence. Existence is already given thereby, but the mode in which I am to determine this existence, that is, the manifold belonging to it, is not thereby given" (Kant 1929, B158). "The consciousness of self is thus very far from being a knowledge of the self" (ibid.). The self-reflective epistemological ascesis of Descartes is therefore impossible. The self produced as knower is an impossibility but at the same time founds the aesthetic and analytic, which in turn cover apperception.

In the analytic, these two prospective avenues toward knowledge of the self (apperception and inner intuition) do not by their difference suggest a reflexive or split relation that produces the subject of knowledge. What promotes self-reflexivity is reason; the movement from either consciousness of existence and/or knowledge of itself as appearance toward knowledge of the subject-in-itself, constructs the reflexive relation. It is the former on which the paralogisms of pure reason focus.

In the dialectic, "concepts" of understanding become "ideas" of pure reason or transcendent ideas whose function is "to *free* a concept of understanding from the unavoidable limitations of possible experience" (A409). Kant thus undertakes what he calls "a subjective derivation of . . . [these ideas] from the nature of our reason" (B393/A336). What Kant means here by "subjective" is that his analysis of the essential structure of the human subject necessarily includes reason in addition to the faculties of intuition and understanding; that the attempts at objectification—to construct, in effect, a transcendent object which exists parallel to possible experience and corresponding to the idea—are inevitable, built into human nature, and so are necessarily considered. Here we are on the self-reflexive cartesian ground. But it should be noted that self-relation as the producer of (possible) self-knowledge must be posterior to the scientifically produced knowledge of human nature that is the subject matter of the aesthetic and the analytic. In other words, the production of objective knowledge leads to the question of human self-knowledge.

Nearly the whole of the dialectic is appropriate to the concerns here, but the following is limited primarily to the paralogisms and the third antinomy. Paralogism or the pseudo-reasoning that proposes knowledge of the nature of the subject-in-itself derives from apperception or the "I think." The doctrine so derived is called by Kant, in quotation marks, "the rational doctrine of the soul" (A342); it is built upon "the single proposition 'I think'" (ibid.) and nothing else.

But apperception "serves only to introduce all our thought, as belonging to consciousness" (ibid.); or, as previously argued, apperception is consciousness, and consciousness is mere awareness of existence, and not of the mode of that existence. Reason pushes ahead to fill in that nature; yet it cannot be known. The four paralogisms of this rational doctrine are: the soul is substance, is simple substance, is self-identical substance, and is in relation to possible objects in space (A345/B402). Allison says that here "Kant denies that we are entitled to draw any positive metaphysical conclusions" regarding the subject that thinks (1995, 16; see, also, Ameriks 1995, 203–4). If the subject is substance, for example, then it is prior: "in all our thought the 'I' is the subject, in which thoughts inhere only as determination; and thus 'I' cannot be employed as the determination of another thing. Everyone must, therefore, necessarily regard himself as substance, and thought as [consisting] only [in] accidents of his being, determinations of his state" (Kant 1929, A349).

The subject is construed as an origin because it exists prior to thought, which is a momentary if continuing modification of its being. Substance as a category, applied to nonintuition, constructs an object which stands to thought as substance to predicate. This rationally deduced subject is comparable to the Sophist prior Subject as well as to the subject of the aesthetic and the analytic—as prior to and the cause of knowledge. Kant both accepts and refutes this position: "Consciousness is, indeed, that which alone makes all representations to be thoughts, and in it, therefore, as the transcendental subject, all our perceptions must be found; but beyond this logical meaning of the 'I,' we have no knowledge of the subject in itself" (A350). Kant is here opening up the possibility of a self-reflexive position, and at the same time making it clear that the position is "empty." The subject does not know itself simply by being conscious of itself as thinking (A348–B407), although pure speculative reason produces the subject as transcendental object in order to make up for that lack. Consciousness can and cannot think itself prior to itself—that is, prior to the representation "I think" in judgments or determinations of concepts. Etienne Balibar notes the difference between Kant's *subjectum* and Descartes's substantive *res cogitans* (34ff.).

The fourth paralogism, that the soul exists in possible relation to objects in space, speaks equally to the problematic of origin or priority, and to the existence of the thing-in-itself: "I distinguish my own existence as that of a thinking being, from other things outside me—among them my body. . . . I do not thereby learn whether this consciousness of myself would be even possible apart from things outside me through which representations are given to me, and whether, therefore, I could exist merely as thinking being" (B409). The question is whether consciousness supervenes on receptivity and intuition, or whether or not the causality of outer things is the origin of consciousness. Are we awakened as conscious, thinking beings by experience, by what is prior to us? Pure reason uses the fact of consciousness—that is, awareness of existence as thinking—to construct an argument for the originality and priority of the subject as thinking being—in effect, an argument for the self-origination of thinking. The possibility of originality, arbitrary and unexplained, is the crux of the Sophist doctrine, which doctrine for Kant becomes the inevitable work of pure reason repeating the cartesian ascesis as mere speculation.

Kant's conclusion is that analysis "of consciousness of myself in thought in general, yields nothing whatsoever towards the knowledge of myself as object" (ibid.). The logical "I" of consciousness can never be shown to have a determinable content. Thus, it seems, Kant closes down the self-reflexive split opened up in the subject by Descartes, a split which interiorizes the two levels of subjectivity of Sophist theory—where one level of Subject is allowed absolute originality. In Kant, unlike in the "je pense, donc je suis," consciousness is denied the capacity to "see" or to objectify itself—in effect, denied the ability to split itself (see, e.g., Allison 1995 on Kant's *Reflexion* 5661) except speculatively. Yet since pure reason never fails to push toward self-reflection as a potential addition to human knowledge, Kant in effect explains Descartes's insistence on self-reflexive knowledge while maintaining that this "position" remains empty.

The antinomies also spring from the natural tendency of pure reason to extend its domain beyond all limits of experience; the third antinomy is important here because it concerns the notion of the subject. The thesis of the third antinomy is that there exists an uncaused causality, a cause which acts without itself having been caused, or "an *absolute spontaneity* of the cause, whereby a series of appearances, which proceeds in accordance with laws of nature, begins *of itself.* This is transcendental freedom" (A446/B474).

Kant's lengthy treatment of the third antinomy involves the human subject, the causality of freedom, and practical reason. Because this section serves in one sense to introduce the *Critique of Practical Reason,* much of the analysis may be deferred. Here in the first critique Kant articulates what is at stake in the third antinomy:

> the causality of the cause, which *itself happens* or comes to be, must itself in turn have a cause; and thus the entire field of experience, however far it may extend, is transformed into a sum total of the merely natural [that is, natural causality or determinism]. But since in this way no absolute totality of conditions determining causal relation can be obtained, reason creates for itself the idea of a spontaneity which can begin to act of itself, without being determined to action by an antecedent cause in accordance with the law of causality. (A533/B561)

The notion of origin is the key. According to the first antinomy, it cannot be known whether the world has a beginning in time and a limit in space; the causal regress will never arrive at the unconditioned (or the "absolute totality" of conditions). It cannot, at the very least for the reason that cause applies to appearances, and appearances are by definition conditioned by human receptivity. Pure reason simply supplies this deficiency, proposing an origin. Kant's shift to practical reason or "the practical concept of freedom [that] is based on this transcendental idea" (ibid.) of a spontaneous cause marks the move from a general notion of a cause that acts of itself to the notion of the freedom of the human subject. Kant poses the question of human freedom by placing the subject in the context of its receptivity to appearances: "Freedom in the practical sense is the will's independence of coercion through sensuous impulses. . . . sensibility does not necessitate its action. There is in man a power of self-determination, independently of any coercion through sensuous impulses" (A534/B562).

Once the human subject becomes the focus, it is clear that the text has returned to the perspective of the "scientific" or philosophic observer in whose purview the human subject appears as an object. Kant's earlier concern with apperception and self-consciousness, especially in the paralogisms, shifted the perspective to a failed self-scrutiny (from the "inside," so to speak) raised by the recognition of necessity of self-consciousness in the "I think" for intuition and cognition; but now the original perspective returns. This is important because exactly the same problems concerning self-reflexivity seem to be at issue: Self-consciousness does not lead to self-knowledge, so Kant rejects that perspective for the original objective position in the attempt to reconcile human freedom and natural necessity. This is of course the unproduced perspective that warrants the aesthetic and analytic. Hence: "Man is one of the appearances of the sensible world" (A546/B574).

Kant does not demonstrate the necessity of freedom. He shows "that causality through freedom is at least *not incompatible with* nature" (A558/B586) in the following way: causal necessity applies only to appearances, not to noumena or intelligible objects. Appearances alone are subject to time (as inner intuition) and causality is one of the concepts which bears on the relations of appearances in time. Yet appearances also bear some relation to noumena—there is, according to Kant, something outside experience, of which the appearances are representations. Since there is no incompatibility between these two relations, then neither is there incompatibility between the intelligible subject (if it exists) as an origin of appearances and the causal relation of appearances.

Kant specifically does not demonstrate either the "reality" or even the "possibility" of freedom (ibid.), but merely its compatibility. The subject may be treated as an intelligible cause of sensible effects only if we shift from theoretical to practical reason, that is, reason as a pure, self-originating cause which determines the will toward action. From the perspective of theoretical reason, practical reason represents an aberrant or bastard sort of knowledge; it is in one sense not incompatible with theoretical knowledge, but is actually not knowledge, in the theoretical sense, at all; that is, it is incapable of being known. The subject cannot know itself or reflect upon itself as a noumenon: the external perspective of scientific observation as a position of the noumenon and/or as a position from which to observe itself is closed off, an empty or "logical" rather than a substantive position. This then invalidates the aesthetic and analytic.

《◎》

The *Critique of Practical Reason* is in a sense a reversal of the entire dialectic of the first critique, except for the argument that freedom is compatible with necessity, and this is brought about by the shift in emphasis from theoretical to practical reason. Theoretical reason leaves a "vacant place," the intelligible, which pure practical reason supplies. Reason abstracts the concept of cause from the understanding and theoretical knowledge, and applies it practically, or in terms of human action: now the determination of the will of the subject has its origin in (practical) reason or the moral law, which originates in reason. There is no increase in knowledge: "[T]he concept which reason makes of its own causality as noumenon is significant even though it cannot be defined theoretically for the purpose of knowing its supersensuous existence" (Beck 1963, 159). "I could not," Kant says, "give content to this supposition, i.e., convert it into knowledge even of the possibility of a being acting in this way" (ibid.). Again the denial of the possibility of self-knowledge. Although theoretical knowledge does not increase, its problematic concept of freedom from the first critique now takes on an objective reality, though a reality which is only practical, that is, which can be constituted by the practical faculty, the will (see, e.g., Allison 1995, 25–26).

The result is that practical reason makes a split subject inevitable, as well as a reflexivity that circulates among the "parts" of the subject. This view of the subject is essential to *Critique of Practical Reason*, operating as the materialization of literally every opposition of the text from a priori/empirical to virtue/happiness, but primarily in "the apparent contradiction between the mechanism of nature and freedom" (Kant 1949, 203). For example, the dialectic of pure practical reason derives from this split between the unconditioned, that is, the determination of the will by a priori reason, and the practically conditioned, that is, sensible inclinations and natural need (213–14 and passim). In another of the many places (the analytic) where Kant deals with this contradiction in the second critique: first, necessity impinges on the subject "only so far as the determining grounds of any action of the subject lie in what belongs to the past and is no longer in his power; in this must be counted also his already performed acts and his character as a phenomenon as this is determined for him in his own eyes by those acts" (203). As Kant indicates, this is the phenomenal subject—an appearance among appearances in the sense that the will of the subject is predetermined by the past—the subject's experiences and its consequent habitual actions.

At the other pole of the contradiction—that is, freedom—there is "the same subject, which . . . is conscious also of his own existence as a

thing-in-itself, [and] also views his existence so far as it does not stand under temporal conditions, and to himself as determinable only by laws [that is, the moral law] which he gives to himself through reason" (ibid.). This is the subject that *already* knows itself, although not by means of an ascesis, since this knowledge can't be produced as knowledge by self-inquiry. Self-reflection is not a process but is the grounding of action according to reason or the moral law. This self-reflection with respect to practical reason is parallel to Descartes's self-grounding, but without the production of the subject of knowledge.

This noumenal part of the split subject is by definition outside of time and natural causality. This kind of split, originally treated in the first critique as not incompatible with theoretical knowledge, is the central tenet of the second critique: The causality of freedom entails a subject that transcends time and the phenomenal. For this subject the ground of action must have another kind of cause: Reason as practical is the origin of action in that it determines the will a priori according to the moral law. Thus Kant argues that in the intelligible existence of the subject,

> nothing [phenomenal] is antecedent to the determination of his will; every action and, in general, every changing determination of his existence according to inner sense, even the entire history of his existence as a sensuous being, is seen in the consciousness of his intelligible existence as only a consequence, not as a determining ground of his causality as a noumenon. (ibid.)

For this subject considered as an intelligible cause with sensible effects, any action, "and everything in the past which determined it[,] belong to a single phenomenon of his character, which he himself creates, and according to which he imputes to himself, as a cause independent of all sensibility, the causality of that appearance" (ibid.). The split subject— that is, the subject determinable in time, having a causality under the law of natural necessity versus the subject as self-originating according to its own (practical) reason, and independent of its own phenomenal being— is "absolutely unavoidable if one wishes to maintain both these mutually incompatible concepts" (201) of necessity and freedom. (It is worth noting that what Kant finds not incompatible in the first critique is in the second critique not compatible because in the first Kant already admits noumenal causality based on the assumption that reason is practical—without having any knowledge of what that kind of causality entails. The second critique is simply more explicit about the conditions for its conclusions about a split subjectivity that grounds the subject in its self-knowledge of itself as a noumenon, an origin.)

Splitting the subject opens up a proliferation of reflexivities. In a discussion of the incentive of pure practical reason—that is, subjective respect for the moral law—Kant argues that this incentive "lets us perceive the sublimity of our own supersensuous existence and subjectively effects respect for their higher vocation in men who are conscious of their sensuous existence and of the accompanying dependence on their pathologically affected nature" (194). This appears to locate the position from which the subject sees itself in the phenomenal subject, from which it sees its higher self. In the passages used earlier to open the split in the subject, however, the phenomenal subject sees itself in its phenomenal being; in effect we have a split subject at the phenomenal level, that sees its "character as a phenomenon as this is determined for him in his own eyes by . . . [his prior] acts" (203).

This same subject is also conscious of itself existing as a noumenon in the same quoted passages; from the noumenal position the subject sees the total narrative of its existence as a consequence of its "causality as a noumenon"; and sees itself as self-created. "Personality"—we would say "identity"—is a term Kant uses for what "elevates man above himself as a part of the world of sense, something which connects him with an order of things which only the understanding can think and which has under it the entire world of sense, including the empirically determinable existence of man in time" (193). The split subject here is able to see its sensible existence from its intelligible subject position. As I have said, it *already* knows itself without having produced that knowledge. But for Kant here self-knowledge is necessary to and seamlessly connected with the scientific knowledge of moral behavior.

It is tempting to see a parallel between the freedom of the subject necessary to the second critique and the multiplication of self-reflexivities. The opening of the split in the subject makes each position of subjectivity a viable perspective on the other. But Kant also shifts toward a third perspective, noted in the following attempt to show the unity of the subject—and, perhaps, because of that attempt. Here Kant raises the problem of "mediating the connection of such an intelligible being [as argued by the second dynamical idea, that is, of a necessary being] with the world of sense." Kant continues: There is no problem of connection

> with respect to our own subject so far as it knows itself, on the one hand, as
> an intelligible being determined[,] because of its freedom[,] by the moral law,
> and, on the other, as acting according to this determination in the world of
> sense. . . . [T]he concept of freedom enables us to find the unconditioned for

the conditioned and the intelligible for the sensuous without going outside ourselves. (211)

The subject now stands "outside," in a meta-noumenal position (so to speak), and sees itself as split, as both uncaused or noumenal cause and as articulated within the sensible world. From this third position the subject can, so to speak, put itself back together—although such a strategy has often been shown to involve Kant in an unending regress of subject positions. The kinds of perspectives generated in the second critique raise other interesting problems as well, as will be apparent in a moment.

Kant normalizes human nature, giving it a universal essence, treating the subject as an interiority but not as empirically subjective. He thus collapses the political space between master and pupil (although it is clear that Kant's centralization or "democratization" of the subject feeds directly into the political opposition between center and margin, which concerns us today). But if Kant collapses the distinction of Subject/subject, he also retains the potential for originality which binds the two subjects in Sophist theory, and calls it freedom. Freedom in Kant means only freedom from natural necessity, not absolute freedom, for the moral law is itself a constraint; the Sophist Subject is prior to culture and absolutely arbitrary. Yet since the moral law or practical reason is the identity of the Kantian subject, it is also completely arbitrary, since the nature of the human subject is given. Or, what in human nature is capable of producing the objective is the nature of the subject—among other potential natures.

So Kant simply repeats, in a different venue, the Sophist doctrine of subjectivity: The Subject which stands prior to culture and determines it, or, more precisely, the lower-case split subject produced by culture which is also capable of agency because it can stand outside of that culture. In Kant of course culture is the sensible, material world, and the "outside" is the noumenal position. The third perspective of the subject observing its split self simply shifts the relation of inside/outside in order to unify the split subject; it retains the notion of an external position from which to know the subject. It is the position of the subject of knowledge.

Part of the argument here has been to establish that the split and self-knowing subject is a product of the second critique or of the shift to the practical aspect of reason. From the perspective of theoretical reason the noumenal position is empty, much like Foucault's—and ironically so— panopticon as the figure of regulation of a population historically normalized by cultural institutions. The position from which to observe the unified split subject is also empty according to the same perspective. Theoretical knowledge of noumenal causality, except as an empty form, is impossible, and the existence of the external perspective, either as the origin of the causality of freedom or as the position of the knower or scientific observer is equally impossible. We might then take Kant as saying that the Sophist doctrine of subjective originality is an inevitable one, yet it is one produced only in moral science or practical reason; inevitably, the theoretical critique would deny the claim that the subject is an origin or that it could inhabit the "logical" or empty position outside of culture.

That might be the end of it. Kant proved unable to mark western thought with the recognition that the external or originating perspective of the subject of knowledge is untenable; yet it could be argued that the responsibility for this continuance of the objective position of knowledge lies in the subsequent failure of readers of Kant to distinguish between practical and theoretical reason. The noumenal and meta-noumenal positions produced in practical reason are reintegrated, in questions of theoretical or scientific knowledge, with the prior Subject. (Of course the position of the Subject is also ultimately empty.) Certainly the notion of the subject of knowledge persists long after Kant, coming under attack only lately, in Foucault and others. Kant does claim in *Critique of Practical Reason* that since the production of knowledge is an activity, practical reason is prior to the theoretical. Yet that must be balanced with the fact that in *Critique of Pure Reason* the "knowledge" which enables freedom and practical reason is clearly an untenable form of theoretical knowledge. Each critique incorporates the other, in a sense.

On the other hand, it has already been noted in the first critique that if "objects must conform to our knowledge" then the rational subject is the principle of knowledge: It is prior to knowledge and to objects because it produces both. This is in concert with the paralogical subject which, from consciousness or apperception, constructs itself as prior to its experience. Kant's point is of course that such an external subject cannot be known to exist and that the position of such a subject of knowledge must remain an empty one. The transcendental aesthetic and analytic are narratives which, as noted earlier, depend upon the perspective of the "scientific" observer or the subject that knows, the former of which stands outside in order to objectify and therefore constitute knowledge. Again, what is assumed in these two sections as essential to knowledge is considered a paralogical construction of a substantiality—that is, the subject—and a position which can never be anything but unknowable and untenable. In a sense, then, the *Critique of Pure Reason* has its own split subject, the external objective observer of the aesthetic and analytic, and the immanent subject that paralogically attempts to construct itself as prior to itself or that attempts by means of an inadequate form of theoretical knowledge, practical reason, to construct itself as an origin.

◖◖◎◗◗

Split subjectivity is produced by practical reason and contested by theoretical reason. Yet this comes back to haunt the latter because split subjectivity produces the external position of the subject of knowledge, and that is the only perspective from which knowledge can be produced. So theoretical reason must both utilize that position and at the same time deny its viability.

Kant thus represents the historical ontology of modern human nature in a peculiar way. *Critique of Pure Reason* necessitates the subject of knowledge, yet argues against the possibility of self-knowledge. The second Critique assumes self-knowledge as prior to the scientific knowledge of moral action. Thus *Critique of Practical Reason* seems to have contributed more to the modern notion of a self-reflexive subject, but both Critiques focus on interiority as identity—formal, in this case—and assume the continuity of self-knowledge with objective knowledge.

Let it be noted that this argument is incomplete, since it does not take *Critique of Judgement* into account. There is, of course, the general wisdom that this third critique serves to resolve the antinomies generated between the first two, so we might reasonably expect the question of the self-reflexive subject to be laid to rest there. One common argument is that *Critique of Judgement* produces aspects of the subject left unregarded by the earlier critiques: human nature *subjected to* and part of nature, not the subject as the producer of the regularity of nature or of moral law (yet such a view tends to ignore the opposition between appearances and things in themselves, including the fiction of purposiveness). There is also Kant's "notorious concept" (Bowie 1990, 32) of genius, which is the originary productive knowledge belonging to certain subjects. The concept is clearly a return to the Sophist conception of the singularity of the Subject who institutes culture, noted earlier in the chapter, but in Kant it is the return of the intelligible subject of the second critique as well. On the other hand, the spontaneity of genius most immediately mirrors the cognitive transcendental structures of mind. It is not particularly evident, then, that the *Critique of Judgement* does anything more than continue the oppositional incompatibility of the problem of split subjectivity raised in the first two critiques.

253

Kant's Dehistoricization
of the Subject

There are at least two ways to initiate a discussion on Kant and historic-ization: one, the traditional way, that pays respect to his predecessors, especially Descartes, in establishing a dehistoricized "thought"; second, by way of the late Foucauldian text, "What Is Enlightenment?," written about a text of Kant's of the same title.

This second return to Kant and to the discourse that constitutes the modern subject focuses on the issue of the constitution of a dehistoricized subject of knowledge. This subject, in both Descartes and Kant, though in different ways, is the necessary complement to objective knowledge. I have traced that relation in Descartes and Kant in the last two chapters; here I focus on how in these two thinkers this necessary ahistorical positioning of the subject or object of knowledge occurs. Foucault's claim that Kant recognizes the possibility of the subject's being placed in "the present moment" thus comes under scrutiny, specifically by a return to the analysis of the first two Critiques.

Descartes in the *Discourse* begins as a historical subject, but then at the moment of the *cogito* becomes a transcendentalized subject of knowl-edge. Kant, as usual, reverses Descartes, begins with the normalized and abstract as the subject and object of knowledge; but finally in the *Critique of Practical Reason* he introduces the noumenal subject aware of its own empirical existence. But in each case a transcendental and ahistorical sub-ject is introduced as necessary to the construction of objective knowledge. Thus the link between the two knowledges during modernity can be further clarified and strengthened. The constitution of this subject is an essential part of the modern deployment: to show how this ahistorical subject was constituted sets the stage for the later emergence of the autonomous private subject independent of cultural and historical discourses.

We might pause to remind ourselves why the issue of Kant's dehistoricizing is important. The creation of a universal, transcendent human nature in early modern philosophy led both to the rhetoric of equality and the use of that category to support hegemony. The latter is by now a familiar story: human nature as white, rational, male, European, has usually determined political being and its margins; in order to exist, the individual must form itself as nearly as possible to that nature. Sylviane Agacinski, for example, argues that Kant's a priori subject determines that the (cultural) other will be conceived as the same because the determination takes place within self-consciousness and prior to empirical experience; Agacinski makes the case for reversing the determination (1991, 10). The Constitution of the United States exemplifies the Kantian determination: not everyone is entirely human. On the other hand, this transcendental notion of human nature always haunts political and economic exclusion. The conception shadows every definition of the center and questions every attempt to place the margins at a distance.

Descartes begins his *Discourse on the Method* with an intellectual autobiography about passing through myriad philosophical opinions and learning to doubt them in order to reach knowledge's ground zero; then he gets to the core business of establishing thinking as constitutive of being. At this point the historical subject, Descartes, is transformed into the abstract, transcendental or philosophical subject which is the foundation of knowledge (Judovitz 1988, 116 and passim).

Thus Descartes introduces an ahistorical or transcendentalizing tendency in modern philosophy which determines Kant to a certain degree and does not cease to plague the twentieth-century inheritor of this tradition, phenomenology, in the sense that Husserl, late in his career, attempts to balance transcendentality with the empirical or history, and in that sense Merleau-Ponty attempts to rejuvenate this tradition by reference to empirical perception (Dews 1987, 6–8, 13–19).

The ahistorical Kant of this tradition may be confronted by a historicizing Kant represented by Foucault, one who in the brief "Was ist Aufklarung" "raised the philosophical question of the present day" (Foucault 1984c, 34). That is, Kant is made to appear as the first philosopher who explicitly connected, on the one hand, "the significance of his work with respect to knowledge [here Foucault is referring to the first two critiques] to [on the other,] a reflection on history and a particular analysis of the specific moment at which he is writing and because of which he is writing" (38). Thus from Kant there emerges an "attitude of modernity" which incorporates the view of the present moment "as difference in history" and as "motive" for philosophizing.

Those who know Foucault's text understand it as part of his late attempt to reconcile his genealogy of the modern era (of his *Discipline and Punish* period and afterwards, especially after the final shift in his thinking, as discussed in chapter 5 and the following chapters) with the canon of modern philosophy—in which the subject either as discursive or as autonomous or self-originating is the point at issue. Foucault contrives the reconciliation by seeing self-consciousness and self-reflexivity, in short, the subject's ability to look at itself and determine the manner of its own constitution—not as ontological but as one of the contingent, historical discourses which have constituted the modern subject. This is the positionality which he claims Kant is enacting in relation to the "present moment": he is aware of himself as positioned within historical process.

As striking as Foucault's claim is, it leaves open another reading of Kant's text. For example, the well known distinction between public and private reason seems rather to favor a kind of ahistoricism. The private use of reason, which for Kant is reason used in the performance of the individual's function or role—for example, as military officer, clergyman, or teacher—is allowably restricted to a kind of instrumentality, toward a carrying out of the ends of the individual's institution of employment. Kant, in his own arguments with the censor, distinguished between his lectures (that is, his role as a teacher) and his public role "as a scholar" (that is, his writings addressed to the public at large). Only in this second, public case must freedom be granted; if it is, then, Kant says, "enlightenment is sure to follow" (Beck 1963, 287).

Thus it seems logical that the Critiques become the focus of enlightenment thought—freedom from authority, the coercion of institutions, freedom from history in general—the history that Kant in the Critiques labels the empirical. Both introductions, then, by way of Descartes and Foucault, would lead us to anticipate a profound dehistoricizing tendency at the center of Kant's thought—that is, in the first two Critiques.

In the first section of *Discourse on the Method* Descartes draws an architectural distinction between a city designed ab ovo by a single intelligence and those ancient villages whose development into great cities is the result of successive hands adapting "old walls" to new and unthought-of purposes (1985a, 1:116–17). Descartes thinks of himself as the philosophical architect who likewise builds in a cleared space. This is an explicit refusal of history, or rather an attempt to bring history to an end: those philosophical opinions that have cluttered Descartes's mind and that he clears away by doubt in order to construct a new and unchanging foundation of philosophy in the cogito. This is not another episode in the history of philosophy but its end, and the institution of philosophy proper. On the other hand, Foucault might have adopted this passage as an epigraph to *Discipline and Punish:* the city which emerges from a succession of contingencies and adaptations is history itself, or the genealogical version of it current today. Some recent readings of Descartes have distinguished two subjects in the *Discourse:* the historical subject, Descartes, who in his intellectual autobiography portrays himself as completely subject to doubt and thus led to discover a new foundation for philosophy; and then there is that foundation, which is the human subject, now conceived in an abstract, transcendental, or philosophical way. The process of the first part of the *Discourse* is from this autobiographical and thus supposedly empirical and historical subject to the philosophical one: at the moment of the cogito the actual Descartes becomes the philosophical "I."

The felicity of this narrative relation of subjects has been a matter of debate (a narrative that is similar to an Acker novel in the shift of identity of the narrator—that is, somewhat postmodern). According to one critic, Edmund Husserl notes the absurdity of "Descartes' conflation of the psychological and transcendental subject," that is, making an empirical individual subject into the "axiomatic condition of possibility" of subjectivity in general (Judovitz 1988, 137). What Husserl actually says is that Descartes fails to make the "transcendental turn" of working through the "phenomenological epoché" or doubt in order to arrive at transcendental subjectivity (Husserl 1960, 18); Descartes remains at the level of the empirical and historical ego. The same commentator who quotes Husserl sees the conflation of subjects as the basis of Descartes's considerable success in reorienting philosophy (109).

The autobiographical part of the *Discourse* (that is, his philosophic education and travels, his doubt of the opinions acquired, and his arrival at the cogito) makes clear that there are *already* two subjects: the prior Subject, which stands outside of time or in a continuous, unmarked present, and which narrates the other subject (itself) in and through time. This dual or split subjectivity is equally accessible in Benveniste (that is, the "speaking" subject and the "spoken" subject) and in any sophisticated treatment of narrative convention. The autobiographical subject in Descartes can never be empirical; nor can any subject, since subjectivity is a function of convention, of position, of being inserted into language and/or culture. The possibility of this kind of split subjectivity is grounded in prior traditions of the subject discussed earlier.

The point is twofold: the pattern for the autobiographical convention and for the split in philosophical subjectivity—they are identical—is immediately available, and not in merely peripheral traditions: the primary Subject is never historical, and in fact institutes history; the secondary subject is inside historical process, but its relation to the former allows it the possibility of stepping outside the ground of its own historical constitution. This aspect of the ancient theory of the subject is, as noted, what Foucault grounds in history, or genealogy. Second, as implied by the first point, there is never a single subject, but always a doubling or two subjects in relation, and this relation is central to any description of historical process (or, at least, abstract diachronic process). This is one tradition that must be kept in mind when early modern philosophy is at issue.

There is one other aspect of Descartes's and Kant's presences in history to be considered. Descartes has been accused of solipsism, of seeking "the illusion of some kind of pure, unmediated thought, a perfect transparency of the subject to itself" and of occulting the necessary textual representation of such a subject (Judovitz 1988, 170). Such a claim is accurate, but its implication is ahistorical. What distinguishes Descartes, Kant, Hume, Locke, and so forth, from the prior era, the Renaissance and the baroque, is a shift from a focus on the external text or "book" to its interiorization, the mind or consciousness as the new textual space or temporality. To draw a clear distinction between the interior (of the subject) and the exterior is Kant's most characteristic strategy. The emphasis on the difference of inner perception and outer being is already evident in Descartes. In *Regulae* 12 Descartes distinguishes between the thing itself, a "single and simple entity," and the subject's intellectual intuition of that entity as a composite made up of corporeal nature, extension, and shape—that is, according to "those simple natures which the intellect recognizes by means of a sort of innate light" (1:44).

Hume's skepticism about causality can only be based on a fundamental difference between immediate appearances (that is, presentations within or to consciousness) and what is external. Kant makes the same distinction between *Vorstellungen* (appearances, representations, presentations) and things in themselves, to the latter of which we have no immediate relation. The representation is internal and, moreover, nonlinguistic. In order to proceed in philosophy during this "epistemological" era (which seems to persist at least through Husserlian phenomenology) one must ask: how is the subject constituted? how does it know, if it is capable of knowledge? and so on. The subject of philosophy is thus conceived of as prior, that is, as the necessary ground or structure within which the notion of "appearance" and "exterior/interior" have significance (although, as noted in the previous chapter, this is a complex issue of speculative reason in Kant). Subjectivity usually comes to be defined in terms of the essential constitution of the human subject, and this subject tends, as the ground of epistemology, to be autonomous and independent of historical and cultural determination; it is no longer individual and contingent, but now a necessarily abstract, philosophical subject.

For example, a recent rereading of Freud summarizes the general idea in the following interiorized and self-reflexive way:

> the subject of the moderns is first and foremost a subject of representation . . . the subject as representation and representation as subject. I would recall that it is by representing itself, by posing itself, in the mode of the *cogito* me cogitare, "with" all the representation it poses before itself, that the Cartesian ego establishes itself as the basis of all possible truth, i.e., as subjectum of the total being. (Borch-Jacobsen 1991, 64)

The tendency toward self-reflexive ahistoricism is thus built into the historical structure of conducting philosophy during this era. Finally, the doubling of the subject evident in the Sophist tradition takes place within interiority in a continuing and ahistorical present.

To return now to the cogito. The "je pense, donc je suis" is seen as the moment of transition from the empirical to the transcendental subject. By an abstraction, that is, a movement from *what* is being thought (the material or content—opinion, matters subject to doubt) to the self-reflexive recognition, by the subject, that it is engaged in a generic process called thinking—this shift amounts to the self-understanding, on the part of the subject, of the form of its consciousness and the warrant of its existence (Husserl calls this an incipient but incomplete phenomenological reduction).

The doubled autobiographical subject reappears in parallel within the *cogito* (inevitably, I would say, according to the Subject/subject tradition). One part of the doubled subject is, paradoxically, positioned outside of and independent of opinion, doubt and thinking, so that it can see itself thinking and conclude from this that thinking logically implies intellectual and non-empirical existence. This self-reflexive Subject/subject relation is identical to the doubled subject of autobiography except that here temporality and history are almost completely foreshortened into the continuous present (that is, I am thinking, thus as long as this persists I am existing). The prior diachronic relation of subjects becomes, because of the focus on interiority, a synchronic relation, and interiority itself is doubled to accommodate this doubled simultaneous subject relation.

Thus the supposed transition from individual and contingent to abstract subjectivity occurs; what actually occurs is a transition from a subject constituted according to literary convention to a subject constituted by philosophic convention, with a specific intensification of the abstraction typical of philosophy (this is part of Judovitz's argument). This is the same Descartes as the one described in chapter 7: the one who utilizes interiorized self-relation to constitute a subject of knowledge that is necessarily prior to objective knowledge. In the current chapter I repeat that process, but with the emphasis on the transcendentalizing moment of the subject, which is similarly necessary to objective knowledge.

◦◦◦

Kant maintains the distinction between appearances or "representations of our sensibility" and "things in themselves, which cannot be known" (1929, A30/B45) throughout his work, although intuition for him is, unlike for Descartes, always sensible and never allowably intellectual. Also, in Kant, philosophic analysis focuses from the outset on the abstract subject as the structure of knowledge in an atemporal and continuous present moment.

The famous pronouncement of the second preface to *Critique of Pure Reason,* Kant's Copernican revolution, is a claim that the a priori nature of the human subject determines what we as humans can know. This commits Kant to an analysis of this a priori nature or structure, or in effect of the nature of the transcendental subject—what we "know" prior to experience. He thus is attempting to isolate (that is, abstract from experience) what is given in human nature universally or what in every human subject necessarily conditions experience; this he presents as the foundation of philosophy. The structure of the *Critique of Pure Reason* contains, accordingly, the transcendental aesthetic (space and time as the subjective conditions of sensible experience), the transcendental analytic (the categories and concepts as the subjective conditions of understanding or thinking things), and the dialectic (or the subjective conditions of the transcendence of the empirical). I have noted some of the problems that arise in Kant in relation to the noumenal subject in the previous chapter; but I pass them by here.

Two overall strategies are evident in the text: first, the limitation of the inquiry to the human subject. Kant regularly speaks of the possibility of "other thinking beings" for whom the same conditions of intuition and understanding may not be universally valid: for example, for some beings intellectual intuition may obtain—knowledge without the prior necessity of sensible intuition. In order to proceed in his analysis Kant requires a homogenous group, or in effect a universalized and abstract subject. Kant's (historical) choice of a primary, isolated, and controllable category—the human—has been sustained for so long that only recently have shifts in the historical horizon made this visible as a choice and simultaneously made vulnerable to critique this abstract, homogeneous, and exclusionary human subject as the center of knowledge (for example, Foucault, *The Order of Things*, preface, and recent gender, race, animal, and ecological studies).

The second strategy has to do with the method of universalization of the human subject, given the above categorization, and the already mentioned ahistoricism that it promotes. Kant constitutes a human nature which can be perfectly abstracted from the peculiarities and experiences of individual subjects, the specificities of conditions and contexts of actual experience. For his end is, first of all, regularity and permanence within the historical model of human subjective response—what might be considered the very stuff of variability. Incidentally, neither does historiography or genealogy operate at this fundamental level of particularity, so it is complicit with Descartes's and Kant's construction of a universal human nature, although in often more limited versions such as "the English people," "the plebs," "the middle class," and so on. History appears to demand at least a certain level of abstraction from the particular, except in the anecdote. Individual subjects in historiography tend to be "great men" (gender specific), as subjects who stand outside culture and are positioned to change it; but this "historical" personage is constructed on a model of original subjectivity current in western thought since the Greeks.

To illustrate Kant's construction of the a priori subject: in the transcendental aesthetic, space is characterized as the form or "subjective condition" of the intuition of outer appearances; space is, given the limitation to human nature, also objective and a priori, or, rather, objective because a priori (A26–27/B42–43). Objective means valid for all (normal) human subjects, that is, universal. Time is the second "a priori subjective condition" of intuition, or the form of inner sense (A33ff./B49ff.) by which the subject "represents to . . . [itself] a number of things as existing . . . simultaneously . . . or successively" (A30/B46). History, as chronicle, is thus constituted by the subject, and is in Kant never more than memory based on a kind of secondary experience and recovered in the present moment (A835–38/B863–66), to which certain categorical relations such as cause and effect have already been applied (see Van de Pitte 1971, 94).

Kant puts to one side subjective representations which are not objective and universal, for example, sensations of colors, sounds, and heat, which are "mere sensations and not intuitions" (A28/B44), that is, are the material to which the form of the intuition is applied. Here knowledge is at the limit of the contingent and the variable, for these sensations "cannot rightly be regarded as properties of things"—as if space were!—"but changes in the subject, changes which may, indeed, be different for different men" (A28/B45). (That we have a distinction without a difference here is an indication of how hard Kant is working to construct a stable subject and therefore stable knowledge.)

The stability of knowledge in Kant's system depends on the stability and homogeneity of subjectivity. Kant secures this stability by focusing on the a priori or formal nature of the subject, excluding the materiality, contingency, and variability of the world the subject comes in contact with, and on the nature and condition of its sensible apparatus as well. Whatever makes for difference is excluded, and the result is a stable but ghostly set of forms: that is, formal relations (temporal and spatial positionings, cause and effect, and so forth), formal identities (shape, extension, substantiality), and so on. The material world is excluded, a priori.

But once said, this claim that the system is an empty set of forms must immediately be modified. The a priori forms "allow only of empirical and not of transcendental employment, that is[,] employment extending beyond the limits of [possible] experience" (A296/B352–53). A priori knowledge exists in abstract, but the empirical is its context, and the material and the contingent function as its limit (this is Kant's answer to the rationalists— the reciprocal liminal conditioning of empirical experience). Empirical knowledge is of the actual: for example, that x exists but not that x exists necessarily—that is, contingency.

But now another turn, this time in the third part of *Critique of Pure Reason* (actually the second part of the analytic), the transcendental dialectic: the tendency to transcend the empirical is natural, "inseparable from human reason" (A298/B354). This opens a difference between knowledge and speculation, in which no objects commensurate with the transcendental ideas can ever be constituted from experience: reason projects itself into the realm of things in themselves, transcending any possible empirical verification, leaving behind once more the material and contingent stuff we identify with history. But transcendental reason can provide only a bastard sort of knowledge.

Under the third transcendental idea, however, Kant modifies his stance, shuffling us once again to the other side of the abstract-material opposition. There exists, according to this third transcendental idea, a causality of freedom which is opposed to natural causality. Here Kant conceives of the human subject as both *empirical* (that is, subject to natural necessity, contingent, historical, determined in its action by the empirical "discourses" which constitute it) and *intelligible* (that is, "free from all influence of sensibility and from all determination through appearances" [A541/B569], abstracted from the coercive forces of its particular historical circumstances). Ultimately in the first critique Kant finds the latter claim, that is, that subjects have the capacity for self-origination, unverifiable and still a transcendental idea; yet it is an idea *not* incompatible with theoretical knowledge—that is, not falsifiable.

The practical concept of freedom derives from this transcendental idea (A533/B561) and is the basis of Kant's second critique concerning practical knowledge (as opposed to the theoretical knowledge of the first critique). In this second critique the subject is split between its empirical and intelligible nature, and the dialectic of practical reason is constituted in this split between the conditioned and the unconditioned. As unconditioned, the subject knows itself as a thing in itself, as outside temporal conditions, and as determinable toward action (through the formation of the will) only by the moral law, which is supplied a priori by reason. As a phenomenal subject it is conditioned by its sensible environment, its sensible inclinations and natural needs, as well as by its history or its habits (or, as we might say, the discourses within which it is constituted) (Beck 1963, 109).

Yet patterns of behavior are not cultural and contingent for Kant. They are on the one hand the a priori forms of practical reason, ahistorical and transcendental. On the other, behavior is contingent to a degree, that is, dependent on the sensible environment, but also on that which constitutes the subject as a structure of natural desires and needs. This is as close as Kant gets to our historical subject, and it is not very close. For I suspect that here Kant falls back on some universalized notion of the empirical subject—that is, subject to sexual desire, the desire for power, the desire for comfort, the desire for display; subject to the need for food, for warmth, for the absence of pain and so forth. Still a generic human being.

※

In Kant history and change can only be a function of the empirical or actual, and even that seems to us ahistorical. We trace the enlightenment to Kant, both in terms of the control of human subjects over nature and in the abstract notion of democratic human individuality. In the former: it is a matter of Kant's orientation that the (human) subject controls and even determines nature. Whatever nature is or might be "thought" to be as outside of human experiences (see chapter 8), nature as it can be known is constituted by appearances, which are human constructions of whatever impinges on the subject from the unknown exterior. This means that the subject is conceived of as a priori, that is, before experience and before history. Nature is, in effect, constituted by human nature, and history is similarly a construction.

In the latter case (that is, of equality), however, the constitution of the normal human subject simply makes all subjects available to the "disciplines"; that is, the tendency of philosophy to normalize human nature is the historical counterpart to a disciplinary society which both constitutes and regulates subjects—normal subjects and, by opposition, aberrant ones, who are then subject to further processes of normalization.

It may be an irony (or contingency) of history such as I have just mentioned, but for all of Kant's vacillation between abstract and empirical subject and knowledge, or between totally versus not-so-totally ahistorical subject, the subject which is generally recognized today as Kantian is the ethical subject of the second critique. It is closest to the Cartesian subject, which stands at the end of or outside of history. Kant's is the self-reflexive subject which stands outside itself (as thing in itself) and sees itself (secondarily) as empirical and contingent—in effect the subject of modernism, in history and out of it simultaneously—which is, in fact, the bind in which Foucault finds himself in his own "What Is Enlightenment?" The more undecidable subject of the first critique seems to disappear from the history of thought.

On the other hand Foucault's insight into Kant's "Was ist Aufklarung?" may be the beginning of a counter discourse to the dehistoricized subject that is the necessary foundation of both Descartes's and Kant's philosophies. And it may be in Kant that the partial recognition of the historical or empirical subject in the *Critique of Practical Reason*—as the noumenal subject recognizing itself as enmeshed in history, or causality—is the source of Kant's realization that the philosopher acts within history, and the beginning of the counter discourse that leads to an autonomous subject independent of objectifying knowledge. But that inside/outside positioning of the subject was also available long before in the history of thought on the subject in the west.

Despite his attempt to construct an ahistorical subject, Kant's critiques are clearly historical texts. Reason is gender specific, geographical (Eurocentric), and colored (white). These are determinations of political discourses, with which philosophy is inevitably complicit; they are also discourses within which the historical subject, Immanuel Kant, was constituted, outside of which (to paraphrase Churchill) he cannot get. Kant's philosophy is enabled by these discourses, and limited as well.

These last few sentences summarize in a way dangerously close to cliché our sense of the historical nature of texts; yet we never seem to worry that what is true of Kant's texts is true of our own, that we as subjects are within and constituted by history. What we conceive of as history is specifically the past—what we feel we can get outside of, control, make coherent sense of—in a word, what we construct. And no matter how often new historicists repeat the nostrum that historical truth is always relative to current discourses, there is still an aura of facticity and objectivity about the results of their studies. That may be supplied by us, the readers, but it is still there. We must keep in mind what we are doing.

Conclusion

The chapters in this book are but one more testament to the importance of the problem of human subjectivity. In the human world, and in the human thought about that world, the centrality of subjectivity is hardly surprising. I have begun my analysis in the ancient world, but if we were to consider only the last four hundred years of the west, the (interiorized) subject is clearly the dominant issue. Modern philosophy into the twentieth century continually discovers or constitutes the subject of knowledge as its fundamental task. When philosophers associated with deconstruction appear on the scene beginning in the 1960s, they set up the subject, or the subject as origin, as one of their primary targets: dismantle the primacy of the subject and then the structure of western thought would begin to totter. But the grasp of the subject was not so easily dislodged, as in fact the poststructuralists knew from the outset.

As I have noted earlier, this book is in part a meditation on Foucault: an analysis of his work and its changes; a critical confrontation over some of his insights and methods; and an extension of some parts of his genealogy of self-relation. I have sought through his and my own eyes to understand how the problematics of subjectivity are articulated in particular historical eras.

Most of the second half of the book takes up Foucault's notion of the historical ontology of the modern subject: self-reflexive and self-conscious, self-constituting (as the Subject, or with Descartes inventing himself as knower, or as the subject able to step outside the discourses which constitute it, and so on), and originating (that is, agential). Foucault sees that this form of self-relation in the historical subject both calls for and warrants a genealogy of self-relation. I have seen my task as one of articulating Foucault's strategy in that genealogy and of introducing neglected but important historical issues—such as interiority—and of expanding my notion of his genealogy into historical eras that Foucault simply never got around to, or back to, during his lifetime. I consider the book a joint effort, which at a minimum should keep interest in Foucault's notion of self-relation alive and suggest ways to complete his genealogy. For that genealogy is a key to understanding ourselves, and for setting the stage for the deconstitution of our historical selves.

One might ask what I have learned during this process. In general, very little; as usual, the devil is in the details. But first of all it is clear that the Sophist notion of subjectivity—admittedly a construction—is the one most dominating constructions of the subject in western thought. This theory explains the authority of the Subject, for example, but allows for agency as well in the subject. Almost no statement made about subjectivity in the west escapes its purview and control; in a certain way this ancient notion of the Subject might be said to produce all subsequent thinking about subjectivty. One of my efforts, particularly in the first half of the book, has been to illustrate this phenomenon, and to show that western thought can never quite escape this ancient formulation of the subject.

But poststructuralism, in its historical role, has produced challenging and even disabling attacks on the Sophist notion of the Subject. Derrida, by parodying the metaphysical notion of origin, and of the subject as origin, engages in the process of making both origin and subject disappear. Foucault takes the ontological notion of an originating subjectivity and historicizes it, thereby accounting for the Sophist notion while blocking its recourse to essentiality. Poststructuralism, taking over the task of Nietzsche, thus mounts the first serious and sustained challenge to western thought about the subject.

The emergence of cultural studies in the eighties resulted in the turning away from theory in its deconstructive form and from poststructuralism in general. This turn was largely based on the necessity for agency in the subject, and cultural studies, with notable exceptions, returned to a modified form of the traditional western idea of originating subjectivity. Foucault, whose influence on cultural studies is undeniable if also general, had already explained how we could return to an agential subject without a subsequent acceptance of the traditional notion of the subject's natural capacity to originate. But since cultural studies has made little attempt to justify itself in terms of theory, the connections between its own project and Foucault's argument about the historically constituted subject are rarely noted.

Foucault's turning of the subject toward its historical constitution may be the most striking and productive reconception of the subject since the ancient world. If Derrida dismantled the subject only to have it reappear at another level, Foucault shifted the basis of thinking the subject from ontology to history; and he did this without making use of Kant's distinction between the transcendental and the empirical, which simply returns everything to ontology. Foucault's subject is real without being merely empirical; it has being. Yet this being is a historical "essence," that is, constituted by the various and contingent discourses that impinge on the individual and subjectivate it.

But the subject so constituted—in the case of the modern—is self-reflexive, able to stand outside itself and seek to know itself. Thus the subject regains historically what it has lost ontologically. This subject is an accident really, a result of contingent historical discourses that emerge and merge or conflict over the process of centuries. But this accident of historical construction provides the ground—although not the absolute, ontological ground—for understanding the modern "invention of man" by means of a genealogy of self-relation. This capacity of the modern subject to know itself from outside itself is, then, the "essence" of the subject, the ground of its self-inquiry and also the basis of its claim to a potential for agency.

The modern subject may be specified more precisely. Ever since Descartes utilized interior self-reflection to constitute the knower, the modern subject has been characterized as he conceived it, a subject of knowledge. Along with, and connected with, self-relation, this peculiar modern way of thinking the subject is an important issue in the latter half of the book. The self-reflexive subject of knowledge *is* the modern subject. Modern philosophy needs to be reread in terms of the genealogy of this subject; and not philosophy alone, but in connection with other and more dominant discourses of the period.

Of particular interest in relation to this genealogy is the emergence with the self-knowing subject of the realm of subjective knowledge and the relation of this new kind of knowledge to scientific or objective knowledge. I have begun the task of showing how at times these two knowledges are transparent to each other and reciprocally related, and how at later times self-knowledge becomes opaque and private; and, although I have not developed the point, this self-knowledge and interiority become more and more tied to individual "feeling." These are crucial points in our history as subjects, but the overall narrative of this relation and how it participates in the (self-) construction of the subject, is much more complex and stands to reveal much more about us as subjects. We need, in short, to complete the genealogy of the modern subject over the past four hundred years.

This is what I have not learned about the modern subject, but need to learn.

APPENDIX TO CHAPTER 1

1. There are alternate versions of Freud's *Totem and Taboo* narrative that are very different from the one I am attempting here. Some I have mentioned earlier, especially having to do with Freud's notion of natural sexual difference. One of the most interesting different versions is Mikkel Borch-Jakobsen's; he has been noted earlier but deserves a fuller exposition. His book, *The Freudian Subject,* exposes the abyssal nature of the preexistent Subject that constitutes society according to Freud in the latter part of *Group Psychology*; the same position is summarized in his later article, "The Freudian Subject, from Politics to Ethics." In this article Borch-Jakobsen sets up two related tasks: the teasing into visibility of the Freudian critique of philosophical subjectivity (that is, subjectivity as subjectum or foundation), which critique he finds in Freud's version of narcissistic desire, or the desire to become-ego by assimilating the other prior to representation. This individual psychology is then applied to Freud's anthropological and social-psychology narratives.

Freud always assumed this individual-group relation to hold—as already noted in the subtitle to *Totem and Taboo* or in the title of *Group Psychology and the Analysis of the Ego*—or that individual and social psychology were ultimately homologous (for example, Freud 1955, 69ff.). His purpose is the explicit relation between individual "mental phenomena" and group behavior in *Group Psychology* (for example, 115–16), the former as causal. But in the earlier *Totem and Taboo* narrative, dependent indeed on the feelings and attitudes of the brothers, he makes a much less clear connection between individual psychic behavior and the social. Borch-Jakobsen attempts to adapt the psychic analysis of *Group Psychology* to the earlier narrative (1991, 67, passim). Yet as his work and others' from Lévi-Strauss on make clear, the transition is problematic.

It is noteworthy that Freud makes the "group" (or "crowd") "a revival of the primal horde" (1955, 123) and attempts to map the historical transition from group to individual psychology by reference to some individual who "moves to free himself from the group and take over the father's part" (136)—not incidentally, the individual as subject repeating the originary act of the Subject, but from within discourse. Note also that the Father is originarily an individual subject and that he "forced them [the sons], so to speak, into group psychology" (124).

In his narratives Freud only problematically questions their naturalness or the givenness of subjects. Borch-Jakobsen's conclusion is that the narrative allows for the constitution of the social by the failed attempt at narcissistic identification by the "nonsubjective" brothers with *der Tote,* the dead, nonexistent Father (1991, 75). He comes closest here to my own interest in the a priori Subject in narratives of origin, but the two explanations bear only a certain parallelism. His ultimate concern is to derive the social ethically (from *Totem and Taboo*) in a way that is prior to the political or totalitarian constitution of sociality in *Group Psychology.*

One criticism of his argument might be that he tends to make *Group Psychology* prior to *Totem and Taboo* in the sense that the lack of self-presence of the "individual" nonsubject in the former (that is, that which calls for a Chief-Subject) is carried over into the *Totem and Taboo* "brothers," who thus are desiring-to-be-subject in their devouring of the Father; and the historical inversion is not the worst problem here: for example, identification results in a "partial alteration in itself [the ego] after the model of the lost object" (Freud 1955, 114)—the term "partial" being critical in terms of the assumption of a prior subjectivity. Borch-Jakobsen also fails to mention the importance of repression in the narrative.

Besides, Borch-Jakobsen's concern with the intense "identificatory passion" which exists between brothers and Father excludes, as Freud's analysis does, any reference to women; the killing and consuming are "Not (or only secondarily) to have the women of the flock" (1991, 74) but primarily to identify with the father—the same exclusion of women and the introduction of monogendering or male difference.

See also Phillipe van Haute's reading of *Totem and Taboo* (1996, 189ff.), which assumes the exclusion of women.

《◌》

2. The apriority of the Subject-Father is inevitably attacked by structuralists. Thus "all of our disenchanted modernity, from Lévi-Strauss to Girard, has criticized . . . [Freud]: presupposing the authority of the Father rather than deducing it, *Totem and Taboo* does no more than provide us with a new myth

of origins, a new myth of foundation." In *Group Psychology* the "Führer" is "a Narcissus or Egocrat sprung from nowhere. . . . The Chief self-engenders himself as Subject" (Borch-Jakobsen 1991, 72, 71)—"a Subject founded in itself and based on itself"; this is precisely the original assumption of all theories of origin, since there can be nothing prior to the origin.

BIBLIOGRAPHY

Agacinski, Sylviane. 1991. "Another Experience of the Question, or Experiencing the Question Other-wise." In *Who Comes After the Subject?*, ed. Cadava, Connor, and Nancy, 9–23.

Allison, Henry E. 1995. "Spontaneity and Autonomy in Kant's Conception of the Self." In *The Modern Subject*, ed. Ameriks and Sturma, 11–30.

Ameriks, Karl. 1995. "From Kant to Frank: The Ineliminable Subject." In *The Modern Subject*, ed. Ameriks and Sturma, 217–30.

Ameriks, Karl, and Dieter Sturma, eds. 1995. *The Modern Subject: Conceptions of Self in Modern German Philosophy.* Albany: State University of New York Press.

Arac, Jonathan, ed. 1988. *After Foucault: Humanistic Knowledge, Postmodern Challenges.* New Brunswick, N.J.: Rutgers University Press.

Aristotle. 1941. *Metaphysics.* Trans. W. D. Ross. In *The Basic Works of Aristotle*, ed. Richard McKeon. New York: Random House. 689–934.

Ascham, Roger. 1967. *The Schoolmaster.* Ed. Lawrence V. Ryan. Stanford, Calif.: Stanford University Press.

Ashley, Anthony, Earl of Shaftesbury. 1964. *Characteristics of Men, Manners, Opinions, Times.* Ed. John M. Robertson. Indianapolis and New York: Bobbs-Merrill.

Bailey, Cyril. 1928. *The Greek Atomists and Epicurus.* Oxford: Oxford University Press.

Balaban, Oded. 1990. *Subject and Consciousness: A Philosophical Inquiry into Self-consciousness.* Savage, Md.: Rowman and Littlefield.

Balibar, Etienne. 1991. "Citizen Subject." In *Who Comes After the Subject?*, ed. Cadava, Connor, and Nancy, 33–57.

Banfield, Ann. 1982. *Unspeakable Sentences: Narration and Representation in the Language of Fiction.* Boston and London: Routledge and Kegan Paul.

Barbin, Herculine. 1980. *Herculine Barbin: Being the Recently Discovered Memoirs of a Nineteenth-Century French Hermaphrodite.* Introduction by Michel Foucault. Trans. R. McDougall. New York: Pantheon.

Barker, Philip. 1993. *Michel Foucault: Subversions of the Subject.* New York: St. Martin's Press.

Barthes, Roland. 1974. *S/Z*. Trans. R. Miller. New York: Hill and Wang.

Baudrillard, Jean. 1988. *The Ecstasy of Communication*. Trans. B. and C. Schutze. New York: Semiotext[e].

Bec, C. 1976. "De Pétrarque à Machiavel: A propos d'un topos humanist (Le dialogue lecteur/livre)," *Rinascimento*, 2nd series, 16:3–17.

Beck, Lewis White, ed. 1963. *Immanuel Kant: On History*. Indianapolis and New York: Bobbs-Merrill.

Bembo, Pietro. 1549. *Della volgar lingua*. Florence: Lorenzo Torrentino.

Bernauer, James. 1987. "Michel Foucault's Ecstatic Thinking." In *The Final Foucault*, ed. Bernauer and Rasmussen, 45–82.

———. 1992. "Beyond Life and Death: On Foucault's Post-Auschwitz Ethic." In *Michel Foucault Philosopher*, ed. Ewald, 260–78.

Bernauer, James, and David Rasmussen, eds. 1987. *The Final Foucault*. Cambridge, Mass.: MIT Press.

Bollack, J. 1976. "Momen Mutatum (La dérivation et le plaisir, Lucrèce, II, 184–293)." In *Etudes sur l'epicurisme antique*, ed. J. Bollack and A. Laks. Lille: Publications de l'Université de Lille, III.

Borch-Jakobsen, Mikkel. 1988. *The Freudian Subject*. Trans. Catherine Porter. Stanford, Calif.: Stanford University Press.

———. 1991. "The Freudian Subject, from Politics to Ethics." Trans. Eduardo Cadava. In *Who Comes After the Subject?*, ed. Cadava, Connor, and Nancy, 61–78.

Bordo, Susan. 1987. *The Flight from Objectivity: Essays on Cartesianism and Culture*. Albany, N.Y.: State University of New York Press.

Bouwsma, W. J. 1975. "The Two Faces of Humanism." In *Itinerarium Italicum*, ed. H. A. Oberman and T. Bradey. Leiden: Brill.

Bové, Paul. 1986. *Intellectuals in Power: A Genealogy of Critical Humanism*. New York: Columbia University Press.

Bowie, Andrew. 1990. *Aesthetics and Subjectivity: From Kant to Nietzsche*. Manchester: Manchester University Press.

———. 1996. "Rethinking the History of the Subject: Jacobi, Schelling, and Heidegger." In *Deconstructive Subjectivities*, ed. Critchley and Dews, 105–26.

Butler, Judith. 1990. *Gender Trouble: Feminism and the Subversion of Identity*. New York and London: Routledge.

Cadava, Eduardo, Peter Connor, and Jean-Luc Nancy, eds. 1991. *Who Comes After the Subject?* New York and London: Routledge.

Castiglione, Baldassare. 1964. *Il Libro del Cortegiano*, 2nd ed. Ed. B. Maier. Turin: Unione Tipographico-Editrice Torinese.

Caton, Hiram. 1973. *The Origin of Subjectivity: An Essay on Descartes*. New Haven: Yale University Press.

Chopin, Kate. 1981. *The Awakening and Selected Short Stories*. New York: Bantam.

Cicero, Marcus Tullius. 1925. *De finibus bonorum et malorum*. Ed. J. S. Reid. Cambridge: Cambridge University Press.

———. 1933. *De natura deorum and Academica*. Ed. and trans. H. Rackham. London: William Heinemann.

———. 1949. *De inventione*. Trans. H. M. Hubbell. Cambridge, Mass.: Harvard University Press.

———. 1975. *Cicero: De divinatione, De fato, Timaeus*. Ed. G. Giomini. Leipsig: Teubner.

Clay, Diskin. 1973. "Epicurus' Last Will and Testament." *Archiv für Geschichte der Philosophie* 55:252–80.

Code, Lorraine. 1991. *What Can She Know? Feminist Theory and the Construction of Knowledge*. Ithaca, N.Y.: Cornell University Press.

Conrad, Joseph. 1983. *Heart of Darkness and The Secret Sharer*. New York and London: Signet.

Crane, R. S., ed. 1952. *Critics and Criticism: Ancient and Modern*. Chicago: University of Chicago Press.

Critchley, Simon. 1996. "Prolegomena to Any Post-Deconstructive Subjectivity." In *Deconstructive Subjectivities*, ed. Critchley and Dews, 13–45.

Critchley, Simon, and Peter Dews, eds. 1996. *Deconstructive Subjectivities*. Albany, N.Y.: State University of New York Press.

Deleuze, Giles. 1990. "Lucretius and the Simulacrum." In *The Logic of Sense*, trans. Mark Lester and Charles Stivale, ed. Constantin V. Boundas. New York: Columbia University Press. 266–79.

Derrida, Jacques. 1972. "Structure, Sign, and Play in the Discourse of the Human Sciences." In *The Structuralist Controversy*, ed. Richard Macksey and Eugenio Donato. Baltimore: Johns Hopkins University Press.

Descartes, René. 1970. *Descartes: Philosophical Letters*. Trans. and ed. Anthony Kenny. Minneapolis: University of Minnesota Press.

———. 1985a. *Discourse on the Method . . .* In *The Philosophical Writings of Descartes*, 2 vols. Trans. J. Cottingham, R. Stoothoff, and D. Murdoch. Cambridge: Cambridge University Press. 1:111–51.

———. 1985b. "Meditations on First Philosophy." In *The Philosophical Writings of Descartes*, 2:3–62.

Descombes, Vincent. 1991. "A Propos of the 'Critique of the Subject' and the Critique of This Critique." In *Who Comes After the Subject?*, ed. Cadava, Connor, and Nancy, 120–34.

Dews, Peter. 1987. *Logics of Disintegration: Post-structuralist Thought and the Claims of Critical Theory*. London: Verso.

Diamond, Irene, and Lee Quinby, eds. 1988. *Feminism and Foucault: Reflections on Resistance*. Boston: Northeastern University Press.

Dickens, Charles. 1965. *Great Expectations*. Ed. R. D. McMaster. New York: Odyssey.

Diogenes Laertius. 1925. *Lives of Eminent Philosophers,* 2 vols. Trans. R. D. Hicks. London: William Heinemann.

Epictetus. 1928. *The Discourses . . .* Trans. W. A. Oldfather. London and New York: William Heinemann and G. P. Putnam's Sons.

Epicurus. 1973. *Opere.* Ed. G. Arrighetti. Turin: Einaudi.

Erasmus, Desiderius. 1971. *Dialogus Ciceronianus.* Ed. Pierre Mesnard. In *Opera omnia Desiderii Erasmi Roterodami.* Amsterdam: North Holland. I-2, 581– 710.

Ewald, François. 1992. *Michel Foucault, Philosopher.* Trans. Timothy J. Armstrong. New York: Harvester Wheatsheaf.

Fehn, Ann, Ingeborg Hoestery, and Maria Tatar, eds. 1992. *Neverending Stories: Toward a Critical Narratology.* Princeton, N.J.: Princeton University Press.

Fielding, Henry. 1961. *Joseph Andrews.* Ed. Martin C. Battestin. Boston: Houghton Mifflin.

Flynn, Thomas. 1987. "Foucault as Parrhesiast: His Last Course at the Collège de France." In *The Final Foucault,* ed. Bernauer and Rasmussen, 102–18.

Foucault, Michel. 1970. *The Order of Things.* New York: Random House.

———. 1972. *The Archaeology of Knowledge.* Trans. A. M. Sheridan-Smith. New York: Pantheon.

———. 1973. *The Birth of the Clinic: An Archaeology of Medical Perception.* Trans. A. M. Sheridan-Smith. New York: Random House.

———. 1977. *Michel Foucault: Language, Counter-Memory, Practice.* Ed. D. Bouchard. Trans. D. Bouchard and S. Simon. Ithaca, N.Y.: Cornell University Press.

———. 1979a. *Discipline and Punish: The Birth of the Prison.* Trans. Alan Sheridan. New York: Vintage.

———. 1979b. *Michel Foucault: Power, Truth, Strategy.* Ed. M. Morris and P. Patton. Sydney: Feral Publications.

———. 1980a. *The History of Sexuality,* vol. 1: *An Introduction.* Trans. R. Hurley. New York: Vintage.

———. 1980b. *Power/Knowledge.* Ed. Colin Gordon. Trans. Colin Gordon et al. New York: Pantheon.

———. 1984a. *The Foucault Reader.* Ed. Paul Rabinow. New York: Pantheon.

———. 1984b. "On the Genealogy of Ethics: An Overview of Work in Progress." In *The Foucault Reader,* ed. Rabinow.

———. 1984c. "What Is Enlightenment?" Trans. Catherine Porter. In *The Foucault Reader,* ed. Rabinow.

———. 1985a. "The Battle for Chastity." In *Western Sexuality: Practice and Precept in Past and Present Times,* ed. Philippe Ariès and André Béjin. Oxford: Basil Blackwell. 14–25.

———. 1985b. *The Use of Pleasure.* Trans. Robert Hurley. New York: Random House.

———. 1986. *The Care of the Self.* Trans. R. Hurley. New York: Random House.

———. 1987. "The Ethic for the Care of the Self as a Practice of Freedom." Trans. J. D. Gauthier. In *The Final Foucault*, ed. Bernauer and Rasmussen, 1–20.

———. 1988. *Michel Foucault: Politics, Philosophy, Culture: Interviews and Other Writings, 1977–1984.* Ed. Lawrence D. Kritzman. Trans. Alan Sheridan et al. London and New York: Routledge.

Foucault, Michel, and Richard Sennett. 1982. "Sexuality and Solitude." In *Humanities in Review*, vol. 1. Ed. David Rieff. Cambridge: Cambridge University Press. 3–21.

Frank, Manfred. 1989. *What Is Neostructuralism?* Trans. S. Wilke and R. Gray. Minneapolis: University of Minnesota Press.

———. 1995. "Is Subjectivity a Non-Thing, an Absurdity [Unding]? On Some Difficulties in Naturalistic Reductions of Self-Consciousness." Trans. Karl Ameriks. In *The Modern Subject*, ed. Ameriks and Sturma, 177–97.

———. 1996. "Identity and Subjectivity." In *Deconstructive Subjectivities*, ed. Critchley and Dews, 127–48.

Freud, Sigmund. 1953a. *Three Essays on the Theory of Sexuality.* In *The Standard Edition of the Complete Psychological Works*, trans. and ed. James Strachey. London: Hogarth Press. 7:123–243.

———. 1953b. *Totem and Taboo.* In *Standard Edition*, 13:1–161.

———. 1955. *Group Psychology and the Analysis of the Ego.* In *Standard Edition*, 18:65–143.

———. 1961. *Civilization and Its Discontents.* In *Standard Edition*, 21:57–145.

Furley, David J. 1967. *Two Studies in the Greek Atomists.* Princeton, N.J.: Princeton University Press.

Fuss, Diana. 1989. *Essentially Speaking: Feminism, Nature, and Difference.* New York and London: Routledge.

Garin, Eugenio. 1965. *Italian Humanism.* Trans. P. Munz. Oxford: Oxford University Press.

Gillan, Garth. 1987. "Foucault's Philosophy." In *The Final Foucault*, ed. Bernauer and Rasmussen, 34–44.

Gray, H. H. 1963. "Renaissance Humanism: The Pursuit of Eloquence." *Journal of the History of Ideas* 24:497–514.

Greenblatt, Stephen. 1980. *Renaissance Self-Fashioning: From More to Shakespeare.* Chicago: University of Chicago Press, 1980.

Greene, Thomas. 1976. "Petrarch and the Humanist Hermeneutic." In *Italian Literature: Roots and Branches*, ed. G. Rimanelli and K. Atchity. New Haven: Yale University Press. 201–24. (Also published in a chapter of Thomas Greene, *The Light in Troy: Imitation and Discovery in Renaissance Poetry* [New Haven: Yale University Press, 1982.])

Guthrie, W. K. C. 1960. *The Greek Philosophers: From Thales to Aristotle.* New York: Harper and Row.

———. 1967–78. *A History of Greek Philosophy*, 5 vols. Cambridge: Cambridge University Press.

Guzzoni, Ute. 1996. "Do We Still Want to Be Subjects?" In *Deconstructive Subjectivities*, ed. Critchley and Dews, 201–16.

Hadot, Pierre. 1992. "Reflections on the Notion of 'the Cultivation of the Self.'" In *Michel Foucault, Philosopher*, ed. Ewald, 225–31.

Harootunian, H. D. 1988. "Foucault, Genealogy, History: The Pursuit of Otherness." In *After Foucault*, ed. Arac, 110–37.

Hoy, David Couzens. 1988. "Foucault: Modern or Postmodern?" In *After Foucault*, ed. Arac, 12–41.

Husserl, Edmund. 1960. *Cartesian Meditations: An Introduction to Phenomenology.* Trans. Dorion Cairns. The Hague: Martinus Nijhoff.

Irigaray, Luce. 1985. *The Sex Which Is Not One.* Trans. Catherine Porter et al. Ithaca, N.Y.: Cornell University Press.

Isocrates. 1945a. *Against the Sophists.* In *Isocrates*, ed. and trans. George Norlin. London: William Heineman. 2:160–80.

———. 1945b. *Antidosis.* In *Isocrates*, ed. Norlin, 2:181–367.

Jaeger, Werner. 1944. *Paideia: The Ideals of Greek Culture*, 3 vols. Trans. Gilbert Highet. New York: Oxford University Press.

Judovitz, Dalia. 1988. *Subjectivity and Representation in Descartes: The Origins of Modernity.* Cambridge: Cambridge University Press.

Kant, Immanuel. 1929 [1781, 1787]. *Critique of Pure Reason.* Trans. N. K. Smith. London: Macmillan.

———. 1949 [1788]. *Critique of Practical Reason and Other Writings in Moral Philosophy.* Ed. and trans. L. W. Beck. Chicago: University of Chicago Press.

———. 1963 [1786]. "Conjectural Beginnings of Human History." Trans. Emil L. Fackenheim. In *Immanuel Kant: On History*, ed. Beck, 53–68.

Lentricchia, Frank. 1988. *Ariel and the Police: Michel Foucault, William James, Wallace Stevens.* Madison: University of Wisconsin Press.

Lerner, Gerda. 1986. *The Creation of Patriarchy.* New York: Oxford University Press.

Lloyd, A. C. 1978. "Emotion and Decision in Stoic Logic." In *The Stoics*, ed. Rist, 233–46.

Lucretius. 1963. *T. Lucreti Cari De rerum natura.* Ed. J. Martin. Leipzig: Teubner.

McKeon, Richard. 1952. "Literary Criticism and the Concept of Imitation in Antiquity." In *Critics and Criticism*, ed. Crane, 147–75.

———. 1954. *Thought, Action, and Passion.* Chicago: University of Chicago Press.

McNay, Lois. 1992. *Foucault and Feminism: Power, Gender, and the Self.* London: Polity Press.

Melanchthon, Philipp. 1963. "Philippi Melanthonis Opera quae super sunt omnia." Ed. Carolus Gottlieb Bretschneider. In *Corpus Reformatorum*. Frankfort: Minerva. 9: cols. 687–703.

Melehy, Hassan. 1997. *Writing Cogito: Montaigne, Descartes, and the Institution of the Modern Subject.* Albany: State University of New York Press.

Miller, James. 1993. *The Passion of Michel Foucault.* New York: Simon and Schuster.

Bibliography

Mitchell, Juliet, and Jacqueline Rose. 1982. *Feminine Sexuality: Jacques Lacan and the "école freudienne."* New York: Norton.

Mohr, Georg. 1995. "Freedom and the Self: From Introspection to Intersubjectivity: Wolff, Kant, Fichte." In *The Modern Subject,* ed. Ameriks and Sturma, 31–42.

Montaigne, Michel de. 1969. *Apologie de Raimond Sebond* in *Les Essais de Michel de Montaigne,* 2 vols. Ed. Samuel de Sacy. Paris: Le Club Français du Livre.

Nagel, Thomas. 1986. *The View from Nowhere.* New York: Oxford University Press.

Pascal, Roy. 1977. *The Dual Voice: Free Indirect Speech and Its Functioning in the Nineteenth-Century European Novel.* Totowa, N.J.: Rowman and Littlefield.

Pavel, Thomas. 1992. "Between History and Fiction: On Dorrit Cohn's Poetics of Prose." In *Neverending Stories,* ed. Fehn, Hoestery, and Tatar, 17–28.

Petrarca, Francesco. 1933–52. *Le familiari,* 4 vols., ed. Vittorio Rossi and Umberto Bosco. Florence: G. C. Sansoni.

———. 1955a. *Prose.* Ed. Guido Martellotti et al. Milan and Naples: Riccardo Ricciardi.

———. 1955b. "Secretum." Ed. Enrico Carrara. In *Prose,* ed. Martellotti et al., 22–217.

———. 1955c. "De sui ipsius et multorum ignorantia." Ed. Pier Giorgio Ricci. In *Prose,* ed. Martelloti et al., 710–67.

———. 1955d. "De viris illustribus." Ed. Guido Martellotti. In *Prose,* ed. Martellotti et al., 218–69.

———. 1955e. "De vita solitaria." Ed. Guido Martellotti. In *Prose,* ed. Martellotti et al., 286–593.

———. 1965. *De remediis utriusque fortunae* in *Opera omnia.* Basle, 1554; Ridgeway, N.J.: Gregg Press. 1:7–254.

Pigman, G. W. 1980. "Versions of Imitation in the Renaissance." *Renaissance Quarterly* 33:1–32.

Poster, Mark. 1989. *Critical Theory and Poststructuralism: In Search of a Context.* Ithaca, N.Y.: Cornell University Press.

Racevskis, Karlis. 1987. "Michel Foucault, Rameau's Nephew, and the Question of Identity." In *The Final Foucault,* ed. Bernauer and Rasmussen, 21–33.

Rajchman, John. 1992. "Foucault: The Ethic and the Work." In *Michel Foucault, Philosopher,* ed. Ewald, 215–23.

Rist, John M. 1978. "The Stoic Concept of Detachment." In *The Stoics,* ed. John M. Rist. Berkeley and Los Angeles: University of California Press. 259–72.

Rochlitz, Rainer. 1992. "The Aesthetics of Existence: Post-Conventional Morality and the Theory of Power in Michel Foucault." In *Michel Foucault, Philosopher,* ed. Ewald, 248–58.

Rorty, Richard. 1979. *Philosophy and the Mirror of Nature.* Princeton, N.J.: Princeton University Press.

Rubin, Gayle. 1975. "The Traffic in Women: Notes on the 'Political Economy' of

Sex." In *Toward an Anthropology of Women,* ed. Rayna R. Reiter. New York and London: Monthly Review Press. 157–210.

Sambursky, S. 1956. *The Physical World of the Greeks.* Trans. M. Dagut. London: Routledge and Paul.

Sandbach, F. H. 1975. *The Stoics.* London: Chatto and Windus.

Saussure, Ferdinand de. 1959. *Course in General Linguistics.* Trans. Wade Baskin. New York: McGraw-Hill.

———. 1968–74. *Cours de linguistique générale,* 2 vols. [4 parts]. Ed. R. Engler. Wiesbaden: Otto Harrassowitz.

———. 1972. *Cours de linguistique générale.* Ed. T. de Mauro. Paris: Payot.

Sawicki, Jana. 1988. "Feminism and the Power of Foucauldian Discourse." In *After Foucault,* ed. Arac, 161–78.

Sedgwick, Eve Kosofsky. 1985. *Between Men: English Literature and Male Homosocial Desire.* New York: Columbia University Press.

———. 1990. *Epistemology of the Closet.* Berkeley and Los Angeles: University of California Press.

Seigel, J. 1966. "'Civic Humanism' or Ciceronian Rhetoric." *Past and Present* 34:3–48.

———. 1968. *Rhetoric and Philosophy in Renaissance Humanism.* Princeton, N.J.: Princeton University Press.

Seneca, Lucius Annaeus. 1925. *Ad Lucilium Epistulae Morales,* 3 vols. Trans. R. G. Gummere. London: William Heinemann.

———. 1928. *De ira* in *Moral Essays,* 3 vols. Trans. J. W. Basore. London: William Heinemann.

———. 1994a. *De tranquillitate animi.* In *Seneca: Four Dialogues,* ed. C. D. N. Costa. Warminster, England: Aris and Phillips.

———. 1994b. *De vita beata.* In *Seneca: Four Dialogues,* ed. Costa.

Serres, Michel. 1982. *Hermes: Literature, Science, Philosophy.* Ed. J. Harari and D. Bell. Baltimore: Johns Hopkins University Press.

Sextus Empiricus. 1905–24. *Sexti Empirici Opera,* 4 vols. Ed. Hermann Mutschmann et al. Leipsig: Teubner.

Sidney, Philip. 1904. *An Apology for Poetry* in *Elizabethan Critical Essays.* Ed. G. G. Smith. Oxford: Oxford University Press. 1:150–207.

Smith, Paul. 1988. *Discerning the Subject.* Minneapolis: University of Minnesota Press.

Stoicorum Veterum Fragmenta. 1903–64. 4 vols. Ed. Hans von Arnim. Leipsig: Teubner [cited in text as SVF].

Stokes, Michael C. 1995. "Cicero on Epicurean Pleasures." In *Cicero the Philosopher,* ed. J. G. F. Powell. Oxford: Clarendon Press. 145–70.

Stough, Charlotte. 1978. "Stoic Determinism and Moral Responsibility." In *The Stoics,* ed. Rist, 203–31.

Strozier, Robert. 1985. *Epicurus and Hellenistic Philosophy.* Lanham, Md.: University Press of America.

————. 1986. "Renaissance Humanist Theory: Petrarch and the Sixteenth Century." *Rinascimento,* 2nd series, 26:193–229.

Sturma, Dieter. 1995. "Self and Reason: A Nonreductionist Approach to the Reflective and Practical Transitions of Self-Consciousness." In *The Modern Subject,* ed. Ameriks and Sturma, 199–215.

Tateo, F. 1960. *"Retorica" e "Poetica" fra Medioevo a Rinascimento.* Bari: Laterza.

Taylor, Charles. 1989. *Sources of the Self: The Making of the Modern Identity.* Cambridge: Harvard University Press.

Too, Yun Lee. 1995. *The Rhetoric of Identity in Isocrates: Text, Power, Pedagogy.* Cambridge: Cambridge University Press.

Trinkaus, Charles. 1960. "A Humanist's Image of Humanism: Inaugural Orations of Bartolomeo della Fonte." *Studies in the Renaissance* 7:90–147.

————. 1970. *In Our Image and Likeness,* 2 vols. Chicago: University of Chicago Press.

————. 1979. *The Poet as Philosopher.* New Haven: Yale University Press.

Tripet, A. 1967. *Pétrarque ou La Connaissance de soi.* Geneva: Droz.

Tuana, Nancy. 1992. "Reading Philosophy as a Woman: A Feminist Critique of the History of Philosophy." In *Against Patriarchal Thinking,* ed. Maja Pellikaan-Engel. Amsterdam: VU University Press.

Van de Pitte, Frederick. 1971. *Kant as Philosophical Anthropologist.* The Hague: Martinus Nijhoff.

Van Haute, Philippe. 1996. "Law, Guilt, and Subjectivity: Reflections on Freud, Nancy, and Derrida." In *Deconstructive Subjectivities,* ed. Critchley and Dews, 185–200.

Vasoli, Cesare. 1968. *La dialettica e la retorica dell'Umanesimo.* Milan: Feltrinelli.

Wilkins, E. H. 1961. *Life of Petrarch.* Chicago: University of Chicago Press.

Wittig, Monique. 1992. *The Straight Mind and Other Essays.* With a foreword by Louise Turcotte. Boston: Beacon Press.

INDEX